WITH ROOTS AND WINGS

ECOLOGY AND JUSTICE
An Orbis Series on Global Ecology

Advisory Board Members
Mary Evelyn Tucker
John A. Grim
Leonardo Boff
Sean McDonagh

The Orbis Series *Ecology and Justice* publishes books that seek to integrate an understanding of the Earth as an interconnected life system with concerns for just and sustainable systems that benefit the entire Earth. Books in the Series concentrate on ways to:
- reexamine the human-Earth relationship in light of contemporary cosmological thought
- develop visions of common life marked by ecological integrity and social justice
- expand on the work of those who are developing such fields as ecotheology, ecojustice, environmental ethics, ecofeminism, deep ecology, social ecology, bioregionalism, and animal rights
- promote inclusive participative strategies that enhance the struggle of the Earth's voiceless poor for justice
- deepen appreciation for and expand dialogue between religious traditions on the issue of ecology
- encourage spiritual discipline, social engagement, and the reform of religion and society toward these ends.

Viewing the present moment as a time for responsible creativity, the Series seeks authors who speak to ecojustice concerns and who bring into dialogue perspectives from the Christian community, from the world's other religions, from secular and scientific circles, and from new paradigms of thought and action.

ECOLOGY AND JUSTICE SERIES

WITH ROOTS AND WINGS

Christianity in an Age of Ecology and Dialogue

Jay B. McDaniel

Michael,
Thank you for
your spirit, kindness,
and guidance. You
embody so much of
what this book is
about. Jay

ORBIS BOOKS

Maryknoll, New York 10545

Portions of Chapter 5 were originally published in "Emerging Options in Ecological Christianity," *Ecological Prospects: Scientific, Religious, and Aesthetic Perspectives*, edited by Christopher Key Chapple. ©1993. By permission of the State University of New York Press.

Library of Congress Cataloging-in-Publication Data

McDaniel, Jay B. (Jay Byrd), 1949-
    With roots and wings : Christianity in an age of ecology and dialogue / Jay B. McDaniel.
        p.   cm. — (Ecology and justice)
    Includes bibliographical references.
    ISBN 1-57075-001-7 (pbk.)
    1. Human ecology—Religious aspects—Christianity.   2. Human ecology—Religious aspects.   3. Spiritual life—Christianity.
I. Title.   II. Series.
BT695.5.M415   1995
261.8'362—dc20   95-3594
                                                                          CIP

Printed on recycled paper

Contents

Acknowledgments

I want to express my gratitude to some friends who have been spiritual guides over the years: John Cobb, Keido Fukushima, Peggy Hays, Rick Clugston, and Cathy Goodwin. John has helped me love God with my mind as well as my heart; Keido has shown me the strength and compassion of Zen mind; Peggy has helped me see the truth of death and resurrection; Rick has shown me that shamans can be Christians too; and Cathy has shown me that good deeds are worth more than theology.

I am also indebted to the Guadalupe River in the Hill Country of Texas; to a tick-infested pine forest near Chidester, Arkansas; to a dog named Edward, who was run over by a car in 1987; to a white-tailed deer whom, I admit with regret, I shot as a young boy; and to two dogs who now grace my backyard: Nathan and Jacob. In different ways, all have shaped the perspective of this book. They, too, have been spiritual guides.

In addition I want to thank my wife, Kathy, and my sons, Matthew and Jason, who are my own most beloved "local community," and whose laughter, tears, and patience are sources of grace in my life. And also my parents, John and Virginia McDaniel, whose support over the years has been unfailing; and my sister, Linda, whose abiding friendship I appreciate.

I want to thank members of the Forum Class at First United Methodist Church in Conway, Arkansas, whose openness to spiritual adventure has been a continued inspiration to me; and worshipers at St. Peter's Episcopal Church in Conway, whose rootedness in tradition has been equally inspiring.

I am grateful to the editors at Orbis Press, whose catholic spirit has shown me Catholicism at its very best; to Joan Laflamme, whose copyediting improved the book considerably; and to Bill Burrows, whose gentle persistence saw this book into completion and whose evangelical liberalism has been an example of healthy roots and strong wings.

Finally, I want to thank the many students I have taught over the years, a few of whose personal stories play a role in this book, and many of whose insights play a role. One in particular—Amy Dunn—read the entire manuscript and helped me with form and content. She said, "It sounds a lot like what we talk about in class all the time." And she was right.

In truth, I am extremely grateful to all my students. Day after day, year after year, they ask honest questions, offer fresh insights, challenge inherited dogmas, and guide me into shared discovery. To illustrate, I mention one other student: Gustavo Zajac.

Gustavo, a Jew of Russian origins whose great-grandparents immigrated to Argentina during anti-Jewish persecutions in the nineteenth century, somehow found his way to Hendrix College in Conway, where I was privileged to be his teacher. In the spring of 1994 he helped me teach a course on Judaism. I learned much more from him, with his love of living Torah and his personal faith in God, than he did from me. He made me very glad there are Jews in the world.

One day, the last class of the term, Gustavo led me and all thirty students in a joy-filled and prayerful adventure in Hasidic dancing. There we were—conservative evangelicals and honest agnostics and liberal Methodists and fun-loving feminists and socially-engaged Buddhists—dancing to Jewish folk songs, with our legs flying and our arms raised, imaginatively returning divine sparks to heaven with flicks of our fingers. Gustavo made clear that none of us had to be Jewish to dance; we just had to be ourselves. Least of all did we need to be "good" at dancing. Gustavo was a professional dancer who had taught many other professionals to do Hasidic dancing. He said that he liked us better than the professionals, because we didn't know what we were doing and we didn't care.

As we were dancing on the lawn of Hendrix College on that hot summer's day, I had the feeling I was experiencing what Christians call church, what Buddhists call *sangha*, and what fun-loving feminists call community. I had the feeling I was participating in the divine Communion, in God. Regardless of personal philosophy or life orientation, every dancer had a place. Even the birds joined in; even the grass. It would be pretentious to dedicate this book to the divine Communion itself. That would be like dedicating it "to the universe, plus more." But I do dedicate it to all my dancing students, in whom that Communion was visibly present. And still is.

WITH ROOTS AND WINGS

Introduction

Roots and Wings

Most of us want to be fully alive, to be whole. The wholeness we seek is more than private pleasure or personal satisfaction. It lies in feeling connected to the larger scheme of things. Drawn by the splendor of Douglas firs and the intricacy of dragonfly wings, by the beauty of animal consciousness and the tenderness of other people's feelings, we seek to be integrated in meaningful ways with the various presences we meet in our lives. We seek to be richly connected with friends and loved ones, plants and animals, hills and rivers, forests and mountains, light and dark, fire and rain, moon and stars, spirits and ancestors.

To be sure, our modes of connection with these presences will differ, relative to their natures and our needs. In relation to other people, for example, we will want to be connected through love and forgiveness and intimacy. In relation to fire, we will want to be connected through awe and wonder and terror. And in relation to the spirits who appear in our dreams, we will want to be connected through amazement and curiosity and understanding. Still, we seek to be attuned to these realities in one way or another. We seek a wholeness of rich connections.

Rich connections are not always happy. Sometimes they are pleasurable, as when we share in the gladness of children at play, or feel the dark presence of a mysterious forest, or take delight in frolicking colts, or swim in the cleansing waters of healthy rivers. But sometimes such connections are painful, as when we share in the sufferings of loved ones, or witness the destruction of healthy forests, or empathize with the terror of slaughtered calves, or witness the pollution of once-living rivers.

Consider, for example, communion with rivers. A leading environmental philosopher, J. Baird Callicott, describes his own experience of a polluted river in poignant terms we might all feel, if not in relation to rivers, then to our own sacred places, whether forests or mountains or oceans or lakes or

1

city parks or historic monuments or aging neighborhoods. Having grown up on the banks of the Mississippi, Callicott returned as an adult to find a different reality.

> As I gazed at the brown silt-choked waters absorbing a black plume of industrial and municipal sewage from Memphis and followed bits of some unknown beige froth floating continually down from Cincinnati, Louisville, or St. Louis, I experienced a palpable pain. It was not distinctly located in any of my extremities, nor was it like a headache or nausea. Still, it was very real. I had no plans to swim in the river, no need to drink from it, no intention of buying real estate on its shores. My narrowly personal interests were not affected, and yet somehow I was personally injured. It occurred to me then, in a flash of self-discovery, that the river was part of me (1989, 114).

Callicott's "self-discovery" that "the river was part of me" is a good example of how roots—in this case, roots in a river—can be painful rather than pleasurable. The meaning of roots, of rich connections, lies not in happiness but in communion. Sometimes, for the sake of communion, we must follow Jesus even unto the cross.[1]

Whether pleasant or painful, experiences of communion are themselves revelatory. They reveal the fact that we are not skin-encapsulated egos cut off from the world by the boundaries of our skin, but rather connected beings, bound together with others in a seamless web of life. After all, we would not delight in frolicking colts and suffer with terrified calves, we would not enjoy swimming in healthy rivers and be pained by their pollution, were we not

---

1. Throughout this book, I refer to Jesus as a historical figure in whom God was enfleshed, who died on a cross for our sins, and who was resurrected. These are things I believe. But I have been trained both in seminary (the School of Theology at Claremont, California) and graduate school (Claremont Graduate School) to recognize that the historical Jesus of first-century Palestine, and the Jesus who speaks in different ways from the pages of the Bible, and into my heart, are not necessarily the same. Much of what we read about Jesus in the Bible is an interpretation of the historical figure, added by the early church, and not necessarily true to his own life. Most liberal Christians have come to assume this discrepancy between Bible and history; many more conservative Christians deny it. I hope that this book might speak to some in both camps. Still, I must confess my more liberal views. When I say Jesus in this book, I am speaking of a living presence in my heart, who has in some ways become a myth over the centuries, beginning with forms of mythicization that occurred in the New Testament itself; that is, Jesus did not necessarily say everything that the Bible says he did.

However, I do not equate such mythicization with falsification. Some forms of mythicizing can be falsifying; but some can be amplifying. As Black Elk once put it in explaining mythical accounts of the peace pipe in his own tradition: "This they tell, and whether it happened so or not I do not know; but if you think about it you can see that it's true" (Neihardt 1972, 5).

In other words, myths can add to rather than subtract from truth. They can even add to the truth of a historical person's life. Just as some who come after us may understand things about us that we ourselves did not understand, so some who came after Jesus may understand things

parts of one another, and of the Earth itself, at a level too deep for words. The wholeness we seek is an affirmation of this connectedness. It is an awakening to the universe as a communion of subjects, not a collection of objects (Berry 1988, 46); to what the Zen poet Thich Nhat Hanh calls the "interbeing" of all things (1993). As we open ourselves to rich connections, we realize that we ourselves, at our deepest core, are interbeings among interbeings.

Still, even as we seek rich connections with others, we also seek the thrill of adventure and the joy of discovery. There is an open-ended feature to life—an open future—that forever beckons us to realize our own creative potential in community with others. We realize this potential not only by creatively solving immediate problems, but also by thinking new thoughts and feeling new feelings, even if the old thoughts and feelings were quite satisfactory. In exercising our creativity, we add our voice, a small but human one, to the unfolding cosmos. We respond to the call of an unrealized future, itself divine.

In adding our voice to the unfolding cosmos, we partake of a larger adventure, itself an endless horizon within us and beyond us. This horizon is, to paraphrase the philosopher Whitehead, the adventure of the universe as One (1967, 295). It is the Sacred Whole, understood as a Communion at the heart of all communions, an Adventure in which all adventures are enfolded.[2] Thus, the wholeness we seek for ourselves and others is a way of being connected to God, even as it is a way of being connected to the rest of creation. Both for our sakes and for God's sake, we seek a wholeness that is creative as well as connected, adventurous as well as communal. We seek a wholeness with roots and wings.

The purpose of this book is to envision a way of living, a life path, that offers nourishing roots and unbound wings. More specifically, I want to imagine my own religious tradition—Christianity—as such a path. Of course, *roots* and *wings* are metaphors. I use *roots* to indicate a sense of spiritual well-

---

about him, that he himself did not understand. My hope is that the image of Jesus that pervades this work is amplifying rather than falsifying.

My own image of the historical Jesus—the Jesus before myth—has been very much shaped by works such as Marcus Borg's *Jesus: A New Vision* (1987), which represents a contemporary synthesis of recent biblical scholarship on the historical Jesus. Borg proposes that, on the basis of recent historical scholarship, the historical Jesus was a healer, a sage who challenged the conventional wisdom of his day, a revitalization movement founder, and a prophet. I see these very activities as ways in which he responded to God in his life and opened himself to God such that the Spirit shown through him like light from a prism (see Chapter 6 for further discussion).

But even Borg's image is a myth of sorts. When it comes to absolute knowledge of the historical Jesus, or any other figure in the past, Paul was right: we "see through a glass darkly" (1 Cor 13:12).

I do not think that absolute knowledge of any sort, concerning Jesus or anything else, is a desirable feature of spiritual life. Reliable knowledge, yes, but absolute knowledge, no. Mythic knowledge, like scientific knowledge, can be reliable, but it is never absolute in the sense of being final and unquestionable. The life of faith lives within and is nourished by some degree of insecurity and uncertainty. Without insecurity and uncertainty, there would be no freedom, no wings.

2. I borrow the phrase *Sacred Whole* from Charlene Spretnak in *States of Grace: The Recovery of Meaning in the Postmodern Age* (1991, 158–161). Spretnak uses the phrase as an alternative

being that comes from being richly connected with the heavens and the earth, and with the God in whom they are enfolded. And I use *wings* to indicate a sense of exploration and freedom that comes from being open to new futures, which are themselves a dimension of God's ongoing life. The basic thesis of the book, then, is that Christianity is, or can be, a way with roots and wings. The more centered we are in God, the more connected we will be to a "very good" creation (Gn 1:31), and the more open we will be to fresh possibilities from the future. They will "know we are Christian," to quote the popular hymn, not only "by our love," but also by our roots and wings.[3]

The Audience of This Book

I borrow the metaphor of roots and wings from a friend, himself a rabbi, who observed that in rearing children we ought to give them roots and wings. The story will be recounted at the opening of the first chapter. For now, suffice it to say that, as soon as he offered the remark, I had a metaphor both for what I seek for myself and for what I seek for others. I suspect that, one way or another, all human beings need roots and wings. Much of the goodness in the world, and much of the evil as well, may stem from our search for connectedness and creativity, for communion and adventure. Sometimes the search is guided, and sometimes misguided. Always it is spiritual.

Although all humans may be searching for roots and wings, I cannot presume to write for all human beings. I write for 1) self-identified Christians who want to follow the way of the Nazarene, but who do not want to be hamstrung by religious authoritarianism; 2) for people who travel other paths—Jews, Buddhists, and Feminist Neo-Pagans,[4] for example—and who do not wish to "become Christian," but who nevertheless want to learn from Christianity, just as Christians can learn from their traditions; and 3) people who

---

to the word *God*. Spretnak's purpose in *States of Grace* to "reclaim the core teachings and practices of the Great wisdom traditions for the well-being of the Earth Community," has been an inspiration to me. Her approach to world religions is from a non-aligned yet religiously sympathetic point of view; mine is from a self-conscious but hopefully open Christian point of view. She takes "the Earth community" as a context for understanding and appropriating insights from various religions: Neo-Pagan, Native American, and Abrahamic. In many ways, I do the same.

3. "They Will Know We Are Christians by Our Love" also goes by "We Are One in the Spirit." It was written by Peter Scholtes (1966). The view of this book, of course, is that roots and wings are themselves dimensions of that love which rightly characterizes the Christian life. Rich connections with things that count are forms of love, or communion; and openness to fresh possibilities from the future, particularly those derived from God, are ways of loving, or being open to, the very Heart of the universe. What makes the latter possibilities "holy" is that they enrich our capacities for still deeper roots in "things that count." They enrich our capacities for love.

4. I use *Feminist Neo-Pagans* to refer to people, mostly but not exclusively women, who are religiously unaffiliated but spiritually interested; who identify with the nature mysticism of "pagan" religions, such as those of pre-Christian European cultures; and who find sacred power in female images of the divine.

are considering "becoming Christian," but who fear that doing so will fore-close possibilities for open-mindedness and open-heartedness.

I identify with all three types of people. While I am a self-identified Chris-tian, I appreciate the truth of other paths, and I understand the reasons, many valid, why some people find other paths preferable to Christianity. I think it is good, not bad, that there are many religions, many paths, and not just one.

In addition, I understand what it can be like to "want" to be Christian, but to fear that doing so will result in becoming more closed rather than more open. I myself was in this situation years ago, while a senior in college. With the help of many Christians wiser than I, I have since come to see Christianity as a path of freedom rather than confinement, of wings as well as roots. Still, I know what it is like to experience it as confining.

In any case, I hope that you—the reader—are among the three types of people I have described. Sometimes my "we" will refer primarily to people in the first category, that is, to the self-identified Christians; in such cases I ask the people in the second two groups to be patient, to glean what can be gleaned, but to ignore the rest. At other times my "we" will refer to people in all three categories, none to the exclusion of the others. After all, all of "us," not just self-identified Christians, need roots and wings.

If I am honest, however, I need to make one more point about who I imag-ine "we" are. If we have the time to read a book such as this, I imagine that, regardless of our religious self-understanding, "we" are college-educated, middle-class people with full stomachs, adequate shelter, sufficient clothing, and access to decent health-care. While you and I may think of ourselves as struggling to make ends meet, "we" are not hungry or cold or homeless. By global standards and by many local standards as well, we are among the privi-leged and powerful of the world.

Of course, our lives are not problem-free. We do indeed have our personal trials and struggles, which are of concern to us, to those who love us, and to God. Some of us are addicted to our jobs, some to alcohol, some to destruc-tive relationships. Some of us are married, some single, and some, married or single, are looking for the "perfect" relationship. Many of us are dangerously obsessed with being liked, or needed, or perfect, or wise, or happy, or secure, or in control. Most of us wrestle with being anxious or afraid or angry. These internal trials and struggles are real and powerful. They are part of an inner journey that takes years to work through. They ought not be dismissed be-cause we are not poor and powerless.

Still, if we have the luxury of reading books such as this, we ought ac-knowledge that our social locations are deeply privileged, that we benefit from social systems in ways others do not. We are not the young black male who will go out tonight and get shot by a rival gang; or the prostitute who will be beaten by her pimp; or the ninety-year-old who will die alone in a nursing home; or the homeless man who will freeze under the bridge during the night. Nor are we the terrified calf being taken to slaughter, or the river being pol-luted by toxic wastes, or the wetland being paved over for a supermarket.

Or are we? To be sure, we may not *think* of ourselves as the young black male or the prostitute or the homeless man. We think of ourselves as different from them, more fortunate than them. If we are typical middle-class liberals, we may also, and rightly, feel guilty about our privileged situations. We may lament our materialism and self-indulgence; we may bemoan our implicit racism or sexism or classism or anthropocentrism. We may wish that we lived in greater solidarity with "them" than we do. Still, if given the option, we would not exchange places. We are too comfortable.

A Christianity with roots and wings will help us overcome this comfort. It will help us simplify our lives, reject the values of consumer culture, and learn to live with less, that others can simply live. It will inspire us to cast our lot with the poor and powerless of the world, cognizant of the fact that in "the least of these" (Mt 25:31) we see not only the face of Christ, but our own faces, too. Here Buddhism can be of help. As we learn from a Buddhist emphasis on interconnectedness, we come to see that, at a level deeper than words, we *are* the gang member and beaten prostitute and the terrified calf and the polluted river, even as we are also Jane Smith and Bill Adams and Sally Jones and John Franklin.

Zen monk Thich Nhat Hanh puts the point well in his poem "Please Call Me by My True Names" (1987, 63-64). I have already mentioned this gentle monk as the person who coined the term *interbeing*. He is a Zen Buddhist from Vietnam who spent years helping Vietnamese people find refuge from the ravages of war and poverty. The poem comes from his experience of helping others; it serves as a good springboard for middle-class people who wish to find a path of our own. The "I" of his poem, I suggest, is our "I" as well.

> Do not say that I'll depart tomorrow
> because even today I still arrive
>
> Look deeply: I arrive in every second
> to be a bud on a spring branch
> to be a tiny bird, with wings still fragile,
>   learning to sing in my new nest,
> to be a caterpillar in the heart of a flower,
> to be a jewel hiding itself in a stone.
>
> I still arrive, in order to laugh and to cry,
>   in order to fear and to hope,
> the rhythm of my heart is the birth and death
>   of all that are alive.
>
> I am the mayfly metamorphosing on the
>   surface of the river,
> and I am the bird which, when spring comes,
>   arrives in time to eat the mayfly.

I am the frog swimming happily in the clear water
    of a pond,
and I am the grass-snake who, approaching,
    in silence, feeds itself on the frog.

I am the child in Uganda, all skin and bones,
    my legs as thin as bamboo sticks,
and I am the arms merchant, selling deadly
    weapons to Uganda.

I am the twelve-year-old-girl, refugee on a
    small boat
who throws herself into the ocean after being
    raped by a sea pirate
and I am the pirate, my heart not yet capable
    of seeing and loving.

I am a member of the politburo, with plenty
    of power in my hands,
and I am the man who has to pay his debt
    of blood to my people,
dying slowly in a forced labor camp.

My joy is like spring, so warm it makes
    flowers bloom in all walks of life.
My pain is like a river of tears, so full it fills
    all four oceans.

Please call me by my true names, so I can hear
    all my cries and laughs at once,
    so I can see that my joy and my pain are one.

Please call me by my true names, so I can wake
    up and so the door of my heart can be left
    open, the door of compassion.

It seems to me that this Zen monk's poem can help all of us who are middle-class seekers, whether Christian or Jewish or Buddhist or Feminist Neo-Pagan. If our Way is Christian, we can hear the voice of Jesus in the poem. As we imagine the man we seek to follow, we rightly imagine a wise and compassionate Jew, himself filled with God, who so identified with the sufferings and sins of those around him that he took them on as his own. He knew that his true name was not simply Jesus, but also "sea pirate" and "raped child." Let our true names correspond to his.

roots   *wings*

In sum, the search for wholeness, for "healthy soils" and "healing skies," is not a search for private fulfillment alone, but rather for communal well-being, for *shalom*. It is a search for ways that we can break out of our self-enclosure, in order to identify with the naked and despised and vulnerable of our world, both human and nonhuman. The search for roots and wings is a search not just for inner wholeness, but for a life of discipleship, of peace-making, in a world both unsustainable and unjust.

The Story

Readers will quickly discover that this is not an academic book. As much as possible I avoid technical language, be it philosophical or theological, and I employ myriad images—such as roots and wings—in order to make my points. Gradually I find that, in my own work, I have felt called to write books that are accessible rather than scholarly.

Readers will also discover that the Christianity of which I speak is normative rather than descriptive. I will indeed draw upon various dimensions of the Christian heritage, creedal and ritualistic. I hope to offer a view of Christianity that is continuous with significant dimensions of the Christian past, such that it is recognizably Christian. Still, my aim is not so much to describe Christianity as it has been, as it is to describe Christianity as it might be and, in my view, should be, if it lives up to the God's call into the future. Religions, no less than people, need wings as well as roots. Christianity is no exception. It is in deep need of adventure at this time in its history, lest it fall into fundamentalist stagnation. As a people, those of us who are self-identified Christians need both to "hear the old, old story" in fresh ways and to tell some new stories, or at least to add some new chapters to the old story.[5] These new chapters are already being added by African Christians and Asian Christians and Latin American Christians and Native American Christians, all of whom are now changing the very face of the Christian religion. This book is by no means a new chapter. At best it is but a sentence in a chapter, representing one hope that, in the end, Christianity can be a Way with wings as well as roots.

Wholeness

I have said that roots and wings are dimensions of wholeness. Wholeness itself consists of "inner wholeness," as felt in a sense of creativity and con-

---

5.   The line "hear the old, old story" comes from a hymn written by Eugene M. Bartlett in 1939, as found in the *United Methodist Hymnal* (1989, 370).

nectedness that permeates our inner lives, and also "outer wholeness," as exemplified in local communities that are socially just, ecologically sustainable, and spiritually satisfying.

Once we have experienced the vicissitudes of life, most of us realize that we will never be completely whole, at least in this life. Our relations will never be perfect, and our creativity will never be complete. We may taste varying degrees of wholeness through love and wisdom, and yet, most of us will never be completely connected and creative, much as we might wish. Most of the wisdom traditions of the world tell us that, for complete wholeness, we will need to wait until the next life, or the one after that. Part of the human condition is to be unwhole as well as whole.

From a Christian perspective, the reality of unwholeness—that is, of blocked creativity and broken connections—is unfortunate. There is a tragic dimension to life. Some but not all of this tragedy is rooted in human sin. Other dimensions of it are accidents of nature.

Still, this tragedy is not the final story. The good news of Christianity is that the heart of the universe—the Sacred Whole—shares in our own incompleteness, like a man on a cross. God shares in tragedy, giving us permission to own our own suffering and brokenness. When we truly understand this point, we realize that it is all right not to be all right. We do not have to be morally perfect, or even whole, in order to be included in the divine Communion. The very heart of the universe accepts us—Christian or Buddhist or Jewish or Feminist Neo-Pagan—even in our incompleteness, even in our brokenness.

Of course, most of us come to accept our incompleteness, not by hearing preachers or teachers, but rather by being loved by other people—and graced by plants, animals, and the Earth—quite apart from our deserts. When we are truly loved by others, when we receive grace through them, they become vessels for an original grace at the very heart of the universe, which welcomes us into its warm embrace, quite apart from what we deserve or have earned. Not when we hear sermons or recite creeds, but rather when we are deeply loved by others, we realize that God, the Sacred Whole, is Christlike.

Our proper response to this realization is not to withdraw from the world, but rather to be more connected and creative, to help others awaken to the grace. It is to seek wholeness for ourselves and others, aware of the fact that the stakes are not heaven or hell, but rather quality of life in the here-and-now. We can partake of this quality, not absolutely but in meaningful degrees, in at least three ways. We can be rooted in the Earth, open to other religions, and centered in God.

To be rooted in the Earth is to enter into communion with other members of the life community, both human and nonhuman. Such communion can include a sense of place with respect to our local bioregions, reverence for life in relation to other animals, attunement to the inner wisdom of our own bodies, forgiving other people even when they have harmed us, and working to create local communities that are both socially just and ecologically respon-sible. All of these are ways in which we can dwell in solidarity with other living beings and affirm our kinship with them. They are ways in which we realize our creative capacities for interbeing.

To be open to other religions is also a way of being richly connected with other members of the Earth community, specifically with people of other faiths. We affirm our kinship with them by honoring the truths they have discovered, from which we can learn. To the degree that we are open, we enjoy a form of creativity and adventure; we spread our wings and fly. My emphasis in this book will be on ways in which Judaism, Buddhism, Hinduism, and Native American religions might teach us to be more rooted in the Earth.

To be centered in God is to be open to the Sacred Whole and sensitive to divine Interbeing. It is to be centered in a relational and healing Spirit by which the universe itself was called into being some fifteen billion years ago, and by which it is called still today. That Spirit is also within each of us as an inner light, an inwardly felt call, toward wisdom and compassion, relative to what is possible for us in the situation at hand. To trust in this Spirit is not to cling to it as if it were an object among objects, but rather to be open to its gentle promptings, cognizant that they are ever-new and ever-fresh. To the degree that we are open to these promptings, we are centered in the living Center of the universe, itself everywhere and nowhere. We are centered in God.

A God with Many Names

God is but one name for the living Center, among which there are others. Indeed, I have already used some others, such as Sacred Whole. I do this purposefully. For some, the word *God* suggests a remote entity who has no real connection with the world. Understood in this way, *God* names a reality that is omni-absent rather than omnipresent.

The idea of an absent God is not entirely wrong. There is wisdom in the idea of an absent God, at least insofar as it rightly reminds us that God is more, much more, than we experience or know. We need not and ought not reduce the living Center of reality to our experience of it. After all, other people may know something of the Center that we may never know, as might other animals, and plants, and the Earth itself. Wherever there is sentience of any sort, there is knowledge of God. Moreover, there is surely more, much more, to the mystery at the Heart of creation than any creature can ever know or feel. At some level the Center is indeed a mystery, absent to experience but present to faith. We do not comprehend it; it comprehends us.

Still, the wisdom of affirming divine absence—divine incomprehensibil-ity—becomes foolishness if it leads us to neglect the immanence of God, the palpable presence of the divine in the world. Sometimes the word *God* leads us to such neglect. It leads to the view, not simply that God is absent in some ways, but that God is omni-absent.

As an antidote to such neglect, we rightly use names other than *God* to name the divine. If we are Christian, we might use names such as *living Christ* and *cosmic Christ* and *Holy Spirit*. To my mind, these phrases often suggest palpable presence in a way *God* does not. So does the phrase *Holy Wisdom.* This is one of my own preferred names for the divine.

The phrase Holy Wisdom comes from Hebrew scripture, where it refers to the self-revelation of God in creation. In Proverbs this Wisdom is personified as female rather than male (Prv 1:20–33; 7; 8; 9:1–12; Sir 24:1–22; Wis 7:22—8:21, Jb 28:12–27). Often in this book I will follow this minority voice in scripture, speaking of God in female rather than male terms. Some scholars such as Rosemary Radford Ruether believe that in the Hebrew tradition Holy Wisdom is subordinated to the male God as a mere attribute (1983, 57); others, such as Elisabeth Schüssler Fiorenza, believe that Holy Wisdom is indeed the God of Hebrew scripture depicted as a goddess (1983, 133). In this book I follow the lead of Schüssler Fiorenza. She may or may not be right concerning what *Holy Wisdom* meant in the Hebrew tradition, but she does point in the direction of what it can and should mean for us. In our time, it seems to me, men and women alike need the presence of God in female as well as male terms, so as to realize the richness of divine nourishment. Female images are not subordinate to male images, they are equal to such images and, in our time, necessary correctives to one-sidedly masculine spiritualities.

Indeed, it seems to me that we now need *many* images of the Divine, some female and some male, some human-like and some organic, some familiar and some strange. We need to speak of God as Father and Mother, Sister and Brother, Bear and Coyote, Earth and Eros, Energy and Fire, Light and Dark, Compassion and Wisdom. Each of these images can be prisms through which divine Light is beheld. Even as we might be mono-theistic, we need also be poly-imagistic.

To be sure, multiple images will not come easy to many of us. So often those of us conditioned by Western monotheism feel a need to reify the divine Mystery, to fix it into certain "acceptable" images that are then distinguished from "unacceptable" images. This desire is understandable if it stems from a desire to free Holy Wisdom from distortion. The living Spirit is not, after all, a cosmic Rapist or a divine Racist. Such images tell us more about ourselves than about the Spirit. They lead us to arrogance rather than openness, violence rather than trust.

Still, there are many images that can be prisms through which the divine Mystery is understood, and to limit these images is to impoverish our access to the mystery. A multiplicity of images reminds us that different people need different images, depending on their circumstances; and that no image is absolute, because none fully captures the divine Mystery at the heart of the cosmos. More important than the images and names is the healing presence itself, as mediated through whatever images are appropriate to the situation at hand. Sometimes images and names must themselves be discarded, not to be replaced by abstract concepts, but rather to be replaced by a living silence, deep within our own hearts.

When we are centered in this silence, we rightly feel secure and safe. We feel rooted, not only in the rest of creation, but in Holy Wisdom herself. We approach our connections with the world from a position of strength rather than weakness, so that our connections themselves can be wise and compassionate rather than compulsive and clinging.

But Holy Wisdom does not simply beckon us into safety and security, into a sense of centeredness. She also calls us to fly and to be vulnerable. Openness to her healing powers makes us more secure, and yet also more adventurous, because we are free from fear. My conviction is that the more centered we are in the healing spirit of God, the more rooted we will be in the Earth itself, and the more open we will be to truth wherever we find it, including religions not our own.

Christian Paganism

I realize that my emphasis on openness runs counter to what some more conservative Christians believe—that fidelity to God requires a rejection of Earth as a source of spiritual strength and a denial of truth in other religions. They fear that openness to the Earth and to other religions will lapse into paganism. I propose, by contrast, that authentic faith in God results in openness to truth, goodness, and beauty wherever they are found, trustful that they are from God and of God. If this be paganism, then I confess to Christian paganism.

My guess, however, is that I am not alone. In an age of religious pluralism, many self-identified Christians feel drawn to learn from other religions. This is particularly true of the more liberal Christians. They realize that Holy Wisdom has revealed truths outside Christianity, even as she has revealed truths within Christianity. Moreover, in an age of massive industrial assault on the Earth, many feel drawn toward greater sensitivity to the Earth. They realize that Holy Wisdom has revealed great truths in the animals and plants, the stars and the galaxies, even as she has revealed truth in human traditions. They realize that the universe itself is a revelation of God.

The good news for such Christians, and for me, is that today there are many writers helping us to open ourselves to other religions and to the universe. There are many "theologies of dialogue" that show how Christians can learn from Buddhism, Hinduism, Judaism, Islam, and native traditions, even as members of these other traditions can learn from Christians.[6] And there are

---

6. One of the most thorough yet accessible introductions to "theologies of dialogue" is Paul Knitter's *No Other Name? A Critical Survey of Christian Attitudes Toward the World Religions* (1985). Readers interested in biblical foundations for interreligious dialogue will find *The Bible and People of Other Faiths* (1985) by Wesley Ariarajah quite helpful.

many "theologies of ecology" that show how Christians can be more responsible to the Earth and its needs, and more sensitive to the spiritual significance of mountains and rivers, plants and animals, bioregions and rain forests.[7] This is a rich time for people interested in dialogue and ecology.

At present, there are few if any books that try to pull the two themes of dialogue and ecology together. This is not my only aim, but it is part of my aim. I cannot separate my own appreciation of "other" religions from my appreciation of the "otherness" of plants and animals, soil and sun. Christian love, it seems to me, rightly delights in such otherness and seeks to "commune" with it, not by denying others their uniqueness, but by respecting and learning from their uniqueness.

Accordingly, I suggest that the Spirit by which the heavens themselves were called into existence, which was itself enfleshed in Jesus of Nazareth, now calls Christians to be more rooted in the Earth and open to other religions. I propose that such openness is our way of responding to the Spirit in our way and our time, as Jesus did in his way and his time. In so doing we extend the healing ministry of Christ.

Rootless Consumerism and Wingless Fundamentalism

In our time there are two obstacles to this extension, two obstacles to following Christ. They are rootless consumerism and wingless fundamentalism. These are the Scylla and Charybdis of our age. Scylla was the six-headed monster described in Greek legend, who lived on an island sailors would pass. Charybdis was a whirlpool in a nearby strait. Trying to avoid Scylla, sailors would drift into Charybdis; trying to avoid Charybdis, they would drift toward Scylla. Similarly, many in our time drift between rootless consumerism and wingless fundamentalism. The challenge is to find a way of living that avoids the Scylla of rootless consumerism, and the Charybdis of wingless fundamentalism, so as to sail through the waters of life toward that wholeness to which the Spirit calls us.

Rootless Consumerism

We learn about rootless consumerism through advertisements. In none too subtle fashion we are told that, if we buy this soap or that deodorant, this beer or that car, everything will be all right with our lives. We will become successful, physically attractive, or both. Success and physical attractiveness are the twin gods of consumer culture.

But what, after all, is success? If we are Christian, we might like to think that success lies in being Christlike. We might like to think that the successful

---

7. For a representative sampling of such theologies, including third-world Christian points of view, see Birch et al. (1990a).

person is one who, like Christ, helps heal broken lives, knows how to forgive, bears crosses with courage, and finds God within and without. But secular culture does not define success this way. From its vantage point, the successful person is one who makes a great deal of money, enjoys the envy of others, and wields control over others. Success means fame, fortune, and power.

Attractiveness, too, is defined in an unchristian way. If we are Christian, we might like to define attractiveness as having the kind of magnetism that Jesus had: a drawing power that comes from humility, compassion for the marginalized of society, and a willingness to speak the truth regardless of the cost. But rootless consumerism does not define attractiveness this way. From its vantage point, the attractive person is one who is young and sexy or old but distinguished. Attractiveness means outer not inner beauty.

Most of us already know that worldly success and physical attractiveness do not yield lasting happiness; they are too ephemeral and too ego-dependent. On this we are in agreement with almost all the world religions, which suggest that we best sink our roots not in success and attractiveness, but rather in deeper things: God, Brahman, the Tao, Nirvana, and the teachings and practices that lead to them. In this sense the great world religions offer roots.

And in this sense consumer culture is itself rootless. It is not shaped by the teachings and practices of the world's spiritual heritages, but rather by the teaching and practices of the marketplace. It is spiritually bankrupt, because it invites no rootedness in the depths that make life worth living. Inasmuch as we allow ourselves to be absorbed in the concerns of consumerist culture, we ourselves become rootless: floating on the surface of life's ocean, never realizing our own potential for spiritual depth or connections with others.

The Pain of Lacking Roots

The problem with rootless consumerism is not simply that it lacks depth, but also that it fails to provide moorings amid life's pain. I witnessed this problem once in the life of a young student whom I will call Bill.[8] Popular among his classmates, he was reared in a middle-class suburb in the Midwest. His parents were business professionals who had little time or interest in organized religion. Both had been raised as Christians, but both had rejected Christianity and anything having to do with "religion" as adults. They themselves had been oppressed by the confines of fundamentalist upbringings. As adults, the purpose of life for them was making money and having fun with the family.

Following in their footsteps, Bill decided to be a business major in college. His aim was to be "successful" like his parents: to have a large home, a fine car, a beautiful family, and lots of opportunities for recreation. His first three

---

8. I have modified several of the circumstances of "Bill's" life in order to protect his privacy. Over the years, I have known many students like him. They have grown up without any form of religion in their lives, and they have suffered the consequences of being spiritually ill-equipped for life's hardships.

years of college were spent partying and trying to acquire the skills that would enable him to get a high-paying job as quickly as possible after graduation. He was taking my course not because he wanted to learn about the world religions, but because the course fulfilled a requirement.

Midway in the semester, tragedy struck. Bill's parents were killed in an automobile accident. Like any twenty year old, he was devastated. He sought me out to explain that he might not be able to concentrate very well during the semester. As we talked, however, I realized that he wanted and needed to talk at a deeper level, so as to work through his feelings. We agreed to meet on a weekly basis.

Strangely, Bill began to concentrate more rather than less on his studies in my course. He began to look at the world religions, not as subjects to master in order to pass tests, but as potential resources for dealing with grief. Amid much pain, he was beginning to discover the divine Spirit, the whole-making process, within his own life. He was beginning to realize that he had a deeper self.

For the most part I did not talk to Bill during our sessions. I just listened. He would take each religion we studied and analyze its helpfulness in the grieving process. This was the first time I had looked at the world religions through the eyes of a griever.

It didn't take long for me to realize that Bill was least attracted to Christianity. He was comforted by its notion of a suffering God, because he liked to think that God suffered with his parents in the horror of the accident and that God suffered with him in his grief. Still, compared to most other religions, Christianity seemed much too exclusivistic to him, too narrow in its insistence that salvation is through Christ alone. After all, his parents had recently died, and neither believed in Jesus Christ at the moment of death. Were they doomed? Bill found the idea spiritually horrifying, and he found this dimension of Christian thought unpalatable. "Christianity doesn't offer me much in my grief."

Thus we found ourselves focusing more on other religions in our discussions. It came as a surprise to me that, after numerous discussions in which Bill had criticized Christian exclusivism in the process of opening himself to other religions, he complained that he wished his parents had taken him to church and to Sunday school as a child. "Why?" I asked. "Don't you think the exclusivism would have bothered you then, as it does now?"

His answer was telling. "Maybe so," he said, "but I still wish they had taken me to church and Sunday school. All my life I have wished I had a foundation, *something* to build upon, even if it's one I had to get rid of later."

I meet many people like Bill—unable to cope with life's tragedies, because they were not given spiritual roots as children. Still, Bill could not accept the confines of a Christianity that clings to traditional exclusivism. He sought a Christianity that had the freedom to repent of features of its past and fly in new directions. Implicitly, he bore witness to the second of the two ills of our time: wingless fundamentalism.

Wingless Fundamentalism

In a Christian setting, wingless fundamentalism is not limited to various forms of Protestant Christianity that stress the inerrancy of scripture, that is, to Protestant fundamentalism. Rather, it includes any form of Christianity that reacts to the rootlessness of secular culture by overemphasizing a return to traditional roots, to "that old time religion," and that, in doing so, ends up absolutizing either the Bible, or the traditional creeds, or a specific set of teachings, or some combination thereof. There are many wingless forms of Christianity today: Episcopalian as well as Southern Baptist, Unitarian as well as Methodist, Catholic as well as Lutheran. They have in common a backward-looking approach to the world.

As the term *wingless* suggests, wingless fundamentalism is enslaved to, rather than nourished by, the past. The roots of this enslavement lie in idolatry: an identification of some feature of the Christian past—the biblical heritage, the creeds, a set of practices—with the living God. In effect, such idolatry confines the Christian pilgrimage to a repetition and reapplication of "what has been," itself understood as "God's will." Idolatry of this sort forecloses any fresh promptings from the Holy Spirit and any capacity to repent of deep-seated problems within the heritage itself, such as exclusivism or sexism or homophobia or, as environmentalists and animal rights advocates rightly emphasize, anthropocentrism. Wingless Christianity in this broad sense offers reified and inflexible roots at the expense of wings.

To be sure, when juxtaposed with the superficialities of consumer culture, there is something right about wingless fundamentalism. It offers people roots in a rootless age, and this is good. The problem, however, is that the roots are inflexible rather than flexible. They fail to resemble the healthy roots of trees.

After all, the roots of healthy trees are not rigid and fixed. Rather they are flexible and mobile. They grow in the soil, extending in directions where richer pockets of water and minerals may occur. The directions in which they grow are partly stimulated by signals they receive from the pockets themselves and partly by their own capacity to grow.

A well-rooted Christianity does the same. It is rooted in the Christian heritage, but its roots are adventurous rather than inflexible. It conserves the Christian past, but in a creative rather than idolatrous way. Its exemplars are themselves "creative conservatives."

Creative conservatives move about within the heritage itself, shifting their roots as they go, in order to find the deepest pockets of faith, hope, and love, and so as to find the kind of nourishment that gives them wings to fly. They are willing to recognize that some pockets, once thought nourishing, were not as healthy as they imagined. Thus, even as they draw nourishment from the heritage, they can also criticize it. Ultimately their faith is not in the heritage, but rather in the living God. This kind of faith gives them wings.

What is needed in our time, then, is a way of understanding the Christian life that creatively conserves the best of the past, but is also open to change and freedom. Only then will people like Bill and his parents find Christianity itself an attractive life option. My aim in this book is to envision that option, with a focus on its implications for dialogue and ecology. I want to envision Christianity as a way of living with both roots and wings.

A Way of Living

A way of living is not just a way of thinking, or of feeling, or of acting. Rather it is all three. The following diagram illustrates the point and offers an overview of my project.

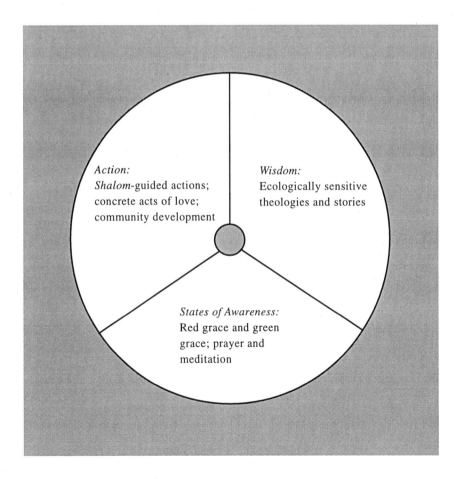

The circle represents a human life—yours or mine—and the sections within the circle represent the three dimensions of our lives: our wisdom, our states of awareness, and our actions. The shaded areas represent God, the divine

Reality, who is an indwelling Spirit within our own lives, and within each and every life on the planet, and also the ultimate context of our lives. To say that God is within us is to say that God is the living Christ, who beckons us toward wholeness and service to others. To say that God is the ultimate context of our lives is to say that God is the place, the home, the reservoir of empathy, in which the universe unfolds. To quote Paul in Acts, we "live and move and have our being" in God (17:28).

The aim of the Christian life, I submit, is to have the three dimensions of our lives—our wisdom, our states of awareness, and our actions—nourished and freed by the Spirit of God, that is, by the living Christ. Inasmuch as they are nourished and freed by divine Love, we participate in what Jesus called the kingdom of God, which is that state of affairs in which the will of God is realized "on Earth as it is in heaven."

As the diagram suggests, our wisdom includes the theologies and philosophies we hold to be true, and also the stories or narratives that shape our imaginations. For example, the beliefs we have about God and Christ are part of our understanding, as well as the biblical stories that shape our imagination. The Christianity with roots and wings that I recommend in this book will emphasize forms of theology and stories that recognize the Earth itself as a primary context for Christian self-understanding, and that see God as a Holy Spirit both within and beyond the Earth community. It will emphasize ecologically sensitive or creation-centered forms of theology and story.

Our states of awareness include our hopes and fears, our loves and hates, and also our deeper modes of consciousness, including prayerful and meditative states. Though these sensibilities are often shaped by, and connected to thoughts and actions, they also have a degree of independence. We can love God with our hearts, even when we do not believe in God with our minds. The Christianity with roots and wings that I recommend in this book will emphasize four kinds of feelings. First are those that are honest to our own inner suffering, our sinfulness, and our brokenness, and that are aware of God's love for us amid, not apart from, such brokenness. These are feelings of what I call "red grace," because they emerge as we awaken to the unconditional love of God as revealed, among other places, in Christ on the cross. The second are feelings of healing and wholeness that occur through the recovery of rich bonds with people, animals, and the Earth. These are feelings of what I call "green grace." The third are those that emerge in various forms of meditation, such as Buddhist mindfulness in which we are "present to the present" in the immediacy of the here-and-now. And fourth are those that emerge in silent and verbal prayer, in which we commune with God in the depths of our hearts. Often these four types of feelings overlap. All are important to an ecologically wise and inwardly rich Christian life.

Our action or behavior includes not only the things we do with our bodies, but also our jobs and relationships, our political involvements, and our language. Our actions are everything we do, in a direct way, to influence others, for good or ill. The Christianity with roots and wings that I recommend in this book will focus on actions that are oriented toward peace with other people, with animals, and with the Earth. I call this peace "green peace," or *shalom*. Its primary aim is not simply to reduce violence and suffering in the world, but to help build vibrant local communities that are socially just, ecologically sustainable, and spiritually satisfying. Thus the active side of the Christian life involves *shalom*-guided action, as embodied in concrete acts of love, aimed at community development.

Structure of Book

The book consists of ten chapters, divided into two parts, plus a Conclusion. Part 1, "Roots in the Earth," comprises Chapters 1 through 6. Chapter 1 develops the theme of roots and wings more explicitly, identifying "healthy soils" and "healing skies" to which we might turn for nourishment in an ecological and pluralistic age. It introduces the basic themes of the rest of the book. Chapter 2 turns to the affective dimension of the Christian life, to the experiences of "red grace" and "green grace" that can inform our innermost depths. Chapter 3 shifts to the active dimension of the Christian life, emphasizing *shalom*-guided action. Chapters 4, 5, and 6 focus on the intellectual dimension of the Christian life, emphasizing creation-centered theologies and a creation-centered reading of biblical stories. Overall, these six chapters accent the importance of the Earth as a context for religious self-understanding and responsible social action.

Part 2, "Adventures in Dialogue," comprises Chapters 7 through 10. Chapter 7 offers an overview of the world religions and proposes one way that Christians can approach such religions. Chapter 8 offers distinctive insights that can be gained by a Christian dialogue with Judaism and Buddhism. Chapter 9 offers insights from Hinduism. And Chapter 10 turns to lessons from Native American religious traditions.[9] Overall, my aim in Part 2 is to show how certain dimensions of selected religions can help Christians be more rooted in the Earth, accepting of diversity, and responsible to local communities.

The Conclusion weaves major themes of the book into a whole, offering final reflections on prayer, community, and resurrection. My proposal is that without a daily practice of prayer and meditation of one sort or another, and without participation in a local community that is both nourishing and spiritually honest, the ideas of this book remain abstract. While community and

---

9. Had I time and talent, I would have treated many other traditions. There is much Christians can learn from other indigenous religions, and from Islam, Confucianism, Taoism, and Shinto. For readers interested in the entire spectrum of religions, as each might contribute both to Christian spirituality and a healthy planet, I recommend *Worldview and Ecology* (1993) by Mary Evelyn Tucker and John Grim. Traditions excluded in this book are included in it.

daily practice are mentioned at the end, they could have as well, and perhaps better, been thematized at the beginning. They form the most practical advice I have to offer, both to myself and to others.

I wrote the book as if it would be read front to back. In successive chapters I try to build upon points made earlier. Still, I do not always read books in this way, and I doubt that you, the reader, do either. I encourage you to read chapters in a freer way if you are so inclined. Readers primarily interested in interreligious dialogue may wish to begin with Chapters 7 through 10 and then turn to other chapters as they see fit. Those primarily interested in social action may wish to turn directly to Chapter 3 and then turn to other chapters as they are inclined. Those most concerned with questions concerning cosmology and God, or with relations between "the Christian story" and the ideas of this book, may wish to begin with Chapters 4 through 6. And those primarily interested in spirituality and prayer may wish to begin with Chapters 2, 8, and the Conclusion.

Throughout the book I offer anecdotes from the lives of students and people I know. In some instances the stories, such as that of "Bill" already shared in this Introduction, are quite personal. For this reason, I have often modified specific circumstances or created composites in order to protect confidentiality. In cases where I have not, I have received prior approval to share the stories. Always I have tried to be faithful to the fundamental concerns and desires of the people and circumstances whose stories I share. I have wanted to speak as they would speak, because their voices are so important, without violating their integrity.

One final word. Entire books can and should be written on each of the subjects I address. My aim here is not to say everything about each of the topics that needs to be said, but rather to indicate how the various topics might be included in the larger purview of a Christianity with roots and wings. I am writing for Christians or for persons interested in Christianity who want to be rooted in the Earth, open to other religions, and faithful to God. I am writing for people who want roots and wings.

Part I

ROOTS IN THE EARTH

Chapter 1

Healthy Soils and Healing Skies

Finding Our Way beyond Consumerism and Fundamentalism

Five days a week I teach world religions and Christian theology to undergraduates at a small, church-related, liberal arts college in Arkansas. Several years ago, while teaching a course on Judaism, I first heard the metaphor of roots and wings. I invited a visitor from Little Rock—Rabbi Eugene Levy from Temple B'Nai Israel—to speak to my class, and somehow, for reasons now forgotten, my class asked him a question concerning family life in Judaism. In the context of responding, he gave me the overall theme for this book.

"As you bring up your children," he said, "you want them to have roots and wings. You want them to feel grounded and secure, to feel connected with things that count. But you also want them to think new thoughts and feel new feelings, to be able to fly in new directions."

"And what if they fly away?" I asked him later, half joking and half serious. My wife and I were parents trying to raise two sons, both of whom were finding their wings.

"You've got to take that risk," he said. "They may even use their wings to abandon the roots you've given them. But you've got to give them wings anyway. Without them they won't grow; they'll suffocate. So give them wings to fly and roots to be nourished by. That's what parents are for."

And that is what Christianity is for, too, I thought to myself. A primary purpose of Christianity is, or should be, to help people become richly connected with things that count and to help them think new thoughts and feel new feelings. It should help make us connected and creative, neither to the exclusion of the other.

Rabbi Levy later explained to me that he did not invent the metaphor of roots and wings. He got it from a friend, who got it from a friend, who got it from a friend. I have since learned that the metaphor is widespread. I hope that it has not become too hackneyed by the time you read this book. Still, it

23

strikes me as no accident that I would first hear the metaphor from a Jew. Memory and imagination: these seem to be the substance of Judaism. Remembering the revelation at Sinai, Jews imagine a Messianic Age in the future, in which that revelation will be fulfilled. My hope is that Christians also can be nourished by the past and open to the future. No less than Jews, we Christians need roots and wings.

When Rabbi Levy used the word *roots*, of course, he meant "being rooted in the wisdom of a human tradition," in his case Judaism. He was encouraging the Christian students in my class to be rooted in their tradition, as he was in his. I think he was right to do so. Unless we are rooted in the wisdom of a human tradition—Jewish, Christian, or otherwise—we lack spiritual moorings. As the Buddha put it, we wander about from this guru to that, this teaching to that, never living with resolve, never finding the depth for which our hearts yearn (Smith 1991, 104). To arrive at even a modest degree of spiritual depth, we must follow a path.

Still, I want to expand the rabbi's meaning. In this book I will emphasize being rooted, not only in the wisdom of human traditions, but also in the silence of God as discovered in prayer and meditation, and in the wisdom of the Earth as discovered in plants and animals, sea and soil. I want to suggest that animals and plants, silence and inwardness, too, can be spiritual guides. My aim is to present a Christianity as a Way with multiple roots and freedom-loving wings.

Perhaps not all Christians need this kind of Christianity. I trust that the Spirit calls Christians to different forms of Christian life, relative to background, temperament, and need. Some Christians are called to more conservative forms of Christian life than that presented in this book, and some to more liberal. Like an ecosystem, Christianity needs diversity to flourish. It is good that the Spirit is herself ecological. It is good that she loves differences.

Indeed, I trust that the Spirit calls many people not to be Christian at all, but rather to be good Jews, or good Muslims, or good Hindus, or good free spirits. As Rabbi Levy spoke in my class, I felt the presence of God in him. In a very different way I have felt that same presence in a warm Zen Master from Kyoto, Japan; a courageous Muslim woman from Louisville, Kentucky; and a kindly Hindu from Little Rock, Arkansas. I have sensed the presence of God's spirit in many people who follow paths other than Christianity, and I am grateful for their witness. In speaking of Christianity as a Way with roots and wings, I do not mean to imply that it is the Way for all people. In the house of God's Spirit, there are many mansions. While all may be called to be Christlike, each in his or her way, not all are called to be Christian.

Still, in this book I speak to Christians, and I hope to invite them—us—to be deeply rooted and adventurously creative, in our path. In my capacity as a college teacher, I sense the need for a Christianity with roots and wings among my students.

Many of my students take courses in world religions because they have a very specific question in mind: How can I live my life? They turn to the world religions not simply for information but for guidance. For many people in the world, of course, the question is irrelevant, because the matter is decided by parents or culture or religion. This has been the way of traditional cultures. In the United States, however, most students are fully aware that there are many ways of living from which they can choose, religious and otherwise. Their problem is not too little choice, but rather too much choice. Amid their confusion, two choices present themselves with overwhelming power: the way of rootless consumerism and that of wingless fundamentalism.

Rootless consumerism is the way of advertising and television, big business and affluence. It tells them that they are "saved" by being as "successful" as they can possibly be, chiefly through the acquisition of fame, fortune, and power; and by being as "attractive" as they can possibly be, chiefly through the acquisition of perfect bodies and eternal youth. In the way of rootless consumerism, all things—even people, animals, and plants—are approached as commodities, as items to be bought and sold in the marketplace. The purpose of life is to get rich, buy toys, and die. Salvation comes through shopping alone.

By contrast, wingless fundamentalism is the way of close-minded and close-hearted religion. It has many versions: Christian, Jewish, Muslim, Buddhist, and Hindu. In its Christian version, particularly on college campuses, wingless fundamentalism has a decidedly Protestant, evangelical cast. It tells students that they are "saved" by accepting Christ as personal lord and savior; by following the Bible as an inerrant authority; by repressing honest doubt in obedience to "the Word"; by rejecting the teachings of other religions, because those teachings are of the devil; and by denying the intrinsic value of the Earth and its creatures, because a recognition of that value borders on "paganism." According to Christian fundamentalism, the purpose of life is to accept Jesus and get saved. Salvation comes, not through good works or even a good heart, but by "believing in Christ" and his atoning death on the cross.

Between consumerism and fundamentalism, I will take fundamentalism. I have known more than a few students whose lives have been made whole through a personal relationship with Jesus Christ. I have seen them come off drugs, escape from depression, find security, and feel grounded. I trust that Christ is present in such life journeys. I trust that God's Spirit is influential in their lives, through the medium of the Jesus who lives in their hearts. When they say that they are "saved by Jesus," I believe them.

Still, I worry about the suppression of honest doubt, the suppression of the truths of their own experience, the rejection of other religions, the rejection of the Earth. I fear that in this kind of fundamentalism, negative attitudes are fostered that lead to repression of other peoples, of animals, and the Earth. I know that in the past and in the present, much violence has issued from such attitudes. For students such as these, I hope for growth beyond fundamentalism, but not beyond Jesus.

In any event, my more fundamentalist students do not exhaust the spectrum. I also meet many students who want to be Christian, but who are looking for an alternative to fundamentalism. They want to follow Christ, but they do not want to reject their hearts and imaginations, or their love of plants and animals, or their appreciation of other peoples, in the process. They hope that being Christian can make them more open, not more closed, to the world. Consider the following example.

"Emma" was a bright young business major taking my course in Christian ethics. In class we had been reading a book called *Following Christ in a Consumer Society* by John Kavanaugh (1991). In powerful terms, Kavanaugh criticized the basic values of consumer culture, such as competition and greed and self-indulgence, showing how these values are hostile to a genuine Christianity. If we truly follow Christ, said Kavanaugh, we will live lives of voluntary and joyful simplicity in service to the poor, not acquisitive and frenetic self-indulgence in service to ourselves.

Kavanaugh's claims especially troubled some of my business majors. For one reason or another, they had come to believe that self-indulgence was good not evil. If we love ourselves enough, they told themselves, if we act in our own consumer-motivated interests, society as a whole will be improved, and everyone will be happy. It is our duty, to ourselves and to the market, to be self-centered and ego-based.

Struck by the contrast between what she was hearing from her friends, and what she was reading in Kavanaugh, Emma approached me and said:

> One of my best friends—another business major—told me that I ought to be a "greedy capitalist pig." He said that I am, and ought to be, as selfish as I can possibly be, because being selfish is what makes capitalism effective. When we look out for number one, he said, everybody benefits. Our selfishness is what makes the market work.

I was troubled but not surprised to hear this account of her conversation. I knew that her friend was mirroring the teachings of economic theory. In many respects, neo-classical economic theory teaches that salvation comes by selfishness, by sin, alone. It makes a virtue of our worst inclinations and a vice of our best.

I tried to tell Emma that there was, and is, hope for capitalism. I think that we can and should move toward a free-enterprise system that is community-based rather than profit-obsessed, relational rather than individualistic, democratic rather than monopolistic. I look for a revised capitalism, transformed by a people who have moved beyond a worship of consumer goods and consumer values to a sense of the common good.

But Emma did not want to hear the views of a religion professor on capitalism. Her eyes glazed over as I gave my brief speech on a revised free-enterprise system. Her concerns were spiritual not economic. She wanted me to hear the cry of her heart, and to respond to that cry. Her words went something like this:

I think my friend was wrong. If that's what my business textbooks teach, then I don't believe them. I see my parents living for themselves and they're miserable. I see my father looking out for number one, and he's as lonely as anyone I know. I see my mother dealing with her failed marriage by shopping, and she's a basket case. I don't want to live like them. I want joy and community, not affluence. I want to be a Christian.

But I don't know where to turn. I'd like to give my life to what Christians call God, but I don't quite know where to find him, or even if "he's" a "he." My conservative friends talk as if God were a policeman in the sky, who condemns everyone to hell unless they are Christian. I can't accept this, because some of my best friends are Jewish and Muslim and postchristian feminists. My liberal friends talk as if God were nonexistent. I can't accept this either, because I do believe in God, or at least in something more than myself. Where can I turn for help? I'm desperate.

In short, she wanted neither wingless fundamentalism nor rootless consumerism. She wanted a Christianity with roots and wings.

I was at a loss for words. As a Christian, I felt that she was looking in the right direction in turning to God. I thought that, for her, Jesus could indeed be a window to the Divine. And yet I also knew that, for her, "God" needed to be more than a focal point in the imagination, more than a policeman, or even a father, in the sky. She wanted a God within her and around her who could be experienced in connections with plants and animals, friends and loved ones. She wanted a Christianity that would require of her a letting go of consumerist values, but also a joyful openness to truth wherever it might be found, including other religions and the Earth. Could I recommend such a God? Could I depict such a Christianity?

This book is that recommendation and depiction. I have needed to answer Emma, and many others, for some years. Accordingly, in the pages of the chapter that follows, I offer a belated response to her forthright question: "Where can I turn for help?" In the process I introduce various themes that are amplified in the remainder of the book. My aim is to identify "healthy soils" and "healing skies" to which prospective Christians such as Emma, and many others besides, might turn in order to find a way between consumerism and fundamentalism. I offer the advice not only to her but also to myself. Most of what I say has come from spiritual guides much wiser than I—a few of whom happen to be trees.

Healthy Soils

Trees can be good teachers. Just as they sink their roots into nourishing soils in order to grow and withstand storms, so most of us need to do the same. If we have food in our stomachs, we need to grow in wisdom and compassion rather than physical size. And if we have shelter to protect us, we may need strength to withstand inner storms, such as fear and temptation, rather than outer storms, such as hail and snow. Still, we need to be anchored and nourished if we are to be of service to the world. Like trees, we need roots to live by.

We also need healthy soils. At one time or another, many of us in consumer societies become planted in unhealthy soils. We become absorbed in dishonest relationships, in alcohol or other substances, in self-centered careers, in mean-spirited forms of religion, in resentments and jealousies, in inflexible plans for the future, in obsessions with perfection, in our own egos. Such soils do not provide the nourishment that we need to become whole or to help others. When we give our lives to them, they become gods who disappoint us and who separate us from a world in need. What we need are deep roots in nourishing soils that help us become whole and helpful. We find ourselves looking for sacred ground. Where can we turn?

Meaningful Relations with Other People

One place we can turn, and perhaps foremost for many of us, is to other people. More specifically, we can be rooted in meaningful relations with other people, such that they are recipients of our care and respect. In learning to love them, our lives are themselves graced. We come to know what Mother Teresa often calls "the joy of loving."

The phrase "joy of loving" is instructive because it reminds us that love in its many expressions does lead to joy. To the degree that we are free of self-preoccupation and rooted in the joy of loving, we are free from anxiety. This does not mean that at all times we should deny ourselves in service to others. Particularly for those who have been taught to love others at the expense of self-love, or who have been conditioned to hate themselves because of their skin color or gender or sexual orientation or ethnic identity, a love of self is important. We need to love ourselves in order to love others. Still, the joy of loving does not end with a sense of positive self-regard. It ends when we reach out to others, realizing that they count, as we do, in the cosmic scheme of things, and that we are connected with them, and they to us, at levels too deep for words.

We hope that many to whom we reach out will love us in return. They will be our friends and family, our co-workers and soul-mates. We will find God in the quiet listening of good friends who hear us and who care enough about us to challenge us when we are wrong; in family members who are kind enough to sacrifice time and energy for our own well-being and who love us beyond our deserts; in lovers with whom we enjoy moments of trust and intimacy and forgiveness. Relationships of friendship and intimacy are essential to the healthy spiritual life, and they are too often neglected in spiritual traditions that emphasize "going it alone" or "finding God all by yourself."

Still, intimacy is not itself a precondition for knowing the joy of loving. We can meet God not only in people who reciprocate our love, but also in people who cannot, or will not, reciprocate that love. Three examples are in order.

First, as the remarkable example of Mother Teresa so well illustrates, and as many other less visible examples also make clear, we can know the joy of loving by serving the needy. Their numbers are legion, and they include the hungry and forgotten, the naked and abandoned, the raped and abused, the lonely and vulnerable. That they are themselves sacred ground is made clear in a story told by the Buddhist writer Joanna Macy.

Macy tells the story of a nurse whom she admired for her strength and devotion in keeping long hours in a children's ward. When she asked the nurse how she found the strength to keep caring, the nurse pointed to the children in the rows of cots and cribs. "It's not my strength, you know. I get it from them. They give me what I need to keep going." Sometimes we are "acted through" by others whom we serve, filled with their energies. We do not love them because they energize us; rather, we love them because they have value in their own right. Still, we often discover that they have more to give us than we have to give them. They, and our relations to them, become sacred soil by which our lives are graced (1991, 24–25).

In addition to the needy, we can meet God in those who are hated and despised by the rest of society. Of course, they too are needy, so they are not really different from those named above. They need our affirmation that they, no less than we, are people who matter, people who count. Recall Jesus' affection for the despised of his day: the tax collectors and harlots and lepers. We too can feel affection for the despised of our society: criminals and street people, for example, or, as targeted by reactionary groups, homosexuals and illegal aliens. In many instances our affection will be quite genuine; we will recognize good features in them which society does not recognize. But even if we cannot manage to like them, as may be the case with hardened criminals, we can nevertheless see Christ in them, for he too was among the neglected and despised at the end of his life. The spiritual writer Kenneth Leech puts it this way: "The ability to see Christ, to see the image and likeness of God, in the faces of the most despised and neglected of humankind is a diagnostic test of true spirituality" (1992, 153).

Third, we can experience the joy of loving in relation to those who have harmed us. Of course, this is not at all easy. Many of us go through life filled with resentment at having been harmed in one way or another. We feel that our resentment is honest and justified. We *like* being resentful. Still, as most of us know, resentment can burn inwardly and block our own capacities for creative connectedness with others, including those we resent. We can burn with anger. The healing balm for this anger is forgiveness. When we realize that we ourselves are sinners, and that Holy Wisdom loves even us, we realize that our "enemies" and we are on the very same level in the divine scheme of things. We come to love them, because we love the One who loves them. We experience God through them.

In short, we can find sacred ground in rich relations not only with friends and family, but also with the needy, with the neglected and despised, and with our own "enemies," whoever they might be. As we sink our roots into relationships with such people, our motives need to be pure. If we love our enemies because it gives us a sense of superiority over them, our motives are not pure; if we care for the needy because it makes us feel "better" than others, our motives are not pure. Other people are healthy soil in which we sink our roots *only* if we respect them as equals, and only if we realize that they are more, much more, than their relationships to us. *If* we give them the space to be themselves, and *if* we honor them as people with integrity of their own, then our connections with them can be grace-filled. For us they become sacred soil. Through them we experience the joy of loving, and through this joy we experience God.

Wisdom Traditions

A second healthy soil to which we can turn in our search for sacred ground is the wisdom of world religions. When we consider the global context of our lives, we realize that the religions from which we can choose are manifold. They include the classical religions, such as Hinduism, Buddhism, Confucianism, Taoism, Judaism, Christianity, Islam, and Bahai, but also the more ancient indigenous traditions, such as African and Asian and Native American religions. We can speak of them as wisdom traditions because they embody partial but time-tested truths, discovered through trial and error, by seekers from the past. When we turn to these traditions, we gain from the experiences of our ancestors.

Few if any of us can learn in any real way from all the traditions. In a given lifetime we can learn from but one or two in a deep way, merely scratching the surfaces of the others. In my own case, I have learned primarily from Christianity, but secondarily from Buddhism. In terms of the tree metaphor, my primary roots are in the soil of the Christian past, but I have secondary roots in the soil of Buddhism.

More specifically, I am rooted in Protestant Christianity. I grew up in the United Methodist Church and am active both in a United Methodist congregation and an Episcopal congregation. I speak of myself as a "Methopalian." My local congregations mean much to me; they give me a sense of community I would otherwise lack. In the context of both I have imbibed, and continue to imbibe, some of the best of the Christian heritage.

Actually, there are five theological traditions that shape this book, all of which I absorbed from family and church. They are:

1. The covenantal tradition, which stresses God as one who enters into covenant with people but also the whole of creation, and which stresses that humans have responsibilities to live up to their side of the covenant.

2. The sacramental tradition, which stresses that the very God who enters into covenant is also immanent within creation itself, revealed in the very material—the plants and animals, the soil and sun—of nature.

3. The peacemaking tradition, which stresses that the Christian life is a life of discipleship to Christ, and which presents the Way of Christ as a Way of nonviolent social activism.

4. The cosmological tradition, exemplified by the cosmic Christologies of the New Testament and also by the early theologian Irenaeus, which sees Christianity in the larger context of the history of creation, and which sees the very purpose of Christianity as that of adding to the history of creation in ways that benefit creation itself.

5. The apophatic mystical traditions—exemplified by John of the Cross, Meister Eckhart, and the author of *The Cloud of Unknowing*—which emphasize that God is found not only in the sounds of creation and the sacraments of community, but also in wordless silence, interior freedom, and a letting go of words and concepts, including concepts of God.

Still, I am also influenced by Buddhism. I was the English teacher for a Zen Buddhist monk from Japan while a seminarian and graduate student in Claremont, California; and his life and wisdom influence me to this day. Even as I sit at the foot of the cross, I also sit on the *zafu*, a Zen meditation cushion.[1] Both shape my life.

Though the particularities of my own spiritual path are unique, my general situation is not. For many people today, including most of my students in the southern state of Arkansas, the time is passing when Christians learn only from Christianity. The world has become a global village, and we find ourselves learning about other religions even as we practice our own. As we learn *about* these religions, we also learn *from* them. Their soils begin to nourish our own souls. We become Christians-influenced-by-Buddhism or Christians-influenced-by-native-traditions or Christians-influenced-by-Judaism.

There is nothing new in this. Even the biblical authors were influenced by alien cultures, often in very helpful ways. The authors of Genesis were Hebrews-influenced-by-Mesopotamian-traditions and the author of the gospel of John was a Christian-influenced-by-Greek-ways-of-thinking. If the Bible is a unity, it is a syncretistic unity. Its various documents gather insights from, and show the influences of, many world traditions: Hellenistic, Roman, Greek, Jewish, Persian, Syrian, and Egyptian.

Later Christian theologians in the West were no less indebted to other ways. Augustine, for example, was a Christian-influenced-by-Plato, and Aquinas was a Christian-influenced-by-Aristotle. Today many Christians in Asia, Af-

---

1. The saying "even as I sit at the foot of the cross, I also sit on the *zafu*" comes from Joanna Macy in private conversation. She was describing her own practice. See Chapter 2 and also Section 1 of the Conclusion for the context.

rica, and Latin America are exercising the same kind of creativity. Native American Christians are combining biblical truths with Native American wisdom; African Christians are combining the truth of Jesus with the wisdom of their ancestors; Asian Christians are combining the truths of Moses with the wisdom of the Tao. All things considered, it is a sign of religious health to be open to truths wherever they are found, trustful that they are of Holy Wisdom and from Holy Wisdom. Such openness can be part of the "wing" dimension of the Christian life.

Of course, we must be careful where we sink our roots. The wisdom traditions all have their failings, Christianity included. If they are inspired by God, they are not completely inspired. For example, many of the classical religions are deeply patriarchal at the expense of including the vision of women, and some have deep tendencies toward violence and intolerance. The failures of religions lie not only in misapplication of teachings but sometimes in teachings themselves. The wisdom of a religion is always partial and often impure. Even as we learn from religions, we ought not absolutize them. We should remember that the living Spirit is always more than, and not limited by, the religious traditions of the world. Somehow, in turning to these traditions, we must separate the wheat from the chaff, the good soil from the bad, cognizant of the fact that our choices are themselves fallible.

Still, the separating process is worth it, for there is indeed wisdom to glean from the best of the past. If we have roots in Christianity, we can draw from the teachings of Jesus, the lives of saints, the wisdom of the mystics, and the courage of martyrs. We can be deepened through worship and prayer and the sacraments, through a study of scripture and an immersion in action aimed to serve the poor. We can be enriched by the teachings of the great theologians: by Origen and Augustine, Bonaventure and Aquinas, Luther and Calvin, Wesley and Kierkegaard. And we can be enriched by the teachings of contemporary Christian theologians as well, many of whom are now women rather than men, and many of whom come from the Third World rather than the First. Once we choose to learn from Christianity, there is much from which to learn, even amid its fallibilities.

At best this learning can occur in the context of a local congregation with which we are involved. Indeed, if we are fortunate enough to find such a community, we might even experience the healing balm of the gospel itself: wholeness through grace. This grace can help us let go of the idea that our worth is dependent on our performance and our achievements. As we enjoy rich relations with other Christians in the context of a Christian community, we begin to understand what it means to be loved by God amid, not apart from, our finitude. We begin to realize that we, and all others besides, are embraced by the very Heart of the universe, by God, in deep compassion and infinite tenderness. We discover the very heart of Christianity.

This, of course, is an ideal. Many today are understandably frustrated because they do not experience Christian congregations as contexts for spiritual growth. Existing Christian congregations are sometimes but a pale reflection of the ideal, and sometimes they are pure travesties. For quite understandable reasons, people turn to other kinds of communities for nourishment: to support groups, advocacy groups, extended families, networks of friends. Though the latter are not "religious," they may nevertheless offer rich soil. Part of the good news of Christianity, I believe, is that communities need not be church-related in order to be grace-inspired. The living God of pure compassion, who accepts us just as we are, lives outside the confines of the church and of Christianity.

Prayer and Meditation

There is still another place that we can find healthy soil, one more inner than outer. We can turn to the quiet presence of God within us. There are many forms of prayer, and people are naturally drawn to different types relative to temperament and need. One form, emphasized by Cistercian priest and monk Thomas Keating, is what is now called "centering prayer" or "silent prayer" (Keating 1986; 1988). This form of prayer has resonances both with contemplative prayer in Roman Catholic monastic communities and with the Quaker tradition. On a daily basis we can still our minds and rest in the presence of a "still, small voice" deep within us, whose essence is divine and whose language is silence. The God of pure compassion rests within us as well as outside us.

As we rest in the presence of this divine silence, we become linked with the compassionate power by which the universe itself was called into existence. This power is the Wisdom by which animals and rivers and mountains and stars were called into existence, and it lies within them as well as within us, though it transcends both. This Wisdom was enfleshed, but not exhausted, in a carpenter from Nazareth, whose life and death revealed its nonviolence, and whose resurrection revealed a new life of which we can partake at every moment of our lives. To be centered in the "still, small voice" is to be centered in Christ and to be involved in a lifelong adventure of openness to new futures. To be centered in Christ is to have both roots and wings.

There are other forms of prayer and meditation of which we can partake. The forms of prayer that are right for us will depend on our personality types. Some prefer to pray by dancing, some by working, some by sitting quietly; some prefer prayer with images, some without images, some with both. I have a daily routine in which, each morning, I do a quiet breathing meditation that I learned from Zen Buddhism, followed by prayer and readings from the lectionary of *The Book of Common Prayer*. The important thing to me is not necessarily the quality of the meditation and prayer and reading, but rather the sheer fact that I do it, daily, whether I feel like it or not. There is wisdom in having a daily spiritual practice of one sort or another, from whatever tradition, that enables us to remember our priorities and affirm what we take to be the center of our lives.

The Earth

A fourth and final "soil" to which we can turn is the Earth itself. We can sink our roots into the healing powers of terrestrial existence, even as we also sink them into meaningful relations with other people, into the wisdom of the world's wisdom traditions, and into daily practices such as prayer and meditation. Indeed, in some ways, our roots in the Earth can serve as a foundation for our roots in human traditions and for our understanding of our own inner lives. The Earth itself is a heritage more ancient than any human tradition we know, and our own inner lives are themselves dimensions and expressions of the Earth's history. We did not drop from heaven; we were born from the Earth. As Genesis puts it, we were made from dust (Gn 2:7).

We were also born from God. At least this is what Christians believe. The dust from which we emerged was itself energized by the Wisdom of heaven. And so was the dust from which all other forms of life emerged. As the Bible recognizes, the breath of God is the very energy by which all living beings, and the whole of creation, are enlivened (Gn 1:2, 2:7). This breath is an aspect of the divine Wisdom. Although more than the universe, she is also within the universe as an enlivening breath. The breath of God is all around us, and it is also within us.

If we are Christian, we see Jesus as a distinctive enfleshment of the divine breath, an incarnation of divine Wisdom. Part of his distinctiveness lies in the fact that he died for our sins, showed us divine forgiveness, and showed us a Way. But even as we rightly see the enfleshment of divine Wisdom in Jesus, even as we rightly speak of him as "the Word become flesh," we can also see that enfleshment in other people, wherever there is love and wisdom. We can see it in other creatures and in the Earth. The Earth reveals the glory and wonder of the divine life, and Jesus reveals the nonviolent Way that we, as humans, can live amid this glory and wonder. Thus, to be centered in Christ and to be rooted in the Earth can be complementary, not contradictory—two sides of one coin.

The Earth

Let me be clear about what I mean by *Earth*. I mean four things at once: 1) the planet on which we live, with its splendid geological formations filled with mysterious and awesome energies; 2) the thin blanket of air, land, and water that lies on the surface of our planet, amid which live myriad forms of life; 3) living beings taken as a whole, as they live in dependence on one another; and 4) each living being individually, considered as valuable in its own right and for its own sake. By *Earth* I mean the planet, its biosphere, the web of life, and each node in the web. You are an instance of the Earth. And so am I.

I capitalize the "E" in Earth to underscore the fact that, in our time, the Earth as a whole is a primary context in terms of which we live. We sometimes speak of the Earth, or at least the environment, as if it were an issue among issues, to be discussed if we have time and inclination. I suggest, by contrast, that the environment, rightly understood, is not an issue among issues, but rather the Earth itself; and that the Earth, rightly understood, is the very context in which we best understand ourselves. As humans, we are members of the Earth community, and we are participants in Earth history. This history has a future as well as a past, and our own actions partly determine that future. We are creatures among creatures on a planet-in-the-making.

Still, if we open ourselves to roots in the Earth, some questions emerge: 1) Why is it so important to be rooted in the Earth, and 2) Where might we begin?

Why Be Rooted in the Earth?

There are at least two reasons why it is important to be rooted in the Earth. First, perhaps obviously, we need to be rooted in the Earth so that we feel a sense of kinship with it and therefore cease exploiting it. Most of us are familiar with the myriad ways in which humans now abuse our fellow creatures and their habitats—topsoil erosion, forest destruction, ozone depletion, groundwater pollution, air pollution, and a host of other ways, all of which result in a diminution of both human and nonhuman life. Consider, for example, a typical day on the planet, as recounted by the environmental philosopher David Orr:

> If today is a typical day on planet earth, we will lose 116 square miles of rain forest, or about an acre a second. We will lose another 72 square miles to encroaching deserts, the results of human mismanagement and overpopulation. We will lose 40 to 250 species, and no one knows whether the number is 40 or 250. Today the human population will increase by 250,000. And today we will add 2,700 tons of chlorofluorocarbons and 15 million tons of carbon dioxide to the atmosphere. Tonight the earth will be a little hotter, its waters more acidic, and the fabric of life more threadbare. By year's end the numbers are staggering: The total loss of rain forest will equal an area the size of the state of Washington; expanding deserts will equal an area the size of the state of West Virginia; and the global population will have risen by more than 90,000,000. By the year 2000 perhaps as much as 20% of the life forms extant on the planet in the year 1900 will be extinct (1994, 7).

It is important that we sink our roots in the Earth so that these "typical days" come to an end.

The second reason to be rooted in the Earth is perhaps more selfish but not less important. Many of us in industrial settings are quite alienated from Earth.

Even if we are not alienated from one another, we are alienated from the nonhuman dimensions of the Earth. We think of ourselves as conquerors of animals and plants and soil and water, not their kin. We are cut off from the healing powers of the Earth and her creatures, and our own souls are impoverished in the process.

Accompanying this impoverishment is an undue and unhealthy emphasis on salvation through human relationships alone. I have noted above that human relations are important and essential for healthy spirituality. They are necessary for wholeness. Still, they are not sufficient. The idea that they are is one of the chief idolatries of our time: the idolatry of assuming that all human needs can be met through inter-human interaction. As a consequence of this idolatry, we place too many stakes in human relationships themselves. Rather than placing *some* of our hope in the possibility of meaningful relationships with other humans, we place *all* our hopes, *all* our trust, on possibilities for communion with people. In the process we neglect possibilities for communion with the Earth and fellow creatures.

One problem with this idolatry is that it causes so much suffering in other animals and so much damage to the Earth as a whole. It leads to the "typical days" described above, in which other forms of life are treated as mere commodities or resources. Another is that it causes so much suffering in people. When we expect all our deepest needs to be met by other people, we impose excessive demands on others and end up frustrated ourselves. Just as in healthy marriages one spouse cannot meet all the needs of the other, so in healthy spirituality humans alone cannot meet all the needs of fellow humans. Rootedness in the nonhuman dimensions of the Earth and in God through prayer are antidotes to this. They free us from relying so heavily on others that others are oppressed by our cravings, and they free us to enter into meaningful relationships of mutuality with them. Thus, we need to be rooted in the Earth, not only for the Earth's sake, but also for our own.

Where Do We Begin?

In seeking to be rooted in the Earth, where might we begin? A first step, itself preliminary to the eight ways of being rooted noted in the next chapter, lies in becoming aware of the ways in which we are *already* rooted by virtue of our very existence. This raising of our consciousness is itself subjective. It is an internal awakening to the sheer givenness of being an earthling among earthlings. Such awakening is itself a form of deep spiritual wisdom. Buddhists might call it being "mindful" of who we are and where we are.

But the state of affairs of which we become aware—namely, our rootedness in the Earth—is quite objective. We would be rooted in the Earth even if we thought we were not. In learning to become more rooted in the Earth, our first task is to come to our senses, to come "down to Earth," to accept the fact that we are already rooted in at least three ways.

Three Ways in Which We Are Already Rooted in the Earth

First, we are rooted in the Earth inasmuch as we depend upon its energies at every moment of our lives. The Earth and its atmospheric gases supply the air we breathe, the food we eat, the water we drink, the materials from which we build our shelters, the energy by which we run our machines, and the repositories into which we place our waste. In a sense, the Earth is like a mother to us, and we are like children who depend upon her at every moment. Without constant nourishment from her vital energies, we would not exist.

Second, we are rooted in the Earth inasmuch as we are made of the Earth's materials. No less than mountains and trees and hills and rivers, our bodies are of the Earth and from the Earth. As the second creation story in Genesis puts it, we are made of the dust of the Earth, and we return to it at death (Gn 3:19).

In our time, what can being "made from dust" mean? At the very least, it can mean that our bodies are made from the materials of the Earth. When we see the mountains and enjoy their splendor, the eyes with which we see are aspects of the Earth itself, as are all aspects of our physical bodies. But it can also mean that our souls—our inner thoughts and feelings—are "made from the Earth" in important respects. Not only are they dependent upon the chemicals in our brains, they are themselves expressive of a kind of interiority, a psychic awareness, that we also see in other creatures of the flesh, particularly in other animals. Thus, both physically and psychologically, we are people of dust. We are rooted in the Earth, not simply as something that exists outside us, but also as something that exists within us. We *are* the Earth, or at least a portion of it.

Third, we are rooted in the Earth inasmuch as we are part of its history. Our feelings and actions are part of a larger history, the history of life on Earth, which is itself part of the history of the cosmos. Whether we act in ways to despoil the Earth or replenish it, we are part of the Earth's history and of the universe's history. We are not simply the Earth being itself; we are also the Earth becoming what it has not been before. Our every thought, feeling, and action adds a chapter, however negligible in importance, to the history of life on Earth.

These three ways of being rooted in the Earth have at least one thing in common. We cannot avoid them. We can choose how we are bonded with environments and our bodies, and how we will participate in the Earth's ongoing history. But, save through death or fantasy or space travel, we cannot choose to sever our bonds altogether. Even if we travel in space, we will doubtless bring earthly ways of thinking with us. And we will bring our bodies. It is our task and pleasure to acknowledge these forms of rootedness and to accept our own role as enfleshed creatures, to become aware of our earthiness, of the creative dust around us and within us, and then to celebrate our participation in the web of life. After all, it is an honor to be such a participant. Much of the healing that can come through the Earth comes through the knowing that we are citizens within, rather than overlords of, a complex and gorgeous life community.

Wings

So far I have suggested that to find some measure of wholeness we need to imitate trees. We need to sink our roots in warm relations with other people, in wisdom traditions, in a daily practice of one sort or another, and in the Earth itself. In such soils we find God, who is like an underground water supply or living stream from which the soils gain their nourishing waters. Without roots in moist and nourishing sources, we die.

Still, roots are not enough. We also need to fly. The divine Spirit is found not only in the dark nourishment of moist soils but also in the openness of indeterminate skies. "I placed you on eagle's wings," God tells Moses in Exodus, "and bore you out myself" (19:4).

The image is of God placing the people of Israel on eagle's wings so as to free them from slavery in Egypt. No less than the people of Israel, we too need to fly, both to escape various forms of enslavement by which we may be bound, whether to other people or to ideologies or to our own egos, and also to enjoy various forms of resurrection, of new life, available to us in the present and future. We too need to pack our bags and journey toward promised lands. Even as we might learn from well-planted trees, so we might also learn from free-flying eagles.

The joy of flying lies not just in the new horizons we discover, but also in the flying itself. We feel zestful and alive when we are free to yearn and to dream, to explore and to wonder; we feel enslaved when these impulses are frustrated. The proper aim of religion, it seems to me, is to give people wings as well as roots.

At least this is, or ought to be, the case with Christianity. When Christianity fails to offer wings, it becomes oppressive. It offers security without adventure, roots without wings. When this happens, roots themselves become problematic; they become fetters rather than feeders, means of enslavement rather than nourishment. Such is the problem of Christian fundamentalism.

In order to avoid fundamentalism, it is best to remind ourselves that the Christian life itself is a pilgrimage, an ongoing process, rather than a static state of perfection. Even our roots must be flexible and creative, like those of trees, rather than rigid and fixed. Sometimes, in the very name of God, certain roots must be severed, such as those that attach us to exclusivism, patriarchy, or anthropocentrism.

Of course, consumer culture makes it difficult to accept life as a pilgrimage. It invites us to think that, if we buy the right car or the right shoes or the right perfume, we will instantly arrive at a perfect state called "happiness." Christians, who ought to know better, can buy into this illusion, and then think of salvation in similar terms. We can think that when we have "purchased" the good news of Christ, we will forevermore be secure and happy. There will be no more surprises. Often it takes years for us to realize that this permanent state never arrives. The Christian life is an ongoing pilgrimage in which new circumstances continually arise calling for new responses, some of which have no precedence in the Bible or tradition. Each moment is a promised land of sorts, a context in which, if we are open, divine grace can be experienced.

How can this grace be experienced? In many ways. We can experience grace through other people, through plants and animals, through the elemental powers of the Earth, and through the wonders of the stars and galaxies. We can experience it through inner dreams, fervent prayers, inner silence, and ecstatic visions. We can experience it through trials and tribulations that we bear with courage, and through joys and pleasures that we enjoy with gratitude. We can experience it through faith, hope, and love; and through a recognition that we are loved by God even in our sinfulness. Last but not least, we can experience grace through the promising possibilities offered to our hearts and imaginations, our "wings."

Our wings are inner rather than outer; they consist of our hearts and imaginations. With their help we discover new and unanticipated possibilities—new ways of thinking, feeling, and acting—that make us more wise and compassionate. The purpose of such possibilities is not to enable us to escape the Earth, but rather to live more richly on the Earth. They help us become fully born, fully aware, fully alive in the here and now.

Where do these possibilities come from? I submit that they come from Holy Wisdom herself, from God. They are invitations to fly, sometimes into new lands, and sometimes over the very lands in which we are planted, so as to behold them in new ways.

Most of us have seen such inspiration in other people's lives. A four-year-old boy suffers from an inferiority complex because he is smaller than others his age, but then finds within himself the courage to develop talents not dependent on size. A thirty-year-old woman suffers from several years of physical abuse from a husband who never loved her, and then finds within herself the courage to leave. A fifty-year-old alcoholic finds within himself the courage to stop drinking. An eighty-year-old woman suffers from loneliness in a nursing home, but then finds within herself the courage to befriend another woman down the hall. These people have discovered within themselves holy possibilities, sacred potentialities, that are avenues for grace in their lives. In their immediate context, they have taken wing.

From the vantage point of this book, every moment contains within itself promising possibilities for responding to the situation at hand. These possibilities well up from a source deep within us, and yet more than us. When we experience them, we experience God as a beckoning presence within us, inviting us. And when we respond to them—in thought, feeling, and action—we help fulfill divine dreams, divine prayer for our lives.

Sometimes the best response is simply to cope with courage. Not all things are possible, not even for God. When we place our trust in a God of possibility, we do not trust that all crosses can be prevented. Instead we trust that, whatever the cross, there is a possibility for resurrection, for some kind of creative response. To believe in God is not necessarily to believe in an all-powerful God who can make things all right. It is to believe that, even when things are not all right, there are possibilities for creative coping and for hope.

Healing Skies

This book deals with two possibilities that are now available to many Christians throughout the world. They are not possibilities for survival, important as they are, but rather for spiritual growth. They are relevant to people who are fortunate enough to have their survival needs taken care of, people who have a responsibility, among other things, to help others have those needs met. One is the possibility of entering into deep and rich dialogue with people of other religions; the other is the possibility of entering into dialogue with the Earth. We might call them "healing skies," because they represent horizons of possibility, of freedom, into which we can fly in order to be more healthily rooted in the Earth and in God.

By *dialogue with other religions* I mean more than tolerance and understanding, important as they are. I mean hearing the truth in other religions and being transformed in the process. Each religion has its distinctive truths, its unique insights, that have emerged over the centuries through trial, error, and revelation from the Spirit. In our time, it seems to me, Christians need to be open to possibilities of learning from others, even as they—we—might also share with others the good news of Jesus Christ. We need to enter into dialogue in ways that enable them to learn from us, and us from them.

By *dialogue with the Earth* I mean more than understanding the Earth, realizing its value, and learning to live in harmony with it. I mean, as well, listening to the Earth, listening to fellow creatures, and learning to feel a deep sense of kinship with them. I mean what the next chapter calls "green grace" and "red grace." To enjoy such grace is to have a sense of place in relation to our bioregions, knowing the plants and animals as well as the people; it is to have a sense of compassion for other living beings, particularly the animals who are our closest biological and spiritual kin; it is to be aware of our own bodies as instruments by which the Earth speaks to us, full of wisdom in their own right. Inasmuch as we surrender to such feelings, we have entered into dialogue with the Earth. We have found something of the *shalom* which God—Holy Wisdom herself—wants for us.

These two dialogues—one with other religions and one with the Earth—are themselves part of the promising possibilities toward which, in my view, Christians are called by the Spirit at every moment of our lives. Christianity is a Way in which we open ourselves to possibilities for healing and peacemaking, thus continuing and advancing the healing ministry of Jesus. Our task is not simply to repeat the beliefs of Jesus. It is to be midwives to the very peace for which his heart yearned and for which he died on the cross. It is to advance the ministry of Jesus by being Christlike ourselves.

Peace is not simply individual or subjective. It is more than peace of mind, important as that is. It is also communal, and its communal dimension includes justice. If we follow the way of peacemaking, we struggle to create communities in which all, and not just a few, enjoy the benefits of grassroots democracy, personal and social responsibility, decentralization, community-based economics, and respect for diversity. Dialogue with other religions is one way, but not the only way, of encouraging justice through respect for diversity. It is one feature of justice for humans.

But justice for humans is not itself enough. The peace to which we are called today must also include justice for other animals and for the Earth. It is important that we treat them justly, not simply for our sakes, but for theirs. Other living beings have value in their own right, quite apart from their usefulness to us. Thus the peace we seek in our local communities and in our world at large must be an ecologically sensitive peace, a green peace. Dialogue with the Earth and dialogue with other religions are themselves ways of working toward green peace.

Many people from many traditions are being called to a peace that includes justice for humans and justice for the Earth. The call is itself an invitation into the healing skies, an immanent possibility, gradually emerging in many hearts and minds, coming from the Spirit itself. Even as many of us might experience more specific possibilities relative to our personal situation, we also experience this more universal possibility of green peace. A central responsibility of religious people throughout the world is to respond to this possibility, to become vessels of a peace that includes justice for humans and for the Earth. The hope is that Christians and others, even as we are rooted in the best of our pasts, can take wing into the healing skies.

Chapter 2

Red Grace and Green Grace

On Being Healed by the Cross and the Earth

Native American peoples sometimes speak of the Earth as inhabited by two-legged creatures, four-legged creatures, winged ones, and crawling ones. We humans are the two-leggeds. We are members of the family of life, participants in the history of life, and manifestations of the Earth's own energies. Biologically and spiritually, we are earthlings among earthlings.

Still, many of us do not realize our earthly status. We sometimes think of ourselves as alien creatures, descended from the heavens, only "passing through" on the way to greater glories. Or, if we do not believe in greater glories, we treat the rest of creation—the plants and animals—as mere commodities for our use, ignoring the fact that we ourselves are kin to other creatures. In either instance we feel separate from that 99 percent of the planet which is not human. We forget that we are mammals among mammals, primates among primates, flesh among flesh.

A Christianity with roots and wings will affirm our enfleshedness. With the Bible, it will remind us that we travel the way of all flesh, which is a way of sensitivity, of mortality, and of receptivity to the divine breath which animates all life. To affirm our fleshly status is not to deny that we have heavenly connections. The first creation story in the Bible reminds us that we are part of a larger creative process that began with the heavens themselves. Recast in contemporary terms, Thomas Berry and Brian Swimme put the point this way:

Tonight on every continent humans will look into the edge of the Milky Way, that band of stars our ancestors compared to a road, a pathway to heaven, a flowing river of milk. Formed by the seemingly insignificant ripples in the birth of the universe, this milky band has been activating its stars with its own fluctuating waves for ten billion years, and when we stare at it, we stare back at our own generative matrix. New ripples in the fabric of space-time, we humans ponder those primal ripples that called us into being (1992, 44).

The point, it seems to me, is that even as we are flesh among flesh, we are connected to a larger galactic whole. Our very selves, like the selves of other living beings, have a cosmic dimension.

Indeed, our very selves have a divine dimension, as do the selves of other creatures of the flesh. From the vantage point of this book, the heavens themselves were beckoned into existence by a Holy Wisdom who resides within each of us and within other creatures as well. Holy Wisdom is an ever-adaptive lure toward the fullness of life, relative to what is possible for the creatures at issue in the situation at hand. We do not always respond to this inwardly felt lure. In biblical terminology we "sin." Still, the divine Spirit is within us as a call into wholeness, wisdom, and compassion. In affirming our earthiness, we can also affirm the inner light, the inner call, that beckons us into the fullness of life.

Even as we recognize our galactic connections, our natural home *is* the Earth. If we imagine Holy Wisdom as the Mother of the universe, then we best realize that we meet her, among other places, on the very planet from which we emerge. We meet her through other people, through inner thoughts and feelings, through plants and animals, through the Earth itself. As the Qu'ran puts it, Holy Wisdom is closer to us "than our own jugular veins." Or, as the New Testament states, Holy Wisdom is Emmanuel, God-with-us.

Holy Wisdom is not only a force but also a consciousness. She is a cosmic consciousness in which the universe is enfolded, and she has dreams or yearnings of her own. One of them, revealed among other places in Jesus Christ, is that we two-legged creatures dwell in communion with one another, just as she dwells in communion with us and with the whole of creation. We respond to her dream in many ways. One way—and not the only way—is to commune with the Earth, to be rooted in the Earth. Of course we are already rooted in the Earth as members of the family of life, as participants in life's history, and as manifestations of the Earth's energies. But, at a spiritual level, we can become *more* rooted than we already are. My aim in this chapter is to present eight ways that we might do this.

We can be more rooted in the Earth 1) by enjoying a sense of place with respect to our local habitats; 2) by revering individual animals as subjects in their own right; 3) by being respectful of and awed by the planet as a whole; 4) by enjoying openness to our own bodies; 5) by becoming inwardly silent, so that we might hear the Earth on its own terms; 6) by feeling the pain of the world, both human and nonhuman; 7) by coming to terms with our own inner violence, which is part of earthly existence; and 8) by recognizing our call from Holy Wisdom to overcome this violence and be peacemakers in a broken world. Each of these eight sensibilities can be part of the inner dimension of a Christianity with roots and wings.

I list these eight ways at the outset, not only to get our bearings, but also to explain the title to the chapter: "Red Grace and Green Grace." The first five ways of becoming more rooted in the Earth I call "green grace." Green grace is the healing that comes to us when we enjoy rich bonds with other people, plants and animals, the Earth. It is the kind of grace celebrated by ecofeminists, native peoples, deep ecologists, and sacramentalists. It is green because, as the color green sometimes suggests, it engenders within us a healing and wholeness, a freshness and renewal, that lead us into the very fullness of life.

For most of us, green grace is experienced first and foremost with other humans. We seek healing through relationships with other people, because without such relationships we feel incomplete. There are many kinds of rich relationships to be enjoyed. There can be rich relations among friends, lovers, colleagues, even competitors. In Christianity, a primary form of rich relationship occurs through forgiveness, which is itself a form of connectedness, a restoration of broken bonds. In a world torn asunder by violence, forgiveness is a most precious form of green grace.

In this chapter, however, my focus is not on community with other people, but rather on community with the other 99 percent of creation so often neglected in human-centered traditions. Through other living beings, too, we can experience green grace, in which case the Earth itself becomes for us a sacred community, a holy communion, a revelation of the Divine. The five forms of green grace can as easily be called five ways of experiencing God through the Earth.

The final three ways of being rooted in the Earth—solidarity with the suffering in life, acceptance of our complicity in violence, and entering into the way of peacemaking—are forms of what I call "red grace." Red grace can be experienced sacramentally, too, in what Christians call holy communion. When, in a spirit of quietness and depth, we taste the wine of the eucharist and feel that we are tasting the very love of Holy Wisdom, we are experiencing red grace. It is red because it was revealed in the spilt blood of Jesus. Red is a metaphor for the blood, and red grace is a name for the healing that can come when we have come to grips with violence, cognizant not only that we have been victims but also victimizers, and that healing is possible even for us. Red grace is a way of coming to grips with our own finitude as earthlings among earthlings.

In truth, red grace is as green as green grace, and as earthly. Blood is as much a part of life on Earth as is the dance of bumblebees and the frolicking of colts. Still, we best begin on a more positive note, with what Matthew Fox calls the "original blessing" of creation itself. Without sensitivity to this blessing, wholeness will not be found.

Green Grace

The healing powers of green grace became clear to me several years ago when I visited a battered women's shelter in Boston. The counselors were deeply influenced by feminist philosophies and theologies, particularly ecofeminism. I had heard that counselors at the shelter made use of ecological spirituality in their therapy, and I wanted to know how they did it. At the shelter I met a counselor who, in a practical way, was an expert on the subject.

For years this counselor had supplemented individual and group counseling with animal-assisted therapy and nature-centered rituals. She would encourage her clients to bond with pets as part of their therapy; to cultivate gardens; to learn about the flora and fauna of nearby parks; to participate in rituals designed to help them know the wonders of the natural world, including the wonders of their own bodies. The results were promising, and she was a firm believer in the healing powers of nature. "The more my clients learn to trust animals and the Earth," she said, "the more they begin to trust themselves. And the more they trust themselves, the better they can free themselves from exploitative relationships."

This counselor was also an agnostic. She trusted the Earth and its web of life, but she was not sure she believed in a cosmic Spider, a cosmic Heart, in whom the web is enfolded. "If grace exists," she said, "it is the grace of rich connections with other nodes in the web. Whether or not it comes from God, I do not know."

She knew that I was a theologian, and she assumed that I believed in a cosmic Spider. She was right. I have spent time, perhaps too much time, developing a Christian understanding of God that emphasizes divine love for the web of life and each node in the web. I believe in a cosmic Life to whom the web of life belongs, who suffered on a cross to show its love for us. I believe in red grace.

But she also knew that I understood her reasons for agnosticism and skepticism. I knew that, for her, the term *God* named a policeman in the sky, a powerful male presence, residing somewhere off the planet, whose primary concern was with being worshiped for his own sake. From years of working with battered women she had had enough of powerful men, human or divine, who were obsessed with being worshiped. They were part of the problem. I didn't blame her for trusting the Earth and being skeptical of "God." For her, the Life in whom I believe was experienced through the Earth, without the use of the word *God*.

The life and work of the counselor are instructive in two ways. First, her perspective shows that people can have a spiritual dimension in their lives without believing in God or using God-language, much less being involved in formal religion. This does not mean that God—the cosmic Spider—is absent from their lives. But it does mean that *belief* in God can be absent from people's lives, at least at a conscious level. They may not "believe in God," yet have a spirituality.

Second, her work reminds us that being rooted in the Earth is important, not only because it instills us with attitudes which can help us protect the Earth and other creatures, but also because it offers us forms of healing we may sorely need. Whether or not we have suffered the pain of sexual abuse, we need rich connections with the web of life and its nodes in order to survive emotionally as well as physically. Like battered women, we need green grace.

What, then, are our opportunities for green grace in relation to the natural world? Consider the following five.

A Sense of Place

The first way is through a sense of place. Most of us already know what it means to have a sense of place, at least with respect to some small portion of the Earth. We can recall a natural setting we enjoyed as a child or one to which we return again and again as adults.

My earliest sense of place emerged in the hill country of Texas, north of Kerrville, on the banks and in the water of Guadalupe River. My parents would take me to the river as a child, and I grew to love the fragrance of the water, the color of the rocks, the smell of the soil, the beauty of the perch swimming just beneath the surface, the turtles and crayfish, and even the water moccasins, whom I feared but respected. If I had to name the spiritual guides of my life, one would be the Guadalupe River. The river was a holy icon for me, a window to God.

I imagine that you have a guide of your own. It may be a river bank, or a cornfield, or a backyard garden. If you spend most of your time indoors, it may be simply a patch of space in which you sit, where you can look outside and let the sun shine on your arm. In any event it is your place, your space, and it has healing power of its own. You feel at home in this place, and you belong to it.

Bioregionalists such as Richard Austin (1988), Wendell Berry (1977, 1981a, 1981b), and Gary Snyder (1990) emphasize that we can expand our senses of place to include larger places, the bioregions, in which we live. They say that if we are to be responsible to the Earth, we must learn to know and love the local cultures, both human and ecological, in which we find ourselves. A series of questions and challenges developed by *Co-Evolution Quarterly* (1981–82) offers a sample of the kind of ecological knowledge most of us need:

- Trace the water you drink from precipitation to tap.
- How many days 'til the moon is full? (Two days slack allowed.)
- What soil series are you standing on?
- What was the rainfall in your area last year? (Slack: one inch for every twenty inches.)
- When was the last time a fire burned in your area?
- What were the primary subsistence techniques of the culture that lived in your area before you.
- Name five native edible plants in your region and their season(s) of availability.
- From what direction do winter storms generally come in your region?

- How long is the growing season where you live?
- On what day of the year are the shadows the shortest where you live?
- When do the deer rut in your region, and when are the young born?
- Name five grasses in your area. Are any of them native?
- Name five resident and five migratory birds in your area.
- What is the land use history of where you live?
- What species have become extinct in your area?
- What are the major plant associations in your region?
- From where you're reading this, point north.
- What spring wildflower is consistently among the first to bloom where you live?

To the degree that we can respond to these questions and challenges, we know where we are with respect to our local bioregions. To the degree that we cannot respond, we do not know where we are. Obviously, the quiz favors country people over urban dwellers, indigenous over industrial. People in rural areas and in indigenous societies are much more knowledgeable of and attuned to the bioregions in which they live than those who live in cities. If we want to know the green grace of knowing where we are, we best sit at their feet.

Reverence for Life

A second way in which we can be rooted in the Earth was also illustrated by the counselor at the women's shelter in Boston. Recall that she encouraged her clients to develop close relations with animals, specifically pets. Close relations of this sort involve knowing animals as living subjects with value in their own right, as opposed to mere objects of value only to others. This kind of knowledge is at the heart of the animal rights and animal protection movements. Following Albert Schweitzer, we can call this knowledge "reverence for life" (1933, 270–72).

The way of reverence focuses not on identifiable geographical regions but rather on individual kindred creatures, particularly animals, who are our closest psychological and biological kin. We have reverence for life when we feel kinship with their joys and sufferings, and when we want for them the kind of happiness that they want for themselves.

Reverence for life is an antidote to points of view that emphasize systems but not individuals. Sometimes the sense of place described above can lapse into such insensitivity. It can celebrate the web of life, as embodied in a local bioregion, but forget the nodes in the web. This is like loving forests but neglecting individual trees, or like loving humanity but hating individual people. To avoid such abstractness, a sense of place needs to be complemented by reverence for life. The "land ethic" of Aldo Leopold (1949), which has been taken up by many an environmentalist, needs to be complemented by the "life ethic" of Albert Schweitzer.

Among the religious traditions of the world, the ones that have been most keenly reverential of life are not the indigenous traditions, important as they are. Rather, they are the classical traditions of Jainism and Jain-influenced Buddhism, with their doctrines of *ahimsa* or non-injury to animals. As these Asian traditions make clear, the life of compassion rightly extends to animals as well as to people. It rightly leads to a progressive disengagement from injury to animals.

Respect for the Planet

A third way of being rooted in the Earth lies in feeling a sense of identity with and reverence for the planet Earth as a whole. Such a feeling is implicit in the idea of trusting the Earth. The planet functions as a subject of loyalty in its own right.

In a certain sense, loyalty to the planet is a new possibility in human history. Many people throughout recorded history have had a special sense for the bioregions in which they lived, but few were able to identify with the planet as a whole, because they had no way of seeing or visualizing the entire planet in its cosmic context.

The picture of the Earth from space has made such visualization possible. When mention is made of the Earth, most of us now imagine a beautiful globe cast in relief against the stars. The Earth as a whole has become a mythic image in our own imaginations. It thus provides food for new mythical sensitivity.

Part of this mythical sensitivity involves seeing the planet as alive. This can mean several things. Some imagine the planet as a living subject in its own right, having awareness of its own, not unlike the way in which an animal has such awareness. Others speak of the Earth as a living subject, but with awareness more diffuse and less centralized than that, say, of a cat or dog. As they see it, the Earth's subjectivity is like that of a living tissue, or a complex plant, rather than like that of an animal. Still others (and I count myself among them) speak of the Earth not as a subject in its own right, but rather as a community of subjects, like a forest whose spirit is the sum total of the spirits of each of its living beings. In each of these instances the Earth itself becomes a subject of respect and loyalty. When we are loyal to the Earth, we are loyal to something that has an identity of its own, one of which we are a part, but which is more than us. We feel connected to and part of a larger whole: our planet, which is itself connected to a still larger whole, namely the cosmos. The natural extension of loyalty to the Earth is cosmic awe.

Awareness of Our Bodies

A fourth way of being rooted in the Earth is closer to home than the loyalty to the Earth. It lies in being aware of our own bodies as living incarnations of the Earth's energies. Our very closest contact with the Earth comes not in our knowledge of our bioregion, or in our allegiance to the planet, or even in our sensitivity to creatures around us; it comes through simple acts of breathing, eating, walking, and sleeping. These acts are instances of the living dynamics of the Earth. As is emphasized in many forms of Buddhist meditation, breathing itself is the self-awakening of the cosmos. We need go no further than our own breathing to experience enlightenment.

Unfortunately, in the West the body has often been considered relatively unimportant in spiritual pursuits. It has even been treated as an enemy to be transcended. Some believe that the more spiritual they are, the less embodied they will be.

Some of us are aware of our own bodies only as objects that we wish conformed to social standards of beauty. We are aware of our bodies only as others see them, as commodities for their consumption. We wish that we were "prettier" or "more virile looking" or that we had less gray hair. We want to look like the models we see on television. The body awareness I have in mind is instead an immediate awareness of the body as subject of trust and as source of wisdom. To trust our bodies is to realize that they are the accumulated wisdom of billions of years of cosmic, geological, and biological evolution. The history of the cosmos has in its own way been a process of trials and errors, amid which things have been learned, such as how to regulate temperature and how to heal wounds and even how to think and feel. We do these things by virtue of our genes, which carry within them the memories and wisdom of the distant past. To be rooted in our bodies is to recognize that our bodies themselves can be spiritual guides. Like all teachers, they are finite. We cannot learn all that we need to know by listening to our bodies. But they may well carry dreams, revelations, which are the voice of God channeled through evolution.

Inner Silence

A fifth and final way we can be more rooted in the Earth, and simultaneously enjoy green grace, is through what might be called inner silence. There are many forms of silence. The kind I have in mind is a silence that has let go of inner preoccupations in order to hear the powers, rhythms, and revelations of the rest of the Earth on their own terms. It is a silence that hears the languages of the Earth.

I borrow my concept of "hearing" from Nelle Morton, a pioneer in feminist theology, who introduced me and many others to the idea of "hearing into speech." Morton describes a consciousness-raising group of which she was a part, in which a woman painfully recalled her life story to some other women who were listening to her in an active, caring way. At one point the woman looked closely at the others and said: "I have a strange feeling you heard me before I started. You heard me to my own story." Morton tells us that when the woman said this, she herself "received a totally new understanding of hearing and speaking" (1985, 127). She saw that genuine listening empowers other people to uncover depths of experience previously unnamed and to express them in ways that are fulfilling. When we truly listen to others on their terms, so Morton says, we "hear them into speech."

Morton's insight can be extended and slightly modified to include experiences we can have in relation to the rest of the Earth and its creatures. Let "hearing" stand for any of our senses: seeing, listening, touching, tasting, smelling. And let "hearing into speech" represent modes of consciousness in which we are aware of the sheer "suchness," the sheer immediacy, of plants, animals, and the elements on their own terms. "Suchness" is the translation of the Buddhist word *tathata*. It means the as-it-is-ness of things, the sheer happening of things as they occur on their own terms (Watts 1957, 67). My suggestion is that, if we allow ourselves to be inwardly silent—that is, to be released from introspective preoccupations—we can sometimes hear the languages of the moon and stars, the forests and oceans, the plants and animals, the elements themselves. Let me offer two examples.

The first is a description by farmer and poet Wendell Berry of his experience of walking into a forest:

> Until we understand what the land is, we are at odds with everything we touch. And to come to that understanding it is necessary, even now, to leave the regions of our conquest—the cleared fields, the towns and cities, the highways—and reenter the woods. For only there can a man encounter the silence and the darkness of his own absence. Only in this silence and darkness can he recover the sense of the world's longevity, of its ability to thrive without him, of his inferiority to it and his dependence on it. Perhaps then, having heard that silence and seen that darkness, he will grow humble before the place and begin to take it in—to learn from it what it is. As its sounds come into his hearing, and its lights and colors come into his vision, and its odors into his nostrils, then he may come into its presence as he never has before, and he will arrive in his place and will want to remain. His life will grow out of the ground like the other lives of the place, and take its place among them. He will be with them—neither ignorant of them, nor indifferent to them, nor against them—and so at least he will grow to be native-born. That is, he must reenter the silence and the darkness, and be born-again (quoted in Tucker 1989, 51).

Berry is describing his experience of hearing the dark forest on its terms, not human terms. He experienced the darkness of his own absence, and the presence of a world of its own. This is one instance of what I mean by "hearing the language of the Earth." Analogous experiences can be felt in relation to mountains, rivers, deserts, lakes, wild animals, plants, wind, ice, and fire. We can see them and feel them in their independence from us, and feel amazed. Gradually we are healed by the amazement itself, and we become born again.

The second example is borrowed from the well-known interpreter of Buddhism, Alan Watts. Watts playfully speculates that the Sanskrit word *tathata* may well have its origins in the sounds of babies as they first discover the sights and sounds of nature (1957, 77). A small child lies in a crib, for example, and her father opens the window. The child looks out the window and sees, for the first time, softly sprinkling rain. The child says "da-da-da," which, Watts speculates, sounds a bit like "tathata." The father thinks that she is saying "da-da" or "daddy," but truly she is saying "look-look-look, look what is there." She is experiencing the rain in its suchness.

Watts's point is that adults can recover the childlike wonder of seeing ordinary realities of the Earth as if for the first time. Some will be pleasant and some unpleasant; some frightening and some pacifying; but all can be amazing, for the Earth and its colors and textures are themselves truly wondrous, if we have eyes to see and ears to hear.

In some ways, Buddhist-influenced poetry such as haiku captures the sensation of seeing things in their suchness. "On a withered branch," Basho writes, "a crow is perched, in the autumn evening" (quoted in Watts 1957, 185). Basho is simply capturing the experience itself, adding no commentary. The silence— that is, the absence of commentary—is as important as the presence of the crow, and both together give us the feeling that Basho was just looking at the crow, not unlike the baby looking at the rain.

The more we are able to hear the languages of the Earth on their terms, the more we tend to lose our own sense of being a separate ego, cut off from the Earth by the boundaries of our skin. One version of this kind of ego-transcending experience is illustrated in J. Baird Callicott's experience of seeing the pollution of the Mississippi River. I quoted this passage in the Introduction, and it is worth quoting again here. Readers will recall that, having grown up on the banks of the Mississippi, he returned as an adult to find a different reality. When he "heard the speech" of the Mississippi as an adult, what he heard was painful:

As I gazed at the brown silt-choked waters absorbing a black plume of industrial and municipal sewage from Memphis and followed bits of some unknown beige froth floating continually down from Cincinnati, Louisville, or St. Louis, I experienced a palpable pain. It was not distinctly located in any of my extremities, nor was it like a headache or nausea. Still, it was very real. I had no plans to swim in the river, no need to drink from it, no intention of buying real estate on its shores. My narrowly personal interests were not affected, and yet somehow I was personally injured. *It occurred to me then, in a flash of self-discovery, that the river was part of me* (1989, 114).

As said in the Introduction, Callicott's description is instructive because it describes a kind of ego-transcendence that sometimes occurs amid the inner silence of hearing the Earth on its own terms, and also because it reminds us that what we hear, see, touch, or taste, may not be pleasant at all. Our authentic response to the Earth may be pain, not pleasure. This takes us, then, to yet another way of being rooted in the Earth: being open to the tragic dimension. Whether the tragedy at issue is human-inflicted or part of natural processes, it is something we must be open to if we are to be deeply rooted in the Earth. One of the best ways I know to be open to the tragic is by realizing that tragedy itself is shared by the Heart of the universe, by Holy Wisdom. Such is the significance of the cross of Christ, of red grace.

Red Grace

I have a friend, an ex-evangelical Christian, who complains that Christianity is too "red" for his liking. "Red is the color of blood," he says, "and Christianity is a religion that focuses on blood." His reference, of course, is to the blood of Jesus on the cross. He is struck by the fact that many evangelical Christians speak of being "washed in the blood" as the very heart of their faith, and that eucharist-centered Christians speak of "drinking the blood of Christ" and "eating his body" as a medium of grace. My friend says that blood-oriented Christians of this sort are very much like people in primal traditions. "They eat their gods in order to gain divine power."

My friend speaks for many Christians who are somewhat repulsed by blood imagery in Christianity and who wish to focus on kinder and gentler themes, like the teachings of Jesus concerning love or the hope of the resurrection. They distrust the blood symbolism in the Christian faith, believing that it too easily lends itself to morbidity and violence.

Perhaps they are right. The Christian heritage is filled with the blood of many victims of Christian fanaticism, whether women, slaves, homosexuals, Jews, or Muslims. Perhaps, in some perverse way, a preoccupation with Christ's blood *has* lent itself to a tendency toward bloodthirstiness among Christians themselves. Perhaps this is particularly the case if the blood is understood to be willed by God.

If this is the case, it is not the whole story. More than a few Christians throughout the ages have become much kinder, not more violent, through an appreciation of Christ's blood on the cross. For them, the blood of Christ has been life-giving and cleansing. They have felt forgiven and loved because God died for them, and then, out of gratitude, they have been able to reach out to others in forgiveness and love. For them, blood has been a means to grace: red grace.

Furthermore, a resistance to blood imagery, even with well-meaning intentions, can betray a false otherworldliness. My friend is right to note that Christianity's fixation on drinking divine blood and on eating divine flesh is related to primal traditions. Primal orientations are often closer to nature, and hence less otherworldly, than classical traditions. There is something mysterious and primordial about blood, even spilt blood. The rabbit being eaten by the fox knows this; we ought to know it as well. Blood, too, is ecological.

Zen writer Gary Snyder puts it this way: "Human beings have made much of purity and are repelled by blood, pollution, and putrefaction." But blood, pollution, and putrefaction, so Snyder insists, are indeed part of life. "Life is not just a diurnal property of large interesting vertebrates; it is also nocturnal, anaerobic, cannibalistic, microscopic, digestive, fermentative: cooking away in the warm dark." A failure to come to grips with blood, including its violent dimension, is itself a flight from the world in which we live. "The other side of the sacred," says Snyder, "is the sight of your beloved in the underworld, dripping with maggots" (1990, 111).

At its best, Christianity—and any other religion—must come to grips with maggots. It must face life squarely, without sentimental blinders. If approached rightly, in a spirit of wisdom and compassion, the blood of Christ provides an occasion for doing this. It helps us to face the violence in our world, including the violence within our own hearts. We see something of ourselves in the people who nailed Jesus to the cross, because often we nail others to crosses. And we can see something of ourselves in the suffering he underwent, because often we ourselves suffer. The cross tells us that we are not alone in our suffering, that it is shared by the very Heart of the universe; it tells us that, as irrational as it may seem by worldly standards, God also receives our violence without responding in kind. The blood of the cross reveals the empathy and nonviolence of God.

The violence and suffering with which we must come to grips are not limited to the human arena. Snyder tells of a friend, Jim Dodge, who "told me how he had watched—with fascinated horror—Orcas methodically batter a Gray Whale to death in the Chukchi Sea" (1990, 110).

The Chukchi Sea is a body of water just north of western Alaska, and orcas are killer whales. If we want to be honest about the natural world, so Snyder seems to say, we must imagine ourselves inside the skin of the gray whale as she is being battered and then eaten by the orcas. And then we must imagine ourselves inside the orcas, knowing that the violence they inflict is not violence from their perspective, but rather the natural satisfaction of hunger.

From a Christian perspective, it seems to me, our proper response to this suffering and violence is not to become bloodthirsty or violent ourselves. Nor is it to wallow in guilt. Rather, it is to be honest and open about the violence around us and within us, not hiding from it; trustful that the very Heart of the universe suffers with each and every living being that suffers; and inspired toward a nonviolent way of living that shares with the world the nonviolence of God. When we have truly felt the significance of the blood of Christ, I submit, we become peacemakers. We enter the Way of peace, not because we will be punished by God otherwise, but because we have been inwardly moved, inwardly healed, by One who loves us more, sometimes much more, than we love ourselves or the surrounding world.

To be sure, many Christians want to make more of the cross than this. They want to see Christ's death on the cross not only as a revelation of divine love, but also as a means of appeasing divine anger, or of satisfying divine honor, or of paying back the devil. I have never been able to make sense of such perspectives. It has never seemed appropriate to me to imagine that God, at a late stage in human history, finally was able to forgive sinners after having been unable or unwilling to do so for countless centuries. This seems to me demeaning of God. Rather, I see the cross as one way, and not the only way, that the Heart of the universe was able to display the love that it felt from the very beginning: a love that accepts us amid our finitude, that forgives us, and that suffers with us, both when we are victims of violence and even when we are perpetrators of it. To understand this love is to be moved by red grace. Christ on the cross can be a vessel for such grace.

Can the experience of red grace help us to become still more rooted in the Earth? I believe it can, and in three ways. It can help us 1) feel the pain of the world, even when we are inclined to hide from it; 2) accept our own complicity in some of the violence from which others suffer; and 3) respond to the divine call to be peacemakers. These are the three additional ways of being rooted in the Earth that I noted in opening this chapter. I will deal with them in order.

Feeling the Pain of the World

Some of the pain in our world is justified and some is not. Ecologists would argue that the pain of the battered whale was justified because it was necessary to the marine ecosystem. Social activists, on the other hand, would argue that the pain of battered women is unjustified, because the violence is a violation of the women's integrity.

A Christianity with roots and wings will certainly agree with the activists, but it will also recognize that—at least from the battered whale's point of view—there is something tragic, or at least unwanted, in her pain as well. There is a tragic dimension to life on Earth, and it is not limited to the injustices inflicted on humans. It is important that we feel the pain from the point of view of its victims. Only then have we truly learned from the wisdom of the cross.

In order to feel the pain of the world, we must first acknowledge its existence. The Buddhist-influenced writer Joanna Macy reminds us just how difficult this can be (1991, 15–28). She speaks of the fact that many people hide from the despair that they feel, not only about individual living beings who suffer, but also about the very possibility of a flourishing planet, given the nuclear proliferation and ecological threats. She notes that many of us hide from this despair, influenced by cultural forces that take "unbridled optimism" as a sign of success and that see openness to despair as depressed and depressing. If we are influenced by conservative forms of Christian faith, we may also think openness to despair signals a loss of faith.

Macy has led workshops throughout the United States in which she helps people to acknowledge and feel their despair and then to do something about it. She invites people to enter imaginatively into the suffering of all living beings and to acknowledge their sadness. One of her aims is to validate the despair, to help people realize that it is all right to feel deeply and painfully about the plight of others, both human and nonhuman.

Macy also points out that despair itself reveals just how interconnected living beings on the planet are. When we feel the suffering of others, and despair over the prospects of life itself, we realize how deeply intertwined our spirits are with theirs. We see through the illusion of the skin-encapsulated ego into the truth of what Buddhists call interconnectedness or *pratitya-samutpada* (Macy 1991, 55–64). We see that they are part of us, and we are part of them.

Though a Buddhist herself, Macy has roots in Christianity, and one of the symbols of the Christian tradition that she appreciates is the cross. "The cross where Jesus died teaches us that it is precisely through openness to pain of our world that redemption and renewal are found" (21–22). Moreover, the cross reminds us that Holy Wisdom shares the pain of the world; the suffering of each and every living being is also the suffering of God.

My suggestion, then, is that openness to the pain of the world—to the pain of battered whales and hungry children, of destroyed forests and denuded landscapes—is itself one way of acknowledging and understanding our connectedness with all who live and suffer, both human and nonhuman. It is a way of affirming that we are flesh among flesh, and that we travel the way of all flesh. When we enter into the spilt blood of Christ on the cross, we enter into the spilt blood of the entire Earth. Only after we have felt this pain, deeply and thoroughly, can we discover the healing and renewal of red grace.

Acknowledging Our Inner Violence

The second dimension of red grace that helps us become more rooted in the Earth has to do with our finitude. We are rooted in the Earth when we accept, rather than hide from, our own limitations, our own finitude.

There are many forms of finitude that we share with other creatures, and that are not necessarily bad. We, like they, grow old and die; we, like they, suffer the ravages of disease; we, like they, experience fear, frustration, and loss.

For most of us, being finite also involves failing to realize various ideals or goals to which we are drawn. This is one of the meanings of "the fall" in Christianity. We are "fallen" creatures inasmuch as we "fall short" of some of our own ideals.

To be sure, some of the ideals we feel drawn toward are not worth realizing. In a consumer society some feel called to be "perfect" in physical appearance, "perfect" in social status, or "perfect" in money-making abilities. Obsession with such ideals can be debilitating and destructive of the natural spontaneity, the happy finitude, of human life.

Still, some ideals are indeed valuable and failing to live up to them can be a cause of genuine guilt. At a deep level many of us feel called to be compassionate, to feel the pain of the world, and to do something about it. We want to be sensitive to the needs of others, respectful of the integrity of others, bonded with others in a spirit of care and solidarity. This "call" is not simply the voice of conscience and society; it is the voice of Holy Wisdom. The very Spirit of God lies within each of us as a call to compassion.

In truth, however, we rather persistently fall short of this deep calling. Despite our own desire to be fully compassionate, we feel resentment and jealousy toward others, and sometimes even hatred. The problem is not simply that we fall short of the ideal, it is that we cannot even acknowledge to ourselves that we fall short. We hide from our moral failings, pretending that they are not part of who we are. This phenomenon is called repression.

As we repress our own moral failings, we begin to think of ourselves in terms of masks with which we identify. We then project our unwanted side onto others. We pretend that "they" are totally evil, whereas "we" are totally good. "They" may be people of other races, religions, or nationalities, or creatures of other species. In any event we have a devil in the making, an evil one who possesses all the traits we foist onto others.

Psychological health requires that we free ourselves of our own pretensions to moral perfection, that we become aware of our own unwanted dimensions. It involves coming to grips with the violence within us; that is, with our inner tendencies to resent, to hate, to scapegoat, and to be jealous. Only when we confront our inner violence can we take its energies and transform them into seeds of compassion and wisdom. The cross of Christ is one way to do this, for it signifies that Holy Wisdom accepts us, indeed loves us, in spite of our own failings. We do not have to be perfect in order to be loved by the Heart of the universe; we are loved amid our finitude. God loves us just as we are.

My point here is that our earthiness includes our failings and that being rooted in the Earth involves awareness of these failings. It involves an awareness of sin. When we understand the cross of Christ on a deep level, identifying not only with Christ on the cross but also with those who hammered the nails, we realize an important dimension of our own earthiness, our own finitude. Other animals need not take responsibility for this finitude, but we must. An awareness both of sin and of the love of Holy Wisdom for us even amid our sinfulness is one way of being rooted in the Earth.

Becoming a Peacemaker in a Broken World

Once we have become aware of our own inner violence, our failure to be fully compassionate, we can use the energies of the violence in more constructive ways. We can hear the call of Holy Wisdom to be peacemakers in a broken world.

Here, it seems to me, we realize something of what it means to be made "in the image of God" (Gn 1:26). To be made in God's image is not to leave our earthiness behind; rather it is to become fully human by realizing our potential for wisdom and compassion. One way that this potential is best realized is evidenced in the nonviolent traditions of the world: certain forms of Buddhism and Jainism, for example (Tobias 1993, 138–49). Buddhists and Jains, no less than some in the Christian community, have felt the cosmic call to nonviolence. My suggestion is that nonviolence is itself a way of being rooted in the Earth. Joanna Macy has pointed out that when we feel the pain of the world, we simultaneously realize our connectedness with the world. I assert that when we respond to this pain with a desire to heal and make whole, we are affirming that connectedness in a positive way. Like Jesus on the cross, we do not respond to violence with violence; rather, we respond to violence with love. Being a peacemaker of this sort is our way, a human way, of participating in the Earth community, of advancing the history of life on Earth. Jesus provides an image, but not the only image, of how we, as humans, might realize our earthly potential for compassion. We can become still more rooted in the Earth by following the prince of peace, who revealed "the Way, the Truth, and the Life" for human beings on Earth (Jn 14:6).

Red Grace and Green Grace Combined

I have suggested eight ways in which we might be more rooted in the Earth. Readers will recall that the Christian life as a way of living involves three dimensions of our lives: our thinking, our feeling, and our acting. The eight ways of being rooted in the Earth can be part of the feeling dimension of our lives. Our deepest consciousness can be infused with feelings and emotions open to red grace and green grace.

Red and green grace are connected in various ways. As noted above, red grace can itself be understood as a form of green grace. If we stretch the notion of green grace to mean "healing connections with the Earth and with earthlings," then red grace can be seen as one form of healing connection that can be enjoyed in relation to one earthling among earthlings, namely, Jesus Christ. After all, Jesus was shaped by genes and environment; he too was part of the history of life on Earth. He was a human being with flesh and blood, as mammalian as a sheep taken to slaughter. To experience the healing power of God through his death is to experience the healing power of God through a fellow instance of that creative energy—that creative Dust—from which all things emerged. To honor Jesus as a human who died for us is not to diminish his distinctiveness, it is to revere his earthiness.

On the other hand, green grace can be seen as an extension of red grace. If the partaking of red grace involves sensing God's unlimited love for us and for the whole creation, the very feelings of divine love that we experience through Christ can themselves be shared with others and with the rest of creation. We can feel the presence of the rest of the world, and in so doing we are bonded with the rest of creation, as we ourselves are felt by God. In this sense the five types of green grace noted above—a sense of place, reverence for life, respect for the planet, awareness of our bodies, and inner silence—are themselves ways in which we live out a love we find in God as revealed in Christ.

However we understand red grace and green grace in relation to one another, both are important to the Christian life. A Christian life that emphasizes red grace alone easily becomes morbid and neglectful of the presence of God in the rest of creation; a Christian life that emphasizes green grace alone easily forgets that all of us are in need of a Love that forgives us and loves us even amid our violence, a love that shares the burden of all suffering. Experientially, red grace and green grace balance each other. They are two sides of a grace-filled life, two sides of that wholeness into which each of us, as two-legged creatures on planet Earth, is called by Holy Wisdom.

Chapter 3

Making Peace in Our Bioregion

Followers of Christ as Midwives to Greenpeace

As a professor of world religions, the most difficult religion for me to teach is Christianity. This is not because I am Christian, though that may indeed be a source of bias. Rather, it is because most of my students live in the Bible Belt and come from Christian backgrounds. They identify "Christianity" with what they learned at First United Methodist Church, or St. Peter's Catholic Church, or Mt. Zion AME Church, or Second Baptist Church. Whether their early experiences were positive or negative, they think they know Christianity, and they arrive in class thinking that they have nothing to learn. As a result, I am constantly on the lookout for readable books that might present Christianity in a new light.

In the 1980s such a book appeared. *Making Peace in the Global Village*, written by popular interpreter of third-world theologies Robert McAfee Brown, is a collection of public lectures delivered by Brown during the heyday of liberation theologies. It was used throughout the United States in churches, seminaries, and colleges to introduce middle-class Christians to the social implications of New Testament Christianity.

Brown's book was an eye-opener. Most of my students were white and middle-class twenty-year-olds. Like so many both then and now, they assumed that being a true Christian and being an upwardly mobile American were two sides of one coin. Softly but firmly, Brown put an end to that illusion. He encouraged readers to question their pledge of allegiance to the American flag and to consider pledging it instead to the God of Jesus Christ, the God of the oppressed.

A Christianity with roots and wings will follow Brown's advice. It will pledge allegiance to the God of Jesus, not to the god of fame, fortune, and power. The pledge is difficult to keep, because there are many voices pulling us in the other directions. Even to make the pledge, much less live up to it, we need the grace of God.

In our time God is conceived in various ways. Some conceive God as an indwelling spirit, others as an external power, and still others, myself included, as both. God is that Holy Wisdom within whose ongoing life the universe lives and moves and has its being. It is as if all the star systems in the universe were organelles within a giant Cell, itself divine; God is the Sacred Whole in whose life all beings dwell. The point of Brown's book is that this Sacred Whole is Christlike. We experience the Sacred Whole, not just as a Life beyond us, but also as a Life within us. Christianity teaches us to experience the divine Spirit as an inward call to follow Jesus and thus to be peacemakers in a broken world.

The purpose of this chapter is to develop this idea of peacemaking as a behavioral dimension of a Christianity with roots and wings. Christian life involves three dimensions: understanding, inner feelings, and conduct or behavior. Chapter 2 emphasized the realm of inner feelings. Chapters 4 through 6 will emphasize understanding. This chapter emphasizes behavior. In the context of discussing this behavioral dimension, I have five proposals to make:

1. That Christianity itself is a way of peacemaking that involves making peace in the global village.

2. That the global village is best understood not simply as a human community with the Earth as backdrop, but rather as a vast web of life—an Earth community—such that peacemaking involves making peace with animals and the Earth as well as with people.

3. That one way we can best make peace with the Earth and its web of life is to be sensitive to the bioregions in which we live, and to make peace with the living beings, nonhuman and human, that dwell within them.

4. That we can make peace in our bioregions only if we participate in the building of healthy communities, which are just in their treatment of people and animals, and sustainable in their relations to the land.

5. That participation in the building of such communities requires *both* lifestyle changes and public policy changes. At the level of public policy, I will focus on the need for community-based economics.

Christianity as a Way of Peacemaking

Making Peace in the Global Village dealt with issues that were timely in the 1980s and timely now: poverty, repression, racism, and violence. In simple and passionate language Brown showed that such issues cannot be addressed simply by overcoming individual pride and self-centeredness. They must also be addressed by criticizing social ideals and public policies that are instruments of evil.

Consider some of the social ideals that Brown thought white, middle-class Christians in the United States ought to criticize: 1) that the United States "should remain number one at all costs," 2) that "blacks ought to be content now" because "we've given them a lot," 3) that "if they don't agree with us" we ought to "bomb the hell out of them," and 4) that, though "we use 40 percent of the world's resources and are only 6 percent of the world's population, we have nothing to be ashamed of; this only shows that we are 'go-getting and efficient' " (1981, 96). Many of my students held such views in the 1980s. Many hold them today.

Ultimately, Brown's aim was not only to challenge existing assumptions, but also to inspire a new way of living among his readers. He wanted to show that there is a meaningful and authentic way to live, an alternative to the way of upward mobility and consumerism that captivates so many imaginations, both young and old. He called this the Way of discipleship to Christ, or, in shortened form, Christianity.

For one reason or another, most of my students did not think of Christianity as a way of living. They envisioned Christianity as a theology or set of beliefs, a blind "faith" requiring assent, even if such assent involves the suppression of honest doubt. By contrast, for Brown, Christianity was not so much an object of belief as it was a path to be followed; the real Christian Way is quite different from the watered-down Christianity of mainline denominations and the narrow-hearted Christianity of fundamentalists. At its very core, he said, the Christian Way is a Way of peace. It involves and requires a commitment to what the Bible calls *shalom*.

As he explained it, *shalom* involves more than inner peace and inner security, important as these are.[1] *Shalom* is a fullness of life that is enjoyed in and through rich relations with others. In terms of the previous chapter, it is a form of green grace, of rich and healing relations with others.

For the poor of the world, Brown emphasized, *shalom* can only be enjoyed once basic needs are met. If we are not among the poor, we must help the poor meet their basic needs if we are to enjoy *shalom* with them and they with us. If we truly want *shalom* in the world, Brown stated, we must work for justice. Peace "has to do with the state of one's belly, whether it is full or empty. . . . It has to do with a security that is physical as well as spiritual" (1981, 14).

Disturbing the Social Order

Brown further insisted that peacemaking involves a willingness to disturb the existing social order. He noted that Jesus, the prince of peace, was himself a disturber. He broke up families, challenged religious and political authorities, and turned over tables in the Temple. He comforted the afflicted and afflicted the comfortable. My students realized that if they told their parents

---

1. In truth, Brown tends to dismiss the importance of inner peace. "*Shalom*," he says, "is much more than the absence of war, and it is much more than inner serenity, which is how Christians often try to spiritualize it" (1981, 14). My aim in this book is to suggest a balance between inner serenity and outward action. Without inner serenity, our outer action loses what Buddhists call "mindfulness," and what Thomas Merton calls "the root of inner wisdom." We too easily burn out (see Conclusion below).

that they intended to follow a man of this sort, their parents would be deeply disturbed. They would assume that the man was leader of a sect. And indeed, so Brown explained, he was: the Jesus sect.

For middle-class Christians, this was a challenging way to see Jesus. Most of my students had only known the comforting Jesus, the Jesus who loved them no matter what they did. Brown introduced them to the afflicter, the one who invited them, as he did the rich young ruler, to "go and sell what you have and give to the poor" (Mt 19:21).

This was tough medicine for those students for whom college was merely a means to the end of getting a good job so as to make enormous sums of money. Still, I sensed that even for them the medicine was efficacious. At a deep level, most of them knew that there was more to life than making money and climbing the ladder of success. They did not want to admit that they knew this, because, at a more superficial level, they thought they were supposed to go after fame, fortune, and power. But at a deeper level many had an untapped idealism, a yearning to serve.

Brown gave them permission to listen to this deeper yearning. He told them that the yearning was from God, that it was God's way of inviting them to travel the Way of peace. If they took this Way seriously, their lives would change. They could no longer be content with private blessings; they also had to be interested in the public good. As Brown explained, peacemaking means "seeing to it that people have enough to eat; that they are not undernourished or malnourished; that they can go to bed at night without fear that someone will spirit them off to prison; that the society will be so planned that there is food enough to go around; that the politics of the country and of the world are so arranged that everybody's basic needs are met" (1981, 14). Being a Christian has political as well as personal consequences, and traveling the Christian Way required a politics all its own: the politics of Jesus.

I will not pretend that after reading Brown's book all my students became nonviolent revolutionaries. To my knowledge, none did. But many did shift their priorities. They came to realize that, in the divine scheme of things, the measure of their lives lies not in how much money they make, or how much fame they achieve, but rather in how much they serve "the least of these." They began to evaluate the public policies of business and government, not in terms of how much affluence they offer the rich, but rather in how well they serve the poor. As these students graduated from college, they sought jobs in helping professions, in socially responsible businesses, and in church work. They had been grasped by Brown's vision of peacemaking as part of one's life work.

The Global Village as an Earth Community

We can be similarly grasped. At least this is the case if we are middle-class Christians in relatively comfortable settings. We too are called to "see to it that people have enough to eat" and to make sure that "the politics of the country . . . are so arranged that everybody's basic needs are met" (Brown 1981, 14). Let us turn, then, to what it might mean for us to be peacemakers today. My suggestion is that peacemaking involves attention not only to our global village but also to our local bioregion.

Recall the title of Brown's book: *Making Peace in the Global Village*. He used the image of a global village to help his readers develop a way of understanding themselves and their world. "It is the task of peacemaking Christians," he said, "to insist that we think and act as citizens of the global village."

Three Dimensions of Global Consciousness

For many of us who are Christian, the idea of living in a global village has already affected our understanding of Christianity. First, we have learned to think of the church as a multicultural family, a community among communities in this village. We have come to realize that today most members of the Christian family live in Asia, Africa, and Latin America; if we are living in North Atlantic nations, we are a minority in the Christian community. Indeed, in many ways we realize that various third-world forms of Christianity are more vital and more promising than much of what is happening in the First World. We welcome missionaries from Asia, Africa, and Latin America, so that the First World can itself be revitalized.

Second, we realize that in addition to the Christian family there are other families in the village—other religions—with truth and beauty of their own. Buddhism and Hinduism and native traditions have truths from which we can learn; they, too, have a place in the global ecology of wisdom traditions. Furthermore, we realize the arrogance of affirming that all truth relevant to salvation is to be found in Christianity alone, and that no truth relevant to salvation is to be found elsewhere. We come to see that the living Spirit of God—the source of truth and goodness—is deeper, richer, and wider than Christianity, and that Christianity is one of many traditions in which this Spirit has been influential.

Third, we realize that our own middle-class lifestyles in industrial nations are immoral when compared with the standards of living of many people in industrializing nations. As Christians, we recognize that peacemaking involves learning to live with less, so that the less fortunate can simply live. We see that peacemaking involves a confession of the sinfulness of affluence, and a willingness to live more simply.

The globalizing of Christian consciousness has involved a recognition of cultural diversity within Christianity itself, of religious diversity beyond Christianity, and of profound disparities in standards of living among rich and poor the world over. The three insights above have become commonplace in much progressive Christian consciousness, though many of us are not sure how to act upon them.

The Ecologization of Global Awareness

But now something new is happening. By virtue of environmental crises and a yearning to recover broken bonds with the Earth, our consciousness is being "ecologized." We are coming to see that the global village is more than a human village, and that the families to which we need be sensitive are not just human families. We see that the village itself is a web of life situated on a small but beautiful planet in a backwater galaxy. We realize that this planet is home to countless plants and animals who are fellow pilgrims in an evolutionary adventure—and that they have as much claim on this home as we. We realize that we live in an Earth community.

With this new image of the global village—as an Earth-community-in-process—we begin to think of our own violence in a new way. We become aware not only of the violence we so often inflict on fellow humans, including indigenous peoples and the poor, but also the violence we inflict on kindred creatures and on the Earth as a whole. What's more, we realize that our violence against people on the one hand, and against the Earth and animals on the other, is linked both inwardly and outwardly.

The inner attitudes that enable us to objectify other people and thus reduce them to commodities for our use are the very attitudes that enable us to objectify other living beings and the Earth and reduce them to commodities as well. Whenever we approach other living beings as commodities—human or animal—we neglect the value they have in and for themselves. We treat them as means to our ends at the expense of recognizing that they are ends in themselves.

Ecofeminists emphasize that these objectifying attitudes are themselves reflections of a patriarchal mindset that has functioned in the West to validate subjugation of women. Theologians such as Rosemary Radford Ruether have shown how patriarchal habits of thought have contributed to oppression of women, the human poor, other animals, and the Earth. If we are truly to be peacemakers, says Ruether, we must learn to think and feel in ways that are post-patriarchal. We must realize that violence against the Earth and animals on the one hand, and against humans on the other, intersect in our own inner attitudes, and that these attitudes are deeply patriarchal. We need post-patriarchal ways of thinking and feeling, and modes of social organization that benefit both women and men.[2]

Violence against people and against the Earth sometimes intersect outwardly in actual patterns of behavior. Consider the following example of such linkage, concerned with meat-consumption among the billion or so well-fed people of the world.

Most of us realize, or should realize, that when we eat meat, we are eating the flesh of animals who wished to live just as we wish to live. In industrial

---

2. My own attempt to articulate the nature of such ways of thinking and feeling, and also the differences they make for Christianity, is presented in *Of God and Pelicans: A Theology of Reverence for Life* (1989, 111–45).

societies these animals are often subjected to severe suffering and deprivation under what have been called intensive rearing systems.

A report to the World Council of Churches puts it this way:

> Corporate animal agriculture relies on what are called "close-confine-
> ment" or "intensive-rearing" methods. The animals are taken off the
> land and raised permanently indoors. There is no sunlight, no fresh air,
> often not even room enough to turn around. In many cases six to eight
> laying hens are packed in a wire-mesh metal cage three-quarters of the
> size of a page of daily newspaper. For up to five years, many breeding
> sows are confined to stalls barely larger than their bodies. Veal calves
> (typically male calves born to dairy herds) routinely are taken from their
> mothers at birth and raised in permanent isolation. Increasingly even
> dairy cattle are being taken off the land and raised indoors (Birch 1990a,
> 285).

On the corporate factory farm "virtually every form of behavior is thwarted,
from preening and dust bathing in chickens to nursing and gamboling in veal
calves. When we purchase the products of corporate factory farming, we support massive animal deprivation and death" (Birch 1990a, 286).

What we may not realize, however, is that we are also contributing to violence against the Earth and poor people. In the case of poor people, our
contribution is indirect but real. Poor people need food, and food must be
grown on land. The meat intake of affluent people requires that enormous
amounts of land be used to grow feed grains for animals; this land could
better be used to grow food for direct consumption by people. Moreover, the
growing of feed grain in the large quantities now required involves chemical-
and energy-intensive forms of agriculture that only rich farmers can afford.
In many instances small farmers, who grow some food for themselves and
others, have been pushed off the land to make room for large-scale enter-
prises that grow grain for animals. According to the Worldwatch Institute,
this is happening throughout the world: "Higher meat consumption among
the affluent frequently creates problems for the poor, as the share of farmland
devoted to feed cultivation expands, reducing production of food staples. In
the economic competition for grain fields, the upper-classes usually win"
(Durnig 1991, 31). Thus, in eating meat we contribute to a system that prevents the poor from owning their own land and that prevents the land itself
from being used to provide food for the poor. Worldwatch points out that in a
world that will soon hold six billion people, affluent peoples must learn to eat
less meat so that the poor can simply eat.

In the case of the Earth, our contributions are again indirect but real. Forests often suffer from livestock production as entire stands are leveled to make
way for pastures. The chemical-intensive forms of agriculture used to grow
grain for animal consumption release dangerous herbicides and pesticides into
the ground and water. The energy and water that are required for large-scale

production are enormously wasteful of precious resources. And the wastes from the factory farms and feedlots release noxious gases into the atmosphere and into the ground. Again, if the Earth is to be a healthy habitat for human and nonhuman life, meat-eating among the affluent must be curbed or eliminated.

Evidence suggests that meat-eating is bad for us. Accumulating medical evidence indicates that even moderate consumption of livestock products can reduce life expectancy. Moreover, as the Worldwatch Institute points out, "meat-rich diets contribute to the diseases of affluence, such as heart disease, stroke, and certain types of cancer, that are leading causes of death in industrial countries" (Durnig 1991, 6). A long-range study of diets in China, sponsored by Columbia University, shows that "Chinese villagers on low-fat, low-meat diets suffered less anemia and osteoporosis than their urban compatriots eating more meat" (Durnig 1991, 28). A cosponsor of the study, Colin Campbell, told the *New York Times*: "We're basically a vegetarian species and should be eating a wide variety of plant foods and minimizing our intake of animal foods." This suggests that violence against animals, the Earth, and poor people is also violence against our own bodies. To reduce or relinquish meat intake can be one way of making peace with animals, the Earth, poor people, and ourselves.

But meat-eating is only one example of the intersection of forms of violence. Others include the destruction of tropical rain forests, which simultaneously destroys the habitats of indigenous peoples; dumping toxic wastes in poor countries, which simultaneously threatens the lives of people and kindred creatures; and the abuses of war, which destroy both animals and people.

There was once a time when environmental and human concerns seemed separate, with the former merely a topic for the middle class. Now we realize that they are inseparable. As the Worldwatch Institute puts it:

> Most of the world's looming environmental threats, from groundwater contamination to climate change, are byproducts of affluence. But poverty can drive ecological deterioration when desperate people overexploit their resource base, sacrificing the future to salvage the present. . . . The once separate issues of environment and development are now inextricably linked. Environmental degradation is driving a growing number of people into poverty. And poverty itself has become an agent of ecological degradation, as desperate people consume the resource bases on which they depend. Rather than a choice between the alleviation of poverty and the reversal of environmental decline, world leaders now face the reality that neither goal is achievable unless the other is pursued as well.[3]

---

3. I am unable to find the source of this quotation, though it comes from Worldwatch materials. I am grateful to Laura Malinowski of Worldwatch Institute for helping me find the sources of the other quotations from Worldwatch.

A Still Greener Peace

Struck by our own complicity in an unjust and unsustainable world order, we begin to yearn for a new kind of peace. We begin to feel that we, as Christians, are called to take ever more seriously the image of *shalom* in the Bible, one that suggests a harmony among people, animals, and the Earth—and between all of them and God. We begin to hope for a still greener peace, one that is more ecologically sensitive. To borrow a term from a well-known environmental organization, we might call it greenpeace. Greenpeace is a state in which maximum cooperation is obtained among people, animals, and the Earth, so that all flourish. To be sure, greenpeace includes justice for people. Those who seek greenpeace must struggle against poverty, racism, and sexism in our world. But it also includes justice for animals and the Earth.

Greenpeace is not static. It is dynamic, enjoyed inwardly as well as outwardly. The spirit of adventure is deepened through cooperative and creative communion with people, animals and the Earth.

Most who yearn for inclusive *shalom*, for greenpeace, do not expect its complete realization in this life; *shalom* will always occur in degrees and with vicissitudes. Nor do we expect the rest of creation to commune with us as we commune with it. We expect rattlesnakes to bite us and earthquakes to rattle us. We understand inclusive *shalom* to be a distinctively human possibility, a way paved by eons of cosmic and biological evolution. To be able to partake of this *shalom* is to live up to the idea that we are made in God's image, a God of nonviolence. Our dream of *shalom* is our way of responding to a divine dream that the will of God might be done "on Earth as it is in heaven."

Making Peace in Our Bioregion

What, then, do we do? The oft-repeated answer is that we should "think globally and act locally." Unfortunately, the phrase has become a cliche, more often repeated than acted upon.

Of course, the word *local* can mean many things. In different contexts our locality can be our family, neighborhood, city, state, or nation. Accordingly, we can "act locally" when we love and respect our children and parents; when we are helpful to our neighbors; when we are involved in the affairs of our cities, making them livable for all; and when we advocate policies for our nations. When such actions are guided by the hope of *shalom*, when they take as their yardstick justice and sustainability, they exemplify the very best of local actions.

Still another locality for which we are responsible is our bioregion. A bioregion is an identifiable geographical region of interacting life-systems that are relatively self-sustaining. I live in a woodland bioregion some fifty miles south of the Ozark mountains. Others live in a plains bioregion, or a seacoast bioregion, or a mountain bioregion. These regions are our habitats, our homes. We are planted in them. If we are to be rooted in the Earth in a meaningful way, we must bloom in these regions.

Bioregionalism is not new. Prior to the coming of Europeans, Native American settlements corresponded roughly with individual bioregions. Each bioregion became a basis for a distinct culture and economy. We need to learn from the first Americans and become responsible to the bioregions in which we live. We need to be rooted in the Earth.

The beginnings of such rootedness lie in acquiring a "sense of place," as described in the previous chapter. Inasmuch as we enjoy a sense of place, we will know about the flora and fauna of our bioregions; we will understand their geographical and biological history; we will appreciate local culture and history; we will be sensitive to local landscapes and forms of life. A sense of place involves amazement at the particular and awe for the ordinary. Only when we accept responsibility for the places we live will the world achieve any degree of inclusive *shalom*.

An inner sense of place is not enough. We need to behave in ways that mirror and express our solidarity with the places in which we live, for example, through community development. From a Christian point of view, we are not simply isolated individuals; our well-being is partly dependent on the well-being of the communities of which we are a part, and vice-versa. Insofar as our local community is impoverished, so we are impoverished. As Edward Schwartz puts it: "It now appears certain that a strong, local community is essential to psychological well-being, personal growth, social order, and a sense of political efficacy" (Daly and Cobb 1989, 17). For Christians interested in making peace in their local bioregion, peacemaking must itself involve a cultivation of meaningful community.

Healthy Communities and Responsible Lifestyles

What kinds of communities, then, ought we strive for in our local settings? Following the Green Party of the United States, I suggest that we seek local communities with the following ten features:

- *Grassroots democracy*, such that people have a role in the decisions that affect their lives.
- *Political decentralization*, such that political decisions are not made from distant, monolithic sources.
- *Respect for diversity*, such that people of different ethnic groups, races, and religious traditions are respected in their differences, and such that other forms of life—animals and plants—are similarly respected in their differences.
- *Nonviolence*, such that people and animals are free from abuse and free to realize their unique potentials.

- *Post-patriarchal values*, such that women are free from being objectified by men, and women and men alike are free from the hierarchical thinking and preoccupation with power that have characterized many patriarchal societies.
- *Personal and social responsibility*, such that people are encouraged to take responsibility for their own lives and also to take responsibility for the common good of their local communities.
- *Global responsibility*, such that people take responsibility for the various ways in which their local actions influence people in other parts of the world.
- *Future focus*, such that the needs of future generations of human beings and other creatures, within and outside the bioregion, are taken into account in the making of decisions.
- *Ecological wisdom*, such that the limits of the bioregion to absorb pollution, supply resources, and carry human population are respected.
- *Community-based economics*, such that local economies are oriented toward self-reliance with regard to basic goods such as energy and agriculture.

Each of these ten values merits extensive discussion.[4] Taken as a whole, they form an image of the kinds of communities we will want to see realized in our neighborhoods, cities, rural areas, and our bioregions. If we are to make peace in our local bioregions, we seek to develop communities that exemplify these values.

Lifestyle Options

For most of us, peacemaking activities involve lifestyle commitments. Consider some of the proposals offered in *Shopping for a Better World* (1991). The book is a shopper's guide to buying from environmentally and socially responsible manufacturers. It helps us go into a local supermarket, for example, and buy products that are produced by companies with good records in the hiring of women and minorities, in charitable giving, companies not involved in animal testing or environmental despoliation. In its introduction, *Shopping for a Better World* lists additional lifestyle activities that can help make our world better. According to its authors, we can:

- Learn to live more simply by reducing consumption and living with less, emphasizing quality not quantity in our life.
- Do volunteer work at a community center, a school, a child care center, a nursing home, a prison, a local congregation.

---

4. I am indebted to Charlene Spretnak (1991, 262) for naming these values for me. For more information on the Green Party and its values, write the Green Committees of Correspondence, National Clearinghouse, P.O. Box 30208, Kansas City, MO 64112.

- Contribute 5 percent or more of our income to charities and/or local communities of faith.
- Become actively involved in local school boards in order to improve the quality of public education.
- Buy products that are produced by companies with good records in minority hiring, charitable giving, environmental responsibility, and so on.
- Encourage our places of work to seek out banks and suppliers owned by women and minorities and to place women and minorities on their own boards of directors and in managerial positions.
- Reduce or eliminate our consumption of meat; buy cosmetics and household products that have not been tested on animals.
- Recycle newspapers, bottles, and cans; reuse containers and products as much as possible; reject disposable products.
- Make sure the household equipment and fixtures in our homes are maximally efficient in their use of electricity and water; weatherize our homes.
- Support legislation aimed at promoting just and ecologically sustainable living within local communities and in the broader world; for example, equal employment opportunity legislation, clean air and water acts.

These are not "commandments" but rather guidelines or suggestions. Perhaps we cannot do all these things; the important thing is to do some of them, preferably in the context and with the help of others who are similarly committed. Thus we build confidence that we can do still more.

We need to realize that actions are external; they need to be qualified and complemented by what is inside us, by our states of consciousness and our understanding. If we think about how we can make peace in our local bioregions, we must try to be the kind of people, with the kinds of perceptions and attitudes, who are aware of our own complicity in unjust and unsustainable social structures; sensitive to the connections between our own lives and other people, plants, animals, and the Earth; nonviolent in spirit and respectful of diversity.

Toward these ends spiritual disciplines, such as worship and prayer and participation in communities of faith, can be as important as other activities. At least they can be important if they are themselves sensitive to the Earth as well as to people, and if they are post-patriarchal. One of the best things we can do in order to be effective in our own local communities is to set aside time each day for a spiritual practice of one sort or another. Such practices give us the centeredness that is required for healthy peacemaking.

Economics for Community

Will the lifestyle options noted above help end the unnecessary violence now inflicted on people, animals, and the Earth? Are they sufficient for Christian peacemaking?

The answer is no. Lifestyle changes are necessary but not sufficient for the kind of world we need today. If they are to make a difference, they must be complemented by structural changes in the economic and political structures of our local communities, nations, and the world.

One problem with emphasizing lifestyle changes alone is that few people are willing to adopt them, and even those who do often find them quite difficult. One example of the latter is the eminent Protestant theologian John Cobb. More than any Protestant theologian in the United States, Cobb has spoken to the need for an ecological dimension to the peace sought by Christians and others. His own story of adopting modest changes in lifestyle and experimenting with communal living can be instructive to all of us, showing the need for structural changes to complement lifestyle changes.

In *Sustainability: Economics, Ecology, and Justice* Cobb relates that, when he became seriously aware of the environmental crisis in 1969, his "first response was to think of the lifestyle changes that would be needed if Americans were to cease to be so destructive a factor on the earth's surface." He felt that "our Christian faith should enable . . . us in the church to shift away from a highly consumptive lifestyle and accustom ourselves to more frugal living so that there would be resources for others to use" (1992, 34).

Cobb and his wife made adjustments in their use of energy, consumption of goods, and recycling. A few years later they joined two other couples in an experiment in communal living.

Cobb's description of this experiment is striking in its candor.

> That experiment had many ups and downs. For us it ended after four years. We had learned much about ourselves and one another. We had probably conserved in terms of resource use. I continue to affirm such experiments, but for us it was not the answer.
>
> Our experience was discouraging. If we, who were well above average in motivation, could change so little, and with such small effect, could appeals to people to change their lifestyles be of much significance in relation to the magnitude of the problem? I doubted it, and still doubt it (1992, 34).

Cobb did not conclude that people will avoid lifestyle changes forever. Indeed, he sees such changes as inevitable. "If the economically privileged pursue our present course, the time will come when we or our descendants will change lifestyles dramatically. There simply will not be the energy and goods available to continue our profligate patterns, or we will be adjusting to drastic changes in our environment." His point, however, is that we will not do so voluntarily. "Voluntary belt-tightening will not go far toward responding to the problem" (1992, 35).

We have come to enjoy the goods and services of modern industrial life, regardless of the fact that such life is immensely unjust in many dimensions and tremendously antagonistic to community life. Cobb's experience led him to "try to envision a society that is at least as enjoyable as this one, that so orders its life as to consume and pollute within sustainable limits" (1992, 35).

The limits of which Cobb speaks include the limits of the Earth to supply nonrenewable resources such as petroleum and minerals, to renew renewable resources such as timber and water, and to absorb pollution. A society is sustainable if it lives within such limits, and unsustainable if it does not. Modern industrial societies are unsustainable.

Modern industrial societies are unsustainable because they are committed to an ever-increasing production and consumption of goods, to economic growth. "Growth" of this sort is the central organizing principle of modern, industrial societies, and, in this sense, the ultimate god of consumer society. The problem with such growth, at local levels or at a global level, is twofold.

Growth-Oriented Economies as Unsustainable

First, economic growth cannot be sustained into the indefinite future, given the reality of ecological limits. In addition to the Earth's limits to absorb pollution, renew renewable resources, and provide nonrenewable resources, there is also an ultimate ecological limit: the limited amount of energy available for human use after photosynthesis. This is called the Net Primary Production, or NPP. It is the amount of energy captured in photosynthesis by plants, minus the energy used in their own growth and reproduction.

Biologists estimate that 25 percent of potential global NPP produced by plants in land and water is now used by human beings; if we take into account land alone, 40 percent is used by human beings, leaving only 60 percent for the other 99 percent of the planet's creatures (Daly and Cobb 1989, 143–44). Humans use this energy not only for food, fiber, fuel, and timber, but also indirectly by reducing potential NPP due to alteration of ecosystems caused by humans (deforestation, desertification, paving over, and human conversion to less productive systems such as agriculture).

Herman Daly and John Cobb point out that, if humans now use 25 percent of NPP, two more doublings of this rate would come to 100 percent, an ecological impossibility. And yet, growth-oriented economies are bent on increasing the human use of such energy indefinitely. This means that growth-oriented economies are on a highway to disaster. In the words of Daly and Cobb: "Unless we awaken to the existence and nearness of scale limits, then the greenhouse effect, ozone layer depletion, and acid rain will be just a preview of disasters to come, not in the vague distant future but in the next generation" (Daly and Cobb 1989, 144).

In sum, growth-oriented economies are incompatible with the ecological wisdom necessary for *shalom*-based, peaceful communities. If they continue, we cannot make peace with the Earth.

Growth-Oriented Economies as Obstacles to Community

The second reason that growth-oriented economies are obstacles to peace is their effects on human communities. It is arguable that, for a time, the industrial revolution was a benefit to humanity even as it was a cost to the Earth. It raised the standard of living for many. Now, so Daly and Cobb argue, the costs of economic growth outweigh its benefits even for humans.

The reason for this is that growth-oriented economies are built upon the assumption that human beings are isolated individuals, needing only to consume and produce, rather than individuals-in-community, needing rich and meaningful connections with other people and the Earth. As isolated individuals, they can be moved around in search of employment, regardless of how disruptive such moves are, as long as such moves contribute to the overall production and consumption of the society. The supposition is that they will be happier for the disruption, because they will reap the benefits of such increased production and consumption.

The costs of this way of thinking in the Third World, particularly Latin America, are well-known. Under the auspices of "development," which means "growth," lands once used by rural peoples to grow their own crops for food are now used to grow cash crops—such as coffee and sugar—for export to wealthy nations. The wealthy landowners and elites justify this in the name of economic growth, which, they argue, will benefit all. Villagers have been forced to migrate to large cities in search of industrial jobs, which often pay wages insufficient for quality living. Wealthy landowners and industrialists have become the primary beneficiaries of "development," rural communities have been destroyed, and countless poor people have wandered into cities in search of jobs that do not exist.

The alternative to "growth" is "community development." Community development takes the village community, rather than the individual or the nation, as the unit of development. It approaches the village holistically, in light of its moral, religious, educational, and political dimensions, as well as its economic dimensions. How can this village best meet its needs? The villagers themselves make their own decisions and determine their own fate. As Daly and Cobb explain: "They may increase the water supply by introducing a pump, or their food production by replacing wooden ploughs with metal ones. Whatever the decision, the community is usually made more productive in doing what it wants to do as a community" (Daly and Cobb 1989, 165). Daly and Cobb suggest that community development ought to be the goal of economic theories, policies, and institutions in urban as well as rural settings, and in the First World as well as the Third World.

The policy implications of an economics for community are manifold. Daly and Cobb specify some of these implications in terms of trade, population, land use, agriculture, industry, labor, income taxes, and national security. In the case of trade, for example, they recommend that nation-states become as self-reliant as possible in terms of basic goods such as agriculture and energy, and then trade only in inessentials. Such self-reliance involves a move toward protectionism, not free trade, so that countries can move toward self-reliance. This involves tariffs on imported goods.

The ideal, however, is not to have a system of nation-states and local communities that are utterly independent of one another. Rather, it is to have a global village, which is not a single, homogenized world order, but rather a community of communities, each enjoying some degree of self-reliance in order to trade on equal terms and enjoy the fruits of cultural interchange.

For Christians interested in peacemaking, the kinds of questions with which Daly and Cobb wrestle are critical. Lifestyle changes alone will not inch our troubled planet toward a greater degree of peace; in addition to such changes, there is a need for a critique of existing social orders and an offering of alternatives such as those proposed by Daly and Cobb. Part of Christian peacemaking must lie in creative yet practical working alternatives to current systems at the level of politics, economics, and social policy.

Of course, part of Christian peacemaking must also lie in the hard work to make those visions a reality. Sometimes there will be pain and despair. The despair is the other side of connectedness, a symptom of just how immanent we are in the lives of other living beings, and they in us. We would not feel the pain of other people, of animals, of the Earth, if we were not so connected. In a Christianity with roots and wings, peacemaking is not all sweetness and light. It knows the pain of being connected to lonely grandfathers, to homeless mothers, to frightened prisoners, to hungry children, to tortured animals, to extinguished species, to a forsaken Earth. But it is also hopeful. Its Way is to follow Jesus, sometimes to the cross, trustful that new life comes even from pain and death.

Chapter 4

Whose Story Shall We Tell?

The New Story and Biblical Story Compared

Several years ago I participated in a workshop on religion and ecology for Jewish and Christian seminarians. I was one of several resource leaders whose task was to help the seminarians better understand the ecological implications of their own faith. In the process I realized just how un-ecological my own point of view could be.

The conference took place at a beautiful conference center in the Hill Country of Texas. A window in our meeting room opened to a gorgeous limestone bluff standing over the Frio River. During breaks all the participants would go outside and stand on a porch gazing at the bluff, imbibing its creative powers and nourished by its quiet energy. We could not keep our eyes off it.

A few at the conference had backgrounds in science, and they were able to explain to us that the bluff had a story of its own, written not in words but in lines, textures, and colors. Various rock layers, clearly distinguishable to the naked eye, revealed millions of years of evolution that had preceded and then been shaped by the river. Various kinds of trees—mountain cedar, sycamores— sat at the water's edge, telling stories of the emergence of life in the area, as did indigenous plants shooting out from crevices in the bluff. And various animals could sometimes be seen grazing at the top of the bluff, particularly white-tailed deer, telling stories of individual animals and their various feeding habits during the day.

These stories were not verbal, but with the help of our naturalist guides, they were readable. Gary Snyder puts it this way: "A text is information stored through time. The stratigraphy of rocks, layers of pollen in a swamp, the outward expanding circles in the trunk of a tree, can be seen as texts. The calligraphy of rivers winding back and forth over the land leaving layer upon layer of traces in previous riverbeds is text" (1990, 66). During breaks at the conference, we read such texts.

But one did not have to be a naturalist in order to be awed by the sheer beauty of the animals and plants and rocks as they disclosed themselves to us.

Throughout the conference we felt God in the Earth, not as a person but as a power. We felt Holy Wisdom through the sheer "suchness" of the bluff in its numinous energies.

During the sessions themselves, however, we failed to acknowledge the suchness. When it came to Christian and Jewish approaches to ecology, the resource leaders referred not to the palpable presence of the bluff, but rather to books written in human languages. We assumed that our only reliable clues for approaching the Earth, our only valid sources of revelation, came from Torah and the Bible. We forgot that the Earth itself could be revelatory.

It is not that we said anything untrue. For my part, I spoke of the goodness of creation, quite apart from its usefulness to humans, as celebrated in Genesis (1:1–25); of second Isaiah's vision of a peaceable kingdom (Is 11:6–9); of Paul's view that the cosmic Christ is a reality in which the whole of creation is held together (Col 1:17). These ideas are important. They can indeed contribute to ecological sensitivity within Christian circles.

Still, they were ideas gained from a human book. They seemed abstract to the seminarians, most of whom were focused on the presence of the bluff as perceived through the plate-glass window. They were all too aware that, in turning to pages of written scripture, I was forgetting the sheer presence of a different kind of scripture, composed of rock rather than ink, with a story of its own. I was forgetting nature as text.

Realizing what was happening, a young woman stood up and said: "Turn around, look out the window, trust the bluff!" Her point was that I was so fixated upon the written word that I was ignoring the deep feelings most of us were experiencing in relation to our beautiful setting. We were failing to allow those feelings to be our guides. We were failing to treat our own experiences, and the natural world that prompted them, as revelatory.

The Earth *is* sacred revelation. We know this fact when we are troubled. Often, when we need to work through a problem, we take a walk in a park, or go outside and sit under a tree, or visit one of our "sacred places" in the natural world, or spend time with our pets, or listen to the wisdom of our own bodies, or gaze at the stars. In so doing we turn to the planet and cosmos—the "other 99 percent of creation"—for assistance. We hear the voices of nature, not in a way that obstructs our critical faculties, but in a way that nourishes them. Such is the way living scriptures—written or non-written—should function.

Still, our religious institutions have not always encouraged us to find guidance in this way. It was in the Hill Country of Texas that I realized the inadequacy of book-centeredness. I realized that attachment to words, even sacred words, is a form of idolatry.

What should we do, given this legacy of word-olatry? Some might argue that we should throw away our books, or at least set them aside for, say, twenty years, and simply learn from the rocks and trees and bluffs. There is some merit in the suggestion, so urgent is our need, as humans, to realize palpable bonds with creation. But such an approach is neither practical nor desirable. It leads to a false dichotomy between verbal revelation and nonverbal revelation. After all, books too are part of creation. Our verbal stories are part of the history of creation, as are the books in which they are contained and the trees and chemicals from which those books are composed. Ultimately, the need is not to throw away our books, but rather to complement our openness to verbal revelation with openness to nonverbal revelation. In part, the latter involves receptivity to opportunities for green grace, described in Chapter 2. We receive nonverbal revelation when we enjoy a sense of place, when we bond with animals, when we listen to our own bodies, and when we experience the silent darkness of wild forests. All of these experiences tell us something about creation, about God, and about ourselves.

Another way of receiving nonverbal revelation, or at least of opening ourselves to the possibility, is by recognizing the power of such revelation in the verbal stories that shape our lives—to use words to help point us beyond words. If, as Gary Snyder insists, the expanding circles of trees tell a story, then perhaps we can learn to tell our own stories in ways that include the expanding circles of trees and, beyond that, the expanding universe. We then can see human stories and tree stories as episodes in the larger Story, the adventure of the universe as One. If we learn to think of ourselves as part of that larger Story, then we are encouraged by our words themselves to attend to and even trust the bluffs and rivers around us.

In order to tell a more inclusive story, however, most of us need help. We have not learned a universe story in Sunday School. Accordingly, one purpose of this chapter is to present the "new story" as it is now told by creative thinkers such as Thomas Berry and Brian Swimme in *The Universe Story* (1992), Rosemary Ruether in *Gaia and God* (1992), Sallie McFague in *The Body of God* (1993), and process theologians such as John Cobb and David Griffin. Swimme is a mathematical cosmologist; Berry is a cultural historian and leading environmental visionary; Ruether is the leading Christian feminist theologian; McFague is a leading ecological theologian; and Cobb and Griffin are philosophical theologians shaped by the natural sciences. In their own ways, all of these thinkers believe that the story of the universe as told by the natural sciences can, if supplemented with spiritual sensitivity and vision, provide a corrective to the fragmented commitments and nihilism that characterize our age. A Christianity with roots and wings can follow their lead. The story of the universe can be part of the wisdom that shapes Christian life and consciousness.

A second purpose of this chapter is to compare and contrast the new story with the biblical story. If a universe story is to shape the lives of Christians, it must somehow be wedded with the story of God and God's love for creation, found in the Bible. In the latter part of this chapter I will present an ecological reading of the biblical story, suggesting that it, in its way, can inspire Christians toward communion with creation, just as the universe story does in its way. In the two chapters that follow I will try to combine the two stories, one biblical and one scientific, into a single story, simply called the Christian story.

Let us begin, then, with the thought of Thomas Berry, with his own reasons for insisting upon a "new story," and with a brief overview of that new story.

Thomas Berry and the New Story

Though he has had profound influence on many Christians, Thomas Berry does not think of himself as a theologian. He is a cultural historian who has also described himself as a "geologian," because he takes the history of the Earth as the primary context in which to understand human history. Berry's thought resonates deeply with traditional Christian themes, and he self-consciously identifies with and is influenced by the cosmological orientations of Thomas Aquinas and Teilhard de Chardin. Moreover, along with his colleague Brian Swimme, he is having an important impact on many Christians in North America and other parts of the world, providing them with a creation-centered way of understanding their faith.

The Need for a New Story

Berry's most important contribution to the Christian community is his insistence that Christians and others need a new story of creation. In emphasizing story, Berry stands in a long Christian tradition. Stories concerning Jesus and the prophets, martyrs and saints, have long been a part of the Christian heritage. Indeed, many North American theologians in our time have come to realize that people's lives are more deeply shaped by stories than by philosophies and theologies. There is a growing movement within Christian ethics today that sees Christianity as a story-based tradition, emphasizing that people learn to be Christians by hearing the Christian story and seeing it embodied in the lives of people living in Christian communities. In theological circles this movement is often called narrative theology, and it is supported by ways of reading the Bible that emphasize seeing many biblical accounts as narratives rather than literal accounts of historical events.

Though Berry does not address the views of narrative theologians, he contributes to their discussions by showing that, among other things, creation stories must shape the Christian consciousness. Creation stories are not simply stories about the past, about how the universe came into existence; they are also stories about the present and future of the universe. Specifically, they give their hearers a sense of their appropriate place in creation in the present, and they offer guidance about how to treat creation in the future. Indeed, they are stories that help their hearers tap into and become parts of the creative processes of creation itself.

Berry points out that most humans throughout history have had functional creation stories. The gatherers and hunters had them; the early agricultural villagers had such stories; and the classical religious civilizations have had them. In each instance the elders would pass down the stories to the children. The stories would be a means by which generations of people would understand their place in relation to animals and plants, the Earth and stars, and (in many instances) the gods and goddesses.

In the Western world of late, Berry suggests, our creation stories have become dysfunctional. The Christian tradition contains creation stories, as recorded in the early chapters of Genesis, which are read in worship services throughout the Christian world. But these stories no longer provide contemporary Christians with a sense of their place in creation. Few Christians "live" in terms of the Genesis creation stories. Whether understood mythically or literally, the biblical stories do not guide us in knowing how to live creatively and responsibly within creation.

The good news is that a new story is emerging. A significant dimension of its plot is being adumbrated, not by priests or theologians, but by scientists. The new story is the story of evolution, whose general outlines Berry draws from the natural sciences and then interprets in a way influenced by Teilhard de Chardin. What interests Berry is that, in one version or another, this story is being told around the world: in Saudi Arabia and in Lithuania, in the United States and in Brazil; in China and in India. For the first time in history we sense the emergence of a common creation story across cultures.

Berry's version of the new story, particularly as told with the help of Brian Swimme in *The Universe Story*, is creative and imaginatively gripping. He divides the new story into four easily understandable, evolutionary phases: 1) the galactic phase, in which the elemental particles and then stars were formed; 2) the geological phase, in which the Earth evolved as a member of the solar system; 3) the biological phase, in which life on Earth came into existence in all its variety; and 4) the human phase, with the rise of consciousness and cultural forms. It is with the human phase that the universe becomes conscious of itself in a unique way. In us the story becomes self-reflexive; we are a chapter in the history of the universe that is able to look back on the other chapters and understand ourselves within the context of the story. But the human phase is quite dependent on the previous phases, which have their own histories independent of human life.

A brief sketch of each phase will provide a sense for the entire scheme.[1]

---

1. In what follows I draw from the work of Berry along with his colleague Brian Swimme in *The Universe Story*, and also from the work of Rosemary Ruether in *Gaia and God* and process theologians. In the case of geological evolution, I draw also from a student of Thomas Berry and creative thinker in her own right, Joanna Macy.

The Galactic Phase

The galactic phase begins with an originating event that occurred fifteen to twenty billion years ago, with a fiery birth, a big bang, a primordial flaring forth. Prior to this, all the matter and energy in the universe was gathered into a dense core of energy that had unimaginable power. The dense core exploded into fragments, which then proceeded to evolve in their own ways into atoms and stars and galaxies and life. Reading these words is itself a creative offshoot, a primal manifestation, of the original flaring forth. So is the page on which the words are printed, and the tree from which the page was made. All beings in the universe are creative manifestations of the original energy in the dense core.

No one knows where the dense core came from. Some believe it was created by God from nothing; others believe it was the tail end of a previous epoch in universe history, which itself was preceded by still earlier epochs, extending into a beginningless past; and still others refuse to speculate. What is agreed upon is that the dense core and its flaring forth formed the beginning of our cosmic epoch, the beginning of our particular universe story. The core of energy was not located in space, because there was no space in which to be located. It was only after the explosion that time and space, particles and light, came into existence. In the beginning, so it seems, there was sheer creative energy, spaceless and timeless.

After the explosion, several major transformations occurred, the first of which took place in the first three minutes of the history of the cosmos. It lay in the emergence of four laws—the gravitational, the electromagnetic, and two laws governing interactions of nuclei within atoms—by which some of the energy from the explosion would be given order. These "laws" were not necessarily imposed from the outside; rather they were "habits" of interaction that emerged amid the chaotic freedom of random energy pulsations emanating from the dense core.

A second major transformation in the galactic phase lay in the emergence of the first elemental particles, ranging from baryons, which emerged in the first millionth of a second, to simple nuclei, which emerged in the first few minutes. These were the first "new things" in the history of the universe. After these elemental particles emerged, the first atoms—helium and hydrogen—came into existence; they planted the seeds for the evolution of stars and galaxies.

For the next fourteen billion years the universe enjoyed the fruits of stellar evolution. By the force of gravity, helium and hydrogen began to form great clouds, which collapsed to form the first stars. These early stars burned and then exploded as supernovas in processes from which the rest of the atomic elements were formed.

The sun of our solar system was one such star, burning in the corner of the Milky Way galaxy. Our galaxy is but one of hundreds of billions of galaxies in the universe, each of which consists of billions of stars. Viewed from the lens of galactic evolution, we live on a small planet in a backwater galaxy, nested in the context of a much larger adventure—that of the universe itself—that continues to this day, with stars emerging, burning, and then dying to produce still more stars. Our own bodies are forged from such elements. We are indeed stardust.

The Geological Phase

The planet Earth emerged out of a cloud surrounding the sun, and quickly became a center of power in its own right.[2] It initiated processes of geological evolution such as the development of atmospheres, continents, and oceans, some of which continue into the present. Similar forms of geological evolution emerged on other planets but for various reasons became frozen. Dynamic evolution seems to have ended on Venus and Mercury some three billion years ago, and on Mars a billion years ago. Apparently only Earth has been the kind of cauldron for geological evolution that made possible the emergence of life.

Early in its history, the surface of the Earth was rock and crystal, beneath which burned tremendous fires. Heavier matter like iron sank to the center, and the lighter elements floated to the surface forming a granite crust. Continuous volcanic activity brought up a rich supply of minerals and lifted up chains of mountains.

Then, about four billion years ago, when the temperature fell below the boiling point of water, it began to rain. The rain fell upon the rocks and the seas emerged: a thin salty soup containing the basic ingredients of life. Finally, a bolt of lightning fertilized the molecular soup, and the first cell was born. The biological phase had begun.

The Biological Phase

From the vantage point of stellar evolution, it is difficult to know what place life on Earth ought to play in cosmic story. On the one hand, the Earth is but a small planet orbiting a small star in a minor galaxy. On the other hand, it is the only planet of which we are presently aware with life on it. As Rosemary Ruether observes: "It seems puzzling that, in the myriad assemblies of billions of planets in billions of galaxies, the particular conditions of life would not have appeared on other planets. Yet, in the absence of evidence for this, Earth continues to be the one planet in all the universe where life is known to have developed" (1992, 42–43).

---

2. Much of the language used to describe the geological phase comes from a guided meditation developed by Joanna Macy and John Seed, in which they invite participants to imagine themselves as the evolving Earth. I participated in the meditation at a retreat. The language comes from an oral tape; I have been unable to find the written version.

For all we know, notes Ruether, Earth is the one planet in the universe that is home to beings such as ourselves, who can contemplate the universe as a whole, and understand the story told above. To our knowledge, "Earth is where the whole cosmic process becomes conscious of itself" (1992, 43). For this reason alone our planet deserves a prominent place in the telling of the cosmic story.

Of course, we humans who can tell the cosmic story are ourselves members of the family of life and products of Earth history. Our self-consciousness and our contemplation of the cosmos itself took several billion years to emerge and are paralleled by other modes of consciousness, including the consciousness enjoyed by other animals. Even as we are cousins to the stars, we are kin to all our fellow earthlings.

The first forms of life emerged some four billion years ago, in the form of bacteria. These were single-celled organisms without nuclei. They prevailed on Earth for approximately two billion years and still compose the largest population of life on Earth. Their earliest forms lived in the oceans, and gradually mutants emerged of various sorts, each of which would play a role in subsequent evolution. Some could feed on the decayed bodies of other bacteria, forming the first ecocommunities; some could even capture photons from the sun and transform them into usable energy. It was with the bacteria that one of the most remarkable achievements of our planet began, namely photosynthesis, by which the sun's energy is converted to carbohydrates, with oxygen being released from the combustion. Ruether notes just how long this process took: "It took about 3.9 billion years, some eight-ninths of earth's history, simply to generate photosynthesizing bacteria" (1992, 45).

After photosynthesizing bacteria emerged, the stage was finally set for multi-celled bacteria, then primitive algae and fish. About five hundred million years ago the first plants emerged from algae gathered on coastal ponds and began to colonize the land. Insects followed to feed on them. Over the next two hundred million years the algae developed into large fern trees and the fish into amphibians, who became egg-laying reptiles and birds. About two hundred twenty-five million years ago the reptiles became dinosaurs, who ruled our planet for some one hundred sixty million years. Mammals also emerged during this period, but were subservient to the reptiles.

The extinction of the giant reptiles sixty million years ago set the stage for the great age of mammals, which continues to this day. The first humans emerged four million years ago as an offshoot of a line that also produced the great apes.

To gain perspective on how late humans appeared in the evolutionary process, we can show biological evolution on Earth as a thirty-day month, with each day representing one hundred fifty million years.[3]

---

3. The calendar is borrowed from Tucker 1989.

Geological Calendar for the History of the Earth

					1	2
(1 day = 150 million years) Homo sapiens appeared 10 minutes ago All recorded history began 30 seconds ago						

3	4	5	6	7	8 Bacteria	9 Bluegreen algae
10	11	12	13	14	15	16
17	18	19	20	21	22	23
24 First nucle-ated cells	25	26	27 Aquatic life; abundant fossils; invertebrates dominant	28 First land plants; first vertebrates; first land animals; first amphibians	29 Vast coal forests; insects; first mammals; reptiles dominant	30 Dinosaurs; first birds; first flowering plants; rise of mammals; Homo sapiens; recorded history

From such a calendar we realize that humans and other mammals are newcomers on the evolutionary scene. As Ruether points out, "Humans occupy . . . less than one-tenth of one percent of earth's history" (1992, 45). When we realize that this "month" is itself but an episode in the larger context of the history of the universe, we are further humbled. Not only are we latecomers temporally, we are minuscule spatially. We are small parts of a much greater whole, itself unfolding in myriad ways, of which life is but one.

The Human Phase

Thomas Berry divides the human phase into five periods: the great age of hunters and gatherers, or the Paleolithic Phase; the age of agricultural villages, or the Neolithic Phase; the age of the classical civilization and the religious cultures of the world; the rise of nations and the emergence of science and technology; and finally, the emerging "Ecozoic" Age (1988, 101; Berry and Swimme 1992, 241–61).

The Paleolithic Phase is the longest and most adaptive phase of human history. It constitutes 98 percent of human history and consists of the time when humans roamed in bands of twenty to fifty as gatherers and hunters. During this period the use of fire emerged (500,000 years ago), followed by ritual burials (100,000 years ago), and cave paintings (18,000 years ago).

As the dominant form of life for humans on the planet, the Paleolithic Phase ended with the agricultural revolution, when humans began to cultivate garden plots and adopt sedentary styles of life. Thus begins the Neolithic Phase, which occurred in various parts of the planet some ten to twelve thousand years ago. It was here that "dominion over the Earth" began for humans, due partly to great increases in human population made possible by increased food supplies.

Part of this dominion lay in a domestication of animals, and part in the cultivation of plants. Sheep and goats were tamed in the Middle East; water buffalo, pigs, and chickens were tamed in Southeast Asia; horses were tamed in Eastern Europe; elephants were tamed in India. Wheat and barley were cultivated in the Middle East; rice in Southeast Asia; and corn, squash, peppers, and beans in the Americas.

But part of dominion also lay in a sense of difference from the rest of creation, a sense that animals and plants are somehow to be tamed in the first place. It was here that, for the first time in human history, it became possible to imagine human beings as separated from the rest of creation by distinctively human powers of control and manipulation.

From the point of view of Berry, such dominion is best understood as a mode of human adaptation rather than divine mandate. Rosemary Ruether agrees: "Clearly anthropocentric claims to have been given 'dominion' over the Earth, and over all its plants and animals, appears absurd in light of 4,599,600,000 years in which Earth got along without humans at all!" (1992, 45).

The third great period of human history—the age of the classical civilizations—emerged as an offshoot of Neolithic villages. It began with the appearance of great urban centers in different parts of the planet. Around 3500 B.C.E., the wheel and cuneiform were invented in ancient Sumeria, and around 3000 B.C.E. civilizations emerged around the Nile in Egypt. Approximately 2800 B.C.E. the Indus Valley civilizations appeared along the Indus River in India; around 2100 B.C.E. Minoan civilizations emerged in Crete; and around 1100 B.C.E. the Olmec civilizations appeared in the Americas. Such events set the stage for the rise of the great religions of the world: Hinduism, Buddhism, Jainism, Confucianism, Taoism, Judaism, Christianity, and Islam. These, of course, are the events studied in what is often called world history.

The fourth great period in human history was the age of science and technology, accompanied by the rise of nation-states. This is the period of the American Revolution, the French Revolution, and the colonization of the world by European powers, with the British assuming control over India and, in the nineteenth century, with European powers dividing Africa into myriad colonies. This is also the age in which Copernicus showed that the Earth revolves around the sun, not vice versa, and in which Newton offered the modern view of the universe. Gradually, there emerged the idea that the Earth, and life on Earth, are themselves the result of an evolutionary process, itself more like an ongoing exploration than fulfillment of a preconceived blueprint. As Berry puts it, "the modern revelation" had begun.

The final age, the Ecozoic Age, does not yet exist, and it may never exist. It is what Berry thinks can exist, if humans learn from the modern revelation, and come to understand themselves as plain citizens of, not exceptions to, the planet and its beauty. Berry uses the word *Ecozoic* to suggest that, at this stage in history, humans assume so much control that we alter the basic chemistry and biology of the planet in ways that form a geological age of its own. His hope is that we will learn to use our control in ways that heal rather than harm, that celebrate rather than dominate. The alternative is a failure to live up to, and into, the dream of the Earth.

Some Spiritual Implications of the New Story

Given the new story noted above, these questions emerge: Does the story itself have an underlying meaning? Is the history of the universe merely a random reshuffling of material elements, or does it have direction and purpose?

Berry's answer is that the unfolding universe *does* have direction and purpose. Along with Teilhard de Chardin and process theologians, he believes that the universe manifests an interiority, an internal aliveness, that is present in each and every creature—and that is capable of responding to general goals and purposes. We sense this interiority in the indeterminate spontaneity of subatomic particles, the self-organizing adaptiveness of living cells, the goal-directed wisdom of individual animals, and the self-reflexive consciousness of human beings. Each and every creature possesses a point of view of its own, a perspective, that is imbued with creativity, awareness, and eros. Each creature is in its own way alive, a subject and not simply an object.

What, then, are the aims or purposes to which, in a general way, the creatures respond? Berry names three. Taken together, these principles form the spirituality of the universe, a spirituality to which we contribute and in which we participate, if we have eyes to see and hearts to feel.

The first is the principle of differentiation. Over vast stretches of time, says Berry, the universe has been drawn toward diversity as something good in its own right. Since the primal flash billions of years ago, countless kinds of creatures have emerged: leptons, neutrons, and protons; proteins, carbohydrates, and lipids; protozoa, plants, and animals; planets, moons, and stars. Moreover, within its own kind, each creature is unique. No two are *exactly* alike. It is as if from the very beginning the universe has yearned for pluralism, for variety, for multiplicity. It has sought to become a diversified Sacred Whole. There is a lesson in this for us. We humans find our rightful place in the cosmos not by denying differences but rather by delighting in them, recognizing that differences need not be divisive, but that they are necessary to the whole. To the degree that we can celebrate otherness we internalize in our hearts the principle of differentiation that has been exemplified throughout cosmic history.

The second is the principle of subjectivity. As just noted, each creature is a subject and not simply an object. The principle of subjectivity adds that, over time, the universe seems drawn toward more sentient forms of subjectivity. The earliest living cells, for example, were sentient. They possessed some degree of awareness, creativity, and desire. But as they bonded together to form complex organs, like the brain, more intense forms of sentience became possible.

Consider a housecat. She feels the presence of her environment in a remarkable way, exhibiting both the alertness of a Zen monk and the vulnerability of a small child. Her subjective states of awareness are dependent on the cells in her brain, and yet they are more than simply the sum of her brain cells. She is a living soul who can suffer more intensely, but also enjoy more richly, than any cell in her body or brain. As an ensouled creature she adds something to the history of creation that was unknown prior to the emergence of multi-celled organisms.

Here, too, there is a lesson for humans. We find our place in the cosmos not by denying the many states of awareness of which we and other creatures are capable but by celebrating them, recognizing that heightened subjectivity is itself one aim of the universe story. To the degree that we are inwardly alive and awake, we add our own distinctive voice to the history of creation. We add subjective richness to the adventure of the universe as One.

The third principle is communion. The universe is not simply a collection of objects, says Berry, it is a communion of subjects. This means that individualized forms of subjectivity become fully themselves not when they luxuriate in isolation, but when they enter into rich bonds with others, forming societies of mutual immanence. In truth, all entities already are communions, whether they know it or not. An atom, for example, is a communion of subatomic particles. Its subatomic particles are mutually present to one another, and mutually immanent in one another, such that they form a mini-church, a micro-*sangha*. Similarly, a living cell is a communion of organelles; a living tissue is a communion of cells; a living body is a communion of tissues; and a living psyche is a communion of feelings, or modes of apprehension, which are themselves in communion with people, plants, and animals, and also the spirits, ancestors, and visions, that they apprehend. Even as the universe seeks diversity and heightened states of awareness, it seeks and embodies communion.

Here too there is a lesson for us. Our task as humans is to extend the principle of communion implicit in the story of the universe by learning better to commune ourselves. Inwardly, this means recognizing our dependence on and indebtedness to the people, plants, and animals that grace our lives. It means knowing green grace. Outwardly, it means struggling to develop local communities—neighborhoods, farms, villages, cities, even nations—that are well integrated into the Earth's ecosystems, humane in their treatment of animals, and compassionate in their inter-human connections. The humane, sustainable communities described in Chapter 3 extend the principle of communion. To the degree that we begin to cultivate such communities, suggests Berry, we add to "the dream of the Earth" (1988, 194-215).

As a Christian and as a human being I find Thomas Berry's perspective compelling. Along with other middle-class Christians in affluent nations I need Berry's message, lest I lapse into a human-centeredness that is forgetful of the other 99 percent of creation and neglectful of that communion into which I am called by the Sacred Whole. Thanks to Berry, I have come to see stars in a new way. When I gaze into the heavens I see not only mystery but also communion. I feel small but also enfolded in a larger whole, and a larger adventure, that I name God.

My seven-year-old son Jason also knows this communion and adventure. He has begun to learn the new story in science classes. Some of his teachers speak to him of a developing cosmos, of stars that are born and then die, of the emergence and evolution of the continents, of the emergence of the first cells, of the great age of the reptiles, and of the earliest humans, our gathering and hunting ancestors. Thanks to these teachers, a host of good books, some wonderful television specials, and a little prodding from his father, he too feels kin to the star. He has a sense of the Sacred Whole and of his place in it.

The problem, however, is that when Jason goes to Sunday School, he hears nothing of this story. His teachers are excellent, but they have not been trained to tell the story of the unfolding cosmos. So Jason hears stories of Adam and Eve, Rebekah and Isaac, Joseph and Mary, all of which are interesting to him, but none of which seems to have any connection with the new story that he is learning in school. For him, and for many adults, there is a gap between the new story and the biblical story. I fear that he someday will feel forced to choose between the two stories, one biblical and one scientific. I hope this does not happen. We need ways of telling both simultaneously, such that each nourishes the other.

Accordingly, my aim in the remainder of this chapter, and also in the two chapters that follow, is to show how the biblical story and the new story might be combined. To begin, let us consider what the biblical story might be when read with ecologically sensitive eyes.

Of course, any postulation of a biblical story is interpretive. It involves a creative and partly subjective gathering of materials that, when first produced, were not necessarily intended to fall into a single story at all, ecological or otherwise. How the materials are gathered together partly depends on the needs and biases of the gatherer. My own biases should be clear. I think that Christians and others are now called to tell our stories with an eye to their implications for the whole of creation, nonhuman as well as human. For Christians, this means reading the Bible, as it were, "like a mountain."

Reading Like a Mountain

Reading the Bible "like a mountain" means at least two things. First, it means seeking themes in the Bible that encourage a sensitivity to the Earth and to life on Earth. Many biblically oriented Christian ecologists have now been doing this for some time. They talk about stewardship of the Earth; they understand *dominion* to mean "kindly use" rather than "exploitation"; they emphasize the important role that the Earth and animals and plants play in the psalms and other forms of wisdom literature; they talk about the whole of creation as subjects of divine redemption. They extract helpful themes for contemporary appropriation.

Second, and less obviously, it means reading the Bible from the imagined vantage point of a creature among creatures and from the vantage point of the Earth itself. Sometimes what we find will not be pleasant. We will be troubled by the divine command to "subdue" the Earth in Genesis, because the Earth itself needs to be respected rather than subdued in our time. We will also be troubled by the story of Noah and the flood, and imagine ourselves inside the skin of the animals left behind—those that were *not* allowed on the ark and that therefore were destroyed in the flood. We will have to face the fact that, as the story goes, their deaths were rather senseless and undeserved. We will have to acknowledge that God could have been less violent. When we read the Bible from an Earth perspective, we will find that in some ways the Bible is wanting.

But there is another way to understand what it might mean to read the Bible from the Earth's point of view. If the Earth is a dynamic process with a history, we might look at the Bible and ask how this history might be understood. If a story of creation emerges from the Bible, might it be juxtaposed with the story of creation that emerges from the natural sciences? Does the Bible itself offer a history of creation?

Significance of Hebrew Scriptures

Any reading of the history of creation in the Bible will emphasize the Hebrew scriptures over the Christian. John Austin Baker, the Anglican Bishop of Salisbury, suggests the following reasons for this:

1. The New Testament was written over a much shorter period of time (fifty years) than the Hebrew scriptures (nine centuries), with much less opportunity on the part of the authors to develop the kinds of "general observations on life and the world-order" found in the Hebrew scriptures.

2. The New Testament was written by urban people and directed to urban audiences, who were not as close to their agricultural roots as many authors of the Hebrew scriptures.

3. Many authors of New Testament documents expected the imminent end of the world, in which case speculations concerning nature were not that relevant.

4. Many New Testament authors generally failed to draw upon ecological insights from the Hebrew scriptures; they approached the latter with the exclusive aim of showing that they pointed to Jesus.

Baker adds: "In seeking for any kind of theology of humanity and nature, the Christian cannot but be grateful that his or her Bible does not consist merely of the New Testament" (1990, 24).

Given the interpretive character of *any* telling of a biblical history of creation, let us now consider what *one* such telling might look like. I choose as my example a rendering of that history as offered by an ecumenical team of theologians who met under the auspices of the World Council of Churches in Annecy, France, in 1990 (Birch et al. 1990a, 276–77). For the sake of understanding, let us imagine the history of creation as a three-act play.

Act I: Primal Harmony

The first act comes from the early chapters of Genesis. Here we learn that, in the beginning, God called into existence the heavens, the Earth, and all that dwell therein. God saw that everything was good. People and animals dwelled in harmony with one another, both eating plants. Animals and humans were commanded to "be fruitful and multiply." Humans, made in the image of God, had special responsibilities to protect the Earth and other creatures, even as they used them for human ends.

Act II: The Fall, the Covenant with Creation, the Sending of Christ

The second act begins when human beings sinned, thus disrupting the harmony of the original creation. This fall began what might be called the interim state of creation, in which violence emerged between animals, between people and animals, and between people and the Earth. During this interim period, in which we ourselves are participants, the whole of creation continued to praise God, but it also groaned in travail under the weight of violence. The violence we see in creation today is a legacy of this primal fall.

Despite the fall of creation, however, God did not abandon creation. God saved Noah from the deluge, commanding Noah to exercise his rightful dominion by saving the animals. God also made a covenant with animals and even with the Earth never to give up on them.

Also during the interim period, God began to plant a seed in the heart of the people of Israel, a longing for universal salvation in which the whole of creation, humans included, would be freed from the violence and reconciled one to another. According to Isaiah their dream for universal salvation was also God's dream: the dream of a "new heaven and new Earth" in which the original intentions of God would be realized.

At one stage (and here we enter the New Testament) God called a particular Jew to show still further the divine will for *shalom* on Earth, particularly as that *shalom* can be realized in the human dimension. As interpreted by his immediate successors, he became the means by which non-Jews could partake of the divine Dream. Not only did he add new themes to the dream, such as loving one's enemy and turning the other cheek, but he opened himself to the Divine such that, at times, he became the dream enfleshed, a living witness of the power of *shalom*.

Act III: The Redemption of Creation

After the man's death, new life emerged, both for him and for us, thus giving us hope that, in a way we can only dimly imagine, the dream of integral creation can be realized. A "new heaven and new Earth" will in some way emerge; violence will cease and the groaning creation, humans included, will be fully redeemed.

Can the biblical history of creation described above also simply be called the biblical story? In other words, is the plot of the Bible itself more cosmological and less human centered than usually imagined? Have Christians been wrongly reading the Bible as if the entire book were but a human story, when in fact the entire book is a creation story? Some biblical scholars say exactly that (Knierim 1981). They suggest that the laws of the Hebrew scriptures are best understood as guidelines by which humans can fit into the history of creation and advance it, rather than escape from it. The laws are best understood within, not outside of, a cosmological context. They come from a God who created the heavens and the Earth, not humans alone, and they represent God's yearnings for humans to be participants in the heavens and the Earth, not exceptions to such participation. The teachings of Jesus and the gospel of the early church also can be understood in a cosmological rather than an anthropocentric way.

The New Story and the Biblical Story Compared

What are we to make of these two stories? Let us first note some differences between the new story and the biblical story.

First, Berry's story has a kind of scientific plausibility that the biblical story lacks. For that matter, the biblical history of creation "rings false" in at least one important way. It suggests that there was a time in the history of life on Earth when perfect harmony obtained: when neither humans nor animals had to rob one another of life in order to live. The scientific account of the history of life on Earth does not bear this out. There has been violence within the experiment of life on Earth from the very beginning of animal life. Berry's story presupposes this violence as a necessary feature of the creative process (1988, 216).

Second, the biblical history of creation has a "character" in the story that Berry's new story does not: the personal God. Berry does speak of God, but rarely. He seems reluctant to "name" God and therefore "objectify" God. When he does speak of an ultimate Source, he speaks as if it is best glimpsed in the creative process itself, rather than as something external to the process. By contrast, the biblical history of creation freely talks about a God who "knows our names," and who is significantly different from creation. (In the next chapter I offer a way of making sense of this personal God.)

Third, the biblical history of creation tends to highlight the special significance of animals in a way that Berry does not. In the biblical history of creation, animals are closer to humans and more valuable than plants. Plants have their primary value in their instrumentality to human and animal purposes, whereas humans and animals seem to have greater value in and for themselves. Thus the individual suffering of animals within nature itself, apart from human intervention, is more problematic in the biblical history of creation than it is in the new story. Berry tends to promote a perspective closely akin to primal religions, wherein violence in nature is seen as part of a natural cycle in which humans participate. The Bible sees violence in nature as indicative of a fall.

Fourth, and related to the point above, Berry often seems to approach the creative processes of evolution (apart from human interference) as if they were unambiguously revelatory of the Divine, whereas those same processes of creation are approached by many biblical authors as part of an interim creation that can reveal God, but only in an ambiguous way. Creation is not as revelatory for biblical authors as it is for Berry.

Despite these differences both stories are now functioning to promote ecological responsibility. Those shaped by Berry's story understand their attempts to live ecologically responsible lives as a way of creatively participating in the creative process of evolution, advancing evolution's own aims for deeper communion between subjects in the Earth community. They are responding to what they call the dream of the Earth.

Those shaped by the biblical history of creation often understand their attempts to live ecologically responsible lives in at least three ways. First, they can understand their attempts as an exercise of stewardship. What is troublesome about this approach, at least to creation-centered critics, including those who follow Thomas Berry, is that it promotes a paternalistic approach of humans to the Earth and to animals. Humans become caretakers of the Earth for an absentee landlord rather than plain citizens of and communers with the Earth.

A second, more promising approach is to understand their attempts as instances of mirroring that unlimited love of creation which God expressed in making a covenant with the Earth and animals. Understood in this way, ecological responsibility and a concern for animal protection is an act of feeling the creation as God feels it—and responding accordingly. This approach, however, still neglects that eros to commune with the Earth and animals which is highlighted by creation-centered Christians.

This takes us to a third way of appropriating the biblical story as a resource for being rooted in the Earth. This is to take the biblical story as a whole as an invitation to participate in God's dreams for *shalom* on Earth. Recall that the biblical story is a three-act play of sorts, and that Acts I and III both illustrate divine hopes for creation. If we internalize this story, we realize that we are connected with a visionary Spirit, a Holy Wisdom, whose very heart yearns for us to dwell in communion with others. To be sure, biblical materials often stress the need for communion with other people. But Acts I and III of the biblical story also suggest communion with the whole of creation. The most promising way for Christians to appropriate the biblical story is to take seriously the idea that there is a divine dream at work in creation. It is to feel called by Holy Wisdom to enter into communion with creation for our own sakes, for the rest of creation's sake, and for God's sake. In responding to this call, we help restore the original hopes of God in creating the universe, and we participate in the "new heaven and new Earth" of Act III. In its fullness, this third act will have to be ushered in by God, because we cannot create a perfect harmony on Earth. But we can taste the harmony, and live out of its richness, in the present. Such tastes are our own ways of participating in the divine dream.

Given this third way of appropriating the biblical story, we see considerable overlap with the new story. Berry's story and the biblical story both invite Christians to feel as if we are participating in a dream, a hope, deeper than our own egos. Both stories suggest that we are lured to commune with the Earth and with animals, to enter into that *shalom* described in the Introduction. The only difference is that Berry's followers understand the alluring agent as the Earth, whereas followers of the biblical story feel called by God to commune with the Earth. Can these differences be reconciled? Let us hope so.

Chapter 5

And God So Loved the Planet

The New Story and the Biblical Story Combined

Christianity is supposed to be good news for all humans on the planet, including children with cancer, homeless people, battered women, schizophrenics, stroke victims, frightened youth in inner city gangs, despised criminals, and middle-class suburbanites. To be truly good, it must also be good news for cramped calves confined in cages, frightened rats undergoing painful experiments, species of birds whose habitats are being destroyed, dying rivers, polluted atmospheres, and the Earth itself. One aim of this book is to suggest how the Christian gospel might indeed be good news for all.

What *is* the good news? Some say that it is summarized in John 3:16: "And God so loved the world that he gave his only Son, so that everyone who believes in him may not perish but have eternal life."

For many quite conservative Christians, mostly but not exclusively Protestant, the meaning of this mini-gospel is clear. It means that God loved the world so much that, when the time was right, he sent Jesus, who lived with him in heaven, to save the world. God's purpose in sending Jesus was to enable people to join God and his resurrected Son in heaven. Those who acknowledge Jesus, who believe in him, will get to go to heaven. Those who fail to acknowledge Jesus will suffer a much worse fate. Because they have not chosen to believe in Jesus, they will suffer eternal damnation in hell.

Four Objections to the Gospel

Like many theologically moderate Christians, I have trouble with this interpretation. First, like others familiar with other religions, I worry about the implications of the gospel, conservatively understood, for people who do not believe in Jesus. Are Jews doomed because they do not believe Jesus is the Son of God? Are Muslims doomed because they believe Jesus was strictly human, a prophet among prophets? Are Buddhists doomed because Jesus plays no central role in their path? Are Hindus doomed because they believe that Jesus is but one of many incarnations of the Divine? I find it difficult to assume such ill of well-meaning people of other paths. I find it difficult if not immoral to say that there is one way, and that this one way requires belief in Jesus.

It *can* be important for some people to undergo a conversion experience. In the later years of my college life I "accepted Jesus as Lord and Savior." I did so not to get to heaven or to receive God's forgiveness, but to set priorities for my life, to commit myself to a Way. I still find the experience meaningful, and one on which I hope to build.

But as I look back, I realize that what was most important about the experience was not that I uttered special words, or even that I pictured Jesus in my imagination, but rather that I decided that, from that point on, I wanted to do my best to give my life to God, and to live from God, rather than my own ego. Of course, like most humans I do not fully do this, and often I fail miserably. If being saved means being healed by God, then I am by no means fully saved. But, like others, I would like to be God-centered. My "born again" experience was a way of saying yes to God, or at least of saying yes to my desire to say yes.

However, I have met people of other paths who, in their way and their time, have undergone similar experiences and undertaken similar commitments. I am thinking of some Jews, Muslims, and Buddhists that I have known. They, too, have wanted to become centered in God, in the Sacred Whole, in Holy Wisdom, rather than centered in self. The fruits of their conversions have been impressive. I find it impossible, therefore, to say that I have given my life to the Heart of the universe, and they have not. I am more prone to say that the Heart of the universe reaches out to all of us in different ways, relative to who and where we are, and relative to the religious and social contexts in which we live. Some by birth have been open to this Heart. They are the natural saints among us. Others have needed a conversion experience of one sort or another, such as the "born again" experience of evangelical Christianity. And most of us need to be converted again and again and again. In my own life it has turned out this way. If I am a "born again" Christian, I have needed to be born again and again and again, in many different ways, relative to different phases of my life. I am still not fully born.

All this leads me to believe that belief in Jesus, deeply understood, is primarily a means to the end of a God-nourished life rather than an end in itself.[1] Buddhists who turn seriously to their Buddhism, taking the Bodhisattva Vow

---

1. This does not mean that "God" is the thematic focus of all religions. The thematic focus of Buddhism, for example, is the sheer presence of things as they are, in their immediacy and interconnectedness, rather than the healing spirit of God, which is but one of the "things" present. As I argue in other contexts (1994, 244-47), different religions can have different thematic centers, different ultimates. It does mean, however, that the God-nourished life seems to be a byproduct of many religions, whatever their thematic focus. In Buddhism, for example, as a person awakens to the sheer presence of things as they are, the healing spirit of God seems to flow from his or her life. He or she becomes more kind and compassionate, more "bodhisattvic," to use the Buddhist term. Even though centered in emptiness, the Buddhist is nourished by God.

to help save all sentient beings, may well be doing much the same as Christians do when they decide to accept Jesus as Lord and Savior. Muslims who begin to take seriously the ideals of submission to Allah, and to follow the way of peace prescribed in the Qu'ran, may well be doing much the same as Jews who turn to Torah. The truth of personal salvation—of wholeness—is deeper than words and formulas and historical references. It is the living presence of Holy Wisdom in people's lives, such that they live from Wisdom's guidance and love, not their own needs for fame, fortune, power, or perfection.

My second objection to the ultra-conservative way of reading John 3:16 comes from training in a liberal seminary. Shaped by a modern worldview and by historical-critical approaches to scripture, I do not think Jesus was "living with God" prior to his birth on Earth. I believe that claims concerning the "preexistence of Christ" were added by the early church, not by Jesus.

I do believe that as the history of life on Earth unfolded, Holy Wisdom may well have hoped for a human being who might reveal her tenderness and vulnerability as well as her power to resurrect and offer hope. The idea of such a being may well have existed prior to the birth of Jesus. But I do not think that Jesus the man existed in heaven, as an individualized self-consciousness, prior to his birth. Rather, I think of Jesus as a Palestinian Jew, flesh among flesh, who was called by God, beckoned by Holy Wisdom herself, to be a vessel of healing love for his people and for us. I think Jesus-the-man "became God" by responding to God's call, by being filled with God's spirit, and by identifying with that spirit such that, for those around him, his life and God's dreams were two sides of one coin.

Third, influenced by feminist theologies, I have problems with the imagery of a male God who sends a male son to the Earth, but who lacks within "himself" female dimensions and who appears only once on the planet, in male form. I believe that women as well as men can enflesh God in certain ways, and that the God whom they enflesh is as appropriately named divine Mother as divine Father. I think that there many be different ways to enflesh God in our lives, and that Jesus did it in a very special way, from which all the world can benefit. But we too might enflesh God in different ways, women as well as men. I think historical Christianity is in sore need of female images of divine enfleshment as a corrective to the one-sidedness of its exclusively male imagery.

Finally, I have problems with the idea that the whole point of Christianity is to help people get to heaven. While I do indeed hope that there is life after death, particularly for the many living beings who die in incompleteness, I also believe that a primary purpose of Christianity, or any other religion for that matter, ought to be to help us live wisely and compassionately in the here-and-now.

I find myself seeking some way of understanding the gospel that avoids these four objections. Is there a way to understand the gospel that makes it a guidepost for wise and compassionate living here-and-now, and not just a prescription for getting to heaven that explicitly excludes people of other religions and that implicitly excludes women?

It helps to know that, from the vantage point of some biblical scholars, "eternal life" does not necessarily mean life-after-death, but rather Spirit-inspired life in the here-and-now. This is how I recommend we understand the phrase. In seeking an ecological version of the gospel, let "eternal life" mean life that is lived from the Spirit, not the ego, and that therefore enjoys communion with God and with that very good creation which God so loves. It is eternal, not necessarily in the sense that it endures forever, though it may, but rather in the sense that it partakes of the timeless quality of divine wisdom and compassion in the immediacy of the present. On this reading, whenever we love others without expectation, or seek truth for its sake, or share in the joys of other living beings, we participate in eternal life.

Given *this* understanding of eternal life, what might a more ecological version of the gospel say? It says that at one stage in the history of life on Earth, the Holy Wisdom at the center of the universe was able to share with the world the very essence of her heart. A young Jew from Palestine named Jesus was the vessel of her sharing. He shared her love, not only by becoming one with her in his own way, but also by being open to others, such that they could energize him and give him the power to heal and to serve. Through their faith, he became, for them, a savior. For us he can be the same.

The question, of course, is saved from what and saved for what? An ecological understanding of the gospel will not insist that we are saved from everlasting damnation, though the possibility of purgative suffering after death ought not be dismissed. For my part, I believe not only in the possibility of purgative suffering, but also in that of spiritual growth after death. For all living beings I hope that there is more to the spiritual pilgrimage than earthly existence.[2] Still, I think the *emphasis* in Christianity ought to be on spiritual pilgrimage *in this life*, not on life after death.

In speaking of salvation our focus, then, ought to be on freedom from the hellish confines of a way of living that is too small for our own human potential, too harmful to ourselves and others, and that misses the mark of God's own hopes for us. That too-small way might be called the way of the skin-encapsulated ego. It is a way that many of us embody in many different ways; it can be called ego-based, because it takes the finite ego as a frame of reference in terms of which the whole of reality, even God, is to be understood. When we live an ego-based existence, we often harm ourselves and others,

---

2. I have proposed one way of understanding such growth in *Earth, Sky, Gods, and Mortals* (1990, 131-32). Drawing from process theology and its idea of a multi-dimensional cosmos, I suggest that human and animal psyches may well survive bodily death, enter into other planes of existence, and further respond to the lure of God in their lives, until wholeness in community with creation is realized, after which they are reabsorbed into the very life of God.

and we fail to respond to God's call toward a wholeness, a salvation, that enjoys deep connections with other people, plants, and animals.

If we are saved *from* ego-based existence, we are saved *for shalom*-based existence, or, as I will speak of it in the next chapter, life in Christ, with Christ understood as the living presence of Holy Wisdom in the cosmos and in our own lives. *Shalom*-based existence is existence that is creative, and yet that is also deeply connected with the rest of creation. It is graced by the energies of others and also by the healing energy of Holy Wisdom. It issues from, and expresses, a deeper self, a true self, that lies within us and beyond us, if we but have eyes to see and hearts to feel.

Subsequent chapters will explain more thoroughly my meaning of true self. My general purpose in this chapter is to situate the mini-gospel just described within a broader theological, cosmological, and biblical context. My aims are 1) to make clear the way of thinking about God that has been implicit in the first four chapters, namely, that of panentheism as developed by process theologians, and 2) to show how this way of thinking might help us integrate the new story and the biblical story into a Christian story.

Panentheism

The way of thinking about God that I have been recommending in this book is called *panentheism.* The term *panentheism* was coined in the nineteenth century by K.F.C. Krause (1781–1832). Literally, the term means "everything in God." As used here, *panentheism* implies an ecological way of thinking about God in which, even as God and creation are distinguished, God is understood to be intimately connected to creation, and vice-versa. God might be called the Interbeing of the universe, in the sense that all things are connected to and make a difference to God, such that God's own Life is deeply and profoundly relational. What makes God "God" is not that God is least connected to the universe, but rather that God is most connected. From a panentheistic perspective, God is the Sacred Whole of the universe, a Life in which all lives are gathered together in wisdom and compassion.

Panentheism is properly distinguished from strict pantheism, which implies an absolute equation of God and creation, and also from strict dualism, which implies an absolute gulf between God and creation. Panentheism is the view that the creation and its processes are somehow "in" God, even though God is "more than" creation. If God is the Sacred Whole, then that Whole is indeed more than the sum of its parts.

Consider a visual image. Imagine the ongoing history of creation as a horizontal spiral. Panentheists would draw a large circle representing God, and then draw within the circle the spiral representing creation. Dualists would draw the divine circle outside the spiral, and pantheists would draw the spiral and no circle at all.

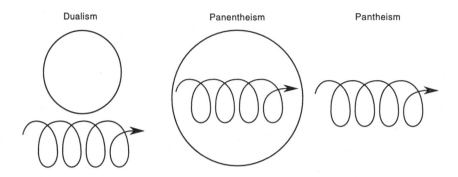

Dualism   Panentheism   Pantheism

But what does it mean to place the spiral of evolution *within* the circle of God? It means that God is a self-conscious Life within whom the unfoldings of the universe occur. Thus God, no less than creatures, is imbued with what Thomas Berry calls interiority. Creatures are immanent within this interiority, and this interiority is immanent within them.

The Presence of Creation in God

In order to understand how creatures are immanent within God's interiority, we might imagine that all the creatures in the universe and on Earth are like fish, endowed with their own interiority, swimming in an ocean called God or the Sacred Whole or Holy Wisdom. Imagine further that this Ocean is not just a watery substance but a living substance. Thus, like the fish, the Ocean feels and perceives and dreams; unlike the fish, however, it is not located in a particular body. It is everywhere at once. It is a living receptacle, an ocean of consciousness, in which the fish, with their consciousness, "live and move and have their being."

Imagine further that this divine Ocean registers each feeling that occurs in each fish as that feeling occurs, and that it registers the feeling empathetically. This means that the Ocean suffers with the sufferings of each and every flounder and whale and shark and perch, and enjoys their joys. Their lives are intimately connected to its Life; what happens to them happens to it. This does not mean that the Ocean controls the fish, although, as we shall see shortly, it influences them. The fish swim according to aims that are at least in part self-chosen. But it does mean that the Ocean shares in their destiny. The divine Ocean is a fellow-sufferer and fellow-enjoyer, who understands.

Finally, imagine that the divine Ocean not only feels each feeling of the creatures who swim within it, but that it also tries to reconcile these feelings, as they occur, into a deeper pattern, a single whole that they might enjoy, inasmuch as they are able, and that it can enjoy. At each and every moment that it receives the feelings of the fish, it integrates those feelings, as much as is possible, into a deeper whole that reconciles their tensions and integrates their contrasts. This deeper whole, forever changing because forever fed by new input from the fish, is the internal life of the Ocean itself. It is divine Interiority understood not only as an empathetic receptacle but also as a self-conscious Subject. The universe is thus a community of subjects within a Subject.

Rough as this analogy is, its images make an important point. Note that the analogy combines two different kinds of images: a non-personal image, that of an Ocean, and a personal image, that of a sentient being with interiority. This combination illustrates one feature of panentheism: it finds truth in both personal and transpersonal imagery for the Divine. God can be an "it" like the Ocean, but also a "she" or "he" like a psyche. Process thinkers suggest that an ecological Christianity can make use of both kinds of images. We can meaningfully speak of the Divine as "the Mystery" and "the Adventure of the Universe as One" and "the ultimate Context" and "the cosmic Ocean," but also as "Mother" and "Father" and "Bear" and "Coyote Trickster." We ought not fixate on particular images, which is a form of idolatry. Rather, we can and should be poly-imagistic, tolerant of others' needs to image the Divine in ways different from our own.

But note further that, inasmuch as God can be envisioned in personal terms, as a psyche, panentheism makes contact with biblical points of view. For panentheists, as for many biblical authors, God is "something like" a person, albeit not located in space or time. God is an omnipresent Life to whom the creatures in the universe ultimately belong, even as they also belong to themselves and to one another. It is as if we creatures are cells in a vast body called the universe, and God is the living Subject to whom the body belongs. The Subject is not exactly outside its body; nor is it precisely the same as its body. It is the unity of the body as a living Soul, the Soul of the universe.

As Christians, process panentheists take this personalist line of thought a step further. Not only is the divine Life "something like" a person, it is "something like" Jesus of Nazareth. The panentheistic image of God, at least that developed by process theologians, is shaped by and indebted to the historical Christian view that God is Jesus-like. This does not necessarily mean that Jesus is the only way to God, or even that Jesus was a sinless being, literally born of a virgin, whose opinions must always be repeated. Rather, it means that in the compassion and forgiveness we see in Jesus, particularly as that compassion and forgiveness are mythically amplified into the figure of an all-compassionate "Christ," we glimpse the very heart of the Divine.

Given this imaginative amplification, the word *Christ* can be used as a name for God, in which case the body of Christ would be not simply the Christian church but the entire universe. The appropriate task of the Christian church would be to protect the body of Christ, to be a healing power in its midst. Among contemporary theologians, Sallie McFague in *The Body of God* has developed this image most thoroughly. She uses the phrase "the cosmic Christ" to name God as present within the history of creation in a healing capacity. Understood as such, God as "Christ" identifies with the suffering of each and every living being on the planet and seeks the well-being of all (1993, 159–91).

To say that God is Jesus-like, or perhaps better Christlike, is not to limit God to the human sphere. The compassion of the God who is Christlike extends to the whole of creation, not simply to human beings. And it extends to each and every living being within creation, not simply the whole. The image is of a compassionate God whose empathy includes not just the totality of creation, but each proton and atom, each molecule and cell, each plant and animal, each Muslim and Jew.

Is this image of a God with interiority, much less Christlike interiority, *too* human-like? It could be argued that even though the love of the panentheistic God well extends to nonhuman beings, the very conception of God as in any way like a person is excessively anthropomorphic. This objection would be particularly telling if humans were the only beings with interiority. If this were the case, then to say that God is "something like" a person would be to say that God is quite unlike animals or plants or protons.

Process panentheists see it differently. Along with Thomas Berry, they believe that even animals and plants and cells and protons are imbued with interiority. Their arguments for pan-experientialism are best presented elsewhere. From their perspective, however, to be "something like" a human is also to be "something like" an animal and "something like" a plant and "something like" a living cell and "something like" a proton. The latter creatures, no less than humans, are expressions of interiority. In this sense at least, panentheism is not anthropomorphic but rather biomorphic and even cosmomorphic. The interiority of God is a supreme expression of, rather than an exception to, what is found throughout the whole of creation. The perspective is anthropomorphic only in the sense that it takes a particular human potentiality, that of compassion, which may well have parallels in other animals, and imagines this potentiality as realized fully, indeed infinitely, in divine interiority.

The Presence of God in Creation

What has been said in the previous section provides an idea of what it means to say that creation is *in* God. I now turn to how, from a panentheistic perspective, God is *in* creation. In terms of the analogy offered above, this is to ask how the divine Ocean might influence, though not control, the fish who swim within it.

The Ocean-fish analogy suggests that creatures have power of their own. From a process perspective, every creature in the universe is endowed not only with interiority, but also with some degree of self-creativity. Examples of this self-creativity range from the spontaneous indeterminacy of quantum events within the depths of inorganic matter, through the moment-by-moment decisions made by animals in natural environments, to the highly complex moral decisions made by human beings in social situations. We live in a creative universe whose direction can be influenced but not commandeered by a creative God, by a Holy Wisdom at the very heart of creation. If God is to be *in* creation at all times, influencing it, then God cannot be a puppeteer pulling strings.

The suggestion of panentheism is that the divine Ocean influences creation as an immanent, ever-adaptive, omni-invitational Lure or Beckoning Presence. Like other creatures, we humans experience this Lure, not necessarily in our conscious minds, but rather in the depths of our preconscious experience. In particular, we experience it in the form of pre-reflective, inwardly felt possibilities or goals, which we ourselves must actualize, and which, if actualized, will yield maximum wholeness or the fullness of life relative to the situation at hand.

Of course, there are many goals, many dreams, within the depths of our preconscious and pre-reflective experience. Many of them are anything but God-infused. Process theologians recognize this. Among the more destructive goals in contemporary culture are those of "success" and "attractiveness," promulgated by rootless forms of consumerism, and also those of "perfect security," fostered by wingless forms of religion. In one case we are drawn to wings without roots, in the other to roots without wings.

But process theologians argue that God, or what Christians often call the Holy Spirit, is also present within each of us at all times. God is present with us through alluring possibilities for the fullness of life, which are themselves God's dreams for our well-being. We experience God through the call to be rooted in healthy soils and to fly into healing skies. Readers will recall that in Chapter 1 I identified some of the healthy soils: meaningful relations with other people, the wisdom of world religions, the silence of God as experienced in prayer, and the Earth itself. I also identified several healing skies: dialogue with other world religions, dialogue with the Earth, and, most importantly, peacemaking. My point here is that we experience the presence of Holy Wisdom, of God, in and through the allurement of such possibilities. When we feel called toward healthy soils and healing skies, we are called by the divine Ocean itself.

Some God-given possibilities are deeply personal. If we are victims of self-doubt, they are possibilities for self-love; if we are victims of pride, they are possibilities for humility; if we are victims of fear, they are possibilities for courage; if we are victims of our own resentment, they are possibilities for forgiveness. Christianity emphasizes that, whatever else they are, they are possibilities for love of self and love of neighbor.

An ecological Christianity emphasizes that these neighbors include non-human as well as human beings. When we feel prompted to conserve land and protect wildlife, to be compassionate toward animals and conversant with plants, to be sensitive to landscapes and awestruck by sunsets, we are prompted by Holy Wisdom, whose very body is creation itself. And when, amid the unnecessary and appalling violence of our human communities, we feel called, sometimes against insurmountable odds, to help create alternative communities that are just in their relations among humans and sustainable in their relations to the Earth, we are likewise called by Holy Wisdom. We are imagining and trying to live into what Paul called a "still more excellent way" of being in the world (1 Cor 12:31).

This "still more excellent way" is in part a human dream. When we feel its presence as a possibility, we are feeling the presence of one of our own deepest hopes. In its own way it is like a prayer. And yet, from a panentheistic point of view, it is also a divine dream, a divine prayer. The Lure of God within us is the dream of God within us. Its given content consists of fresh possibilities, relevant to the immediate situation, to which we may or may not be responsive. When we fail to respond, we "miss the mark" of becoming who we truly want to be and who Holy Wisdom desires that we be. To one degree or another most of us miss the mark all the time. This is the truth of the traditional doctrine of original sin. It is best understood, not as something initiated in a mythical past, but as a name for the fact, all too verifiable, that we perpetually fall short of that wholeness, that fullness of life in communion with others to which we are called. But the divine dreams are within us nevertheless, which is to say that God is within us nevertheless. It is as if within each of us there is a beckoning light—a still, small voice—that calls us to become the best that we can become, whoever and whatever that "best" is.

As process theologians see it, the divine Lure, present in immediately felt possibilities for the fullness of life relative to the situation at hand, is also present in nonhuman creatures. Animals are responsive to the Lure in their ways, as are living cells in plants, and even submicroscopic energy-events within the depths of matter. These creatures are not necessarily called toward the particular forms of fullness toward which humans are called. There are distinctively animal forms of fullness, and distinctively plant forms of fullness, and distinctively protonic and electronic forms of fullness. The divine Ocean is "on the side" of each and every creature as an alluring Presence by which it reaches toward its own distinctive form of self-actualization. This means that, for process thinkers, it is inappropriate to imagine that other creatures were created by God simply to be used by human beings. They were created by God to enjoy their own forms of *shalom*.

Process panentheists use this notion of the Lure to explain how the universe was created. From their perspective the divine Ocean did not create the universe as a potter might mold a pot, through an exercise of manipulative power on a passive substance. Rather, the divine Ocean created the universe, and continues to do so today, as a midwife helping a woman give birth or as an indwelling conductor inspiring musicians to play. Process panentheists believe that there has always been a creative energy within God that God cannot manipulate but can lure into various forms of order and novelty relative to the situations at hand. This creative energy is the very substance of which the universe is made. It is the "creativity" of the fish in the divine Ocean.

Thus, from a panentheistic perspective the universe was created, not by God molding it into existence, but rather by God calling it into existence. The model is not creation out of nothing but rather creation out of chaos. And, of course, this creation did not simply happen in the past; it is happening in the present and will happen in the future. The divine creativity lies in God's steadfast capacity to supply dreams to the creatures in the universe and thereby to call them into forms of order and novelty which yield maximum fulfillment relative to the situation at hand. God is the Dreamer by which the universe was called into existence and by which we are called to enter into inclusive peace with creation.

A Still Newer Story

In light of the explanation of panentheism just offered, I now turn to a constructive task. My aims are to identify ways in which a panentheistic understanding of God might be enriched by and also contribute to the story of the universe as told in Chapter 4, and then to show how a panentheistic telling of this story might also include and be enriched by biblical themes. I will focus particularly on the universe story as told and interpreted by Thomas Berry.

Berry and Panentheism

What does the thought of Thomas Berry add to panentheism? Two things come to mind. In the first place, it adds a *story*. Heretofore, at least as explained by process thinkers, panentheism has lacked a story. It has been a worldview, a way of thinking about God and creation, rather than a narrative that grips the mythic imagination. To be sure, process thinkers have maintained the universe is an unfolding, evolutionary adventure. They have also recognized, with Berry, that each creature in this adventure is imbued with subjectivity and that the universe itself is a community of subjects rather than simply an aggregate of objects. But they have not given historical concreteness to these claims; they have not "told a story" of the evolutionary adventure on its own terms or in its relation to God. They have talked about creation but not the history of creation. Berry talks about the history. He adds a story to the worldview.

Second, Berry's thought adds scope to the panentheist notion of the Lure of God. Process panentheists have usually been content to speak of the Lure of God as something within each individual creature in the cosmos, luring that creature toward its unique forms of wholeness in community with others. They have not often spoken of the Lure of God for the cosmos as a whole. Berry's thought invites process thinkers to recognize that the Lure of God within individual creatures is also a Lure toward differentiation, subjectivity, and communion for the cosmos as a whole. Thus he adds scope, a sense of collective adventure, to what too easily can seem individualistic.

On the other hand, process panentheism offers Berry, or at least those shaped by his new story, a potentially helpful concept of God—potentially helpful because there are contexts in which formal God-talk is not helpful. When formal God-talk leads to a preoccupation with God at the expense of creation, as it often has, then such talk is counterproductive. There is a need within Christianity today for different kinds of stories, some with God-talk and some without. Those without formal God-talk can be understood as correctives to a long history of Christian thinking that has emphasized God, dualistically understood, as the primary focus of Christian piety, and creation as something to be transcended in search for God.

Still, it is doubtful that Christians who are grasped by the new story as told by Thomas Berry will be able to avoid God-talk, at least in the foreseeable future. This is particularly the case with those whose imaginations are shaped by biblical thinking. If biblically based Christians want to internalize the new story told by Thomas Berry, they will need 1) some way of finding "God" in the new story, and 2) some way of understanding the biblical history of creation in light of the new story. To my mind, panentheism can achieve both these ends. It can help us to weave a tale in which God plays an important role, and in which the biblical history of creation can be seen as a mini-story within the larger creation story told by Thomas Berry. This, I believe, is the next step in contemporary Christian ecological theology: a linkage of creation-centered and biblically rooted traditions.

In the following section I will illustrate how I think this new tale might be told, and then, in the final section, I will spell out in a more prosaic way what is implied in the telling.

A Panentheistic Telling of the New Story

In a paper written for the World Council of Churches, Charles Birch tells of watching a television documentary featuring Leonard Bernstein conducting rehearsals for his own composition "West Side Story." During the rehearsals, writes Birch, "the musicians, composer and conductor became one," with the orchestra players responding to the grimaces on Bernstein's face. Sometimes, says Birch, "the orchestra seemed to exceed the conductor's expectations and he responded with intense delight" (1990b, 192).

Birch suggests that the God of panentheism is something like Bernstein the conductor. "An orchestra consists of many creative players. Each player interprets the score in his or her way. But the overall coordination is provided by the conductor" (1990b, 192). God, says Birch, "is like a composer conductor writing the score a few bars ahead of the orchestra, taking into account their harmonies and disharmonies as he proposes the next movement of the music. God does not determine the outcome; the power of God is the power of persuasion to harmonize the whole" (1990b, 192).

If we amplify Birch's analogy, we can see how the biblical history of creation might be included within a panentheistic telling of the new story.

Creation as Unfinished Symphony

Imagine that the history of creation as told by Thomas Berry is an ongoing and as yet unfinished symphony. The symphony begins with the galactic motif, to which is added, at a later date, a geological motif, then a biological motif, and then, as a minor but significant voice, a human motif, itself a voice within the voices rather than a consummating voice.

Let the players be the creatures within creation, and let new players—new creatures—be added to the orchestra as the symphony unfolds. At first, when the music begins, the only players are the elemental particles. Somewhat later molecules enter the orchestra, still later solid masses, and still later, at least in one section of the orchestra, plants and animals, including humans. Imagine that all of these players—the elemental particles no less than the living beings—are creative, though in different degrees. The living beings are capable of much more novelty than the elemental particles, but even the particles are capable of novel expression.

Now imagine that, ingredient in each player, is an inwardly felt aim to play beautiful music in conjunction with the other players. Let *beautiful music* be music that, to use Berry's terms, contributes to 1) a sense of communion among players, 2) an appreciation of diversity among players, and 3) a sense of subjective aliveness in each player. Let *beauty* mean differentiation, communion, and subjectivity, or some combination thereof. Consider these three aspects of beauty as the most desirable themes that can emerge as the symphony unfolds.

Imagine further that this internal aim, felt by each musician, is itself the presence of the conductor. And recognize that this presence is within each creature as something felt by and tailored to the musician's capacities and needs. The conductor is not a musician among musicians or a person standing on a platform; rather, the conductor is an invisible Muse, a holy Spirit. Let this conductor be called God. For our purposes, let us imagine God as "female" rather than "male," in order to avoid the connotation of sheer externality so often characteristic of an exclusively male God. Let her be Holy Wisdom.

In the first few movements of the symphony, the score was for the most part created by the conductor. Indeed, she established the basic themes of differentiation, communion, and subjectivity, toward which the musicians would, at best, be drawn. Early on, she also wrote fairly precise parts for each musician, concerning how these themes might be played. The themes, as specified by the parts, which are themselves felt as aims, were fairly well-defined, with only a small amount of room for improvisation or novelty. The musicians themselves were not really capable of much novelty. Nevertheless, the beauty they enjoyed was rich and amazing, as it is still today.

As the music developed and new musicians entered the orchestra, the musicians became more and more capable of unpredictable spontaneity, some of which would add to the beauty of the symphony, but some of which would not. As this new freedom was emerging in creation, a new dream entered the mind of the conductor. She began to imagine the possibility of a new voice within the music of the spheres which would contribute to the overall effect of the music, not through the playing of well-defined parts, but rather through improvisational amplifications of the three basic themes. This new voice would be a contrapuntal strand: something that supports the main theme yet is different from it. For these musicians, so the conductor imagined, the aims themselves would be the themes. The score for this strand, with its own unique texture and voice, would be co-created by musicians and the conductor.

Indeed, she imagined that this new strand might even mirror her nature in a way the other voices have not. It would be free of violence in a new and unparalleled way, full of *shalom*-like harmony. She began to look for musicians who might be able to play this kind of melody, and she noticed a small collection of new musicians among the animals on Earth who seemed to have the potential. Let these new musicians be Homo sapiens, who emerged some fifty thousand years ago, descendants of ape-like hominids who emerged some two million years ago.

Should she plant the seed of this dream in them? It was risky. In the first place, this new kind of music would involve a relinquishment of her score-writing role and her ability to tell where the symphony might lead. But the promise outweighed the liability, for the joy to be realized in joint creation would be overwhelmingly beautiful. She told herself that, should chaos result, she would always be there suffering with whatever befell them and that she would provide healing aims to bring order out of the chaos and begin anew. She decided to take the risk, and to let them know that, no matter what happened, she would be there with them.

So she planted the seed of her dream amid the internal aims the Homo sapiens felt, and gradually, fleetingly, some of them—at this stage far too few of them—caught the vision, or at least aspects of it. Through their creativity they began to play a distinctive kind of music, a nonviolent music, that contributed more deeply to the music of the spheres. They were called Jains and Buddhists and Hindus and Jews and a host of other names.

Unfortunately, many of their fellow musicians began to play music that was quite discordant. She wondered if she had made a mistake, going so far as to repent of what she had done. But she made a covenant to stick with them no matter what and to keep planting the seeds. She was seed-planting in every culture among the human musicians, always in a way appropriate to their condition and potentiality. In the ancient Near East, she chose a particular set of musicians—call them Israel—to announce the theme in their own distinctive way. She even beckoned one among them to so identify with her tender care that he became for others "the conductor enfleshed." She showed that even in death she would be with them, ever planting seeds of new life.

Her hope, which persists to this day, is that humans will hear the possibility of new music and respond. In her own heart, her own interiority, she can hear it, through her weaving of even discordant notes into harmony. She hopes that someday such music might be heard "on Earth as it is in heaven."

Interpreting the Biblical History of Creation in Light of a Panentheistic Reading of the New Story

Perhaps this extended analogy gives some indication of how a panentheistic reading of the history of creation might be integrated with the biblical history of creation and with Berry's story. Implicit in the story is the idea that the biblical history of creation is itself a story within the history of creation as told by Thomas Berry, and that this mini-story reveals something of God's dreams for us. I conclude by making explicit what was implicit.

From a panentheistic perspective, the biblical history of creation is best understood as a medium through which, if we are sufficiently imaginative, a new evolutionary dream can be heard. The dream is for human musicians who can embody a distinctive sensibility—play a distinctive melody—that might itself be revelatory of the very heart of God and that might serve as an enriching counterpoint, not a substitute, to the other melodies of creation. Just as for Thomas Berry the Earth serves as an embodiment of a dream, so the biblical story can serve as an embodiment of a dream. From a panentheist perspective both dreams are ways in which humans can discover the Divine.

Let us consider what this biblical mini-story might add to Berry's story. Recall the three parts: the original integrity of creation as depicted in the first chapter of Genesis, the interim state in which creation is fallen but nevertheless loved by God, and the final consummation. First, the original integrity of creation.

The Original Integrity of Creation

We rightly recognize at the outset that the integrity of creation depicted in the first creation story of Genesis is not a factual account of a state of affairs that once existed in the history of creation. It is rather a projection back into the past of an idealized state envisioned by biblical authors, who were themselves influenced by a common deposit of ancient Near Eastern creation traditions.

The wisdom of the image of an integral creation lies in the ideal it depicts. This ideal, that of humans who live in peace with animals, with the Earth, and with one another, can itself be understood as a dream of God that was glimpsed by biblical authors, and perhaps by numerous others as well. It was a dream these humans discovered within themselves, but from a panentheist perspective human dreams can make contact with divine yearnings. We are influenced by God in and through new and hopeful possibilities for the fullness of life, discovered within our own imaginations. Thus, the integral creation depicted in the first creation story in Genesis can be understood, at least by those for whom the Bible is a source of religious insight, as a story depicting the original aspirations of God for human beings.

Whether these original intentions were present at the outset of creation is unclear. They may well have emerged in the divine mind only as the history of life on Earth unfolded. In any case the intentions were that humans extend the principle of communion present in creation a step further, toward a creative, nonviolent *shalom* that mirrors the *shalom* of God. The early chapters of Genesis can be understood as a fallible, poetic rendition of this divine dream.

Why were these intentions never realized? This takes us to the second movement in the biblical history of creation, the story of the fall, after which the whole of creation exists in an ambiguous state. It both praises God and groans in travail, and God nevertheless enters into covenant. What can this mean?

Fallen Creation and Covenant

To say that creation is fallen *can* mean simply that much of the nonhuman creation has been infected with forms of despoliation that are the result of human sin. If this is what is meant by a fallen creation, then the image is easily integrated into a contemporary Christian ecology. After all, we *have* despoiled much of earthly creation.

But there is more to be said. The problem for the biblical authors was not just despoliation but violence; for example, the violence of carnivorous animals that kill and eat other animals in order to survive. We realize today that this kind of violence even occurs within given species—that some animals kill and eat their own kind. The biblical authors may have thought that this violence was the result of human sin; if so, we realize that they were wrong. This kind of violence, that of predatory-prey relations, was implicit in creation long before Homo sapiens were on the planet. The question is, should we, in our time, agree with the biblical authors that this violence is in some way indicative of a fallenness, even as we disagree with their view that it was caused by human sin?

There is danger in saying this. It can lead to a moral condemnation of nature that wrongly presupposes that creatures in nature can act otherwise, and it can stimulate the kind of disregard, even hatred, of nature that has plagued much historical Christianity. Nevertheless, I suggest that, if we avoid even the slightest hint of a moral condemnation of nonhuman animals, we can and should agree with the biblical authors for at least two reasons.

The First Reason for Recognizing Fallenness in Creation

First, much of the violence we see in creation falls short of revealing the aims of God *for us*. Violence may well have been a necessary condition for the emergence of the cosmos, and for the emergence of life on Earth, including animal life; this is what panentheists believe, that even God could not have lured the cosmos into existence without violence.

Still, God has a new dream for us, which means that much of the violence we see in creation does not reveal God's dream for us. God's dream is that we become a people of radical nonviolence. While it is unreasonable to want or hope that animals can avoid killing one another, we can reduce the suffering we inflict on them and the numbers we kill, and we can avoid our own wholesale assault on the Earth. We cannot simply turn to violence in creation as an excuse for our own, either in relation to one another, animals, or the Earth. We are beckoned by God toward an amplification of the dream of communion the likes of which the history of life on Earth has not yet seen.

Inasmuch as we affirm the fallenness of creation for this first reason—its falling short of revealing God's full aims for us—we will also recognize that creation, amid its wonder, is not an unfailing source of divine revelation. The fact that creation, at least in some of its violence, falls short of the divine dreams for us means that we cannot turn to the dream of the Earth as our sole source of divine revelation. The *teloi* or aims of the Earth, while revelatory of the principles of communion, subjectivity, and differentiation, are not revelatory in an unambiguous sense. Even if we follow Berry, turning to the pre-rational and instinctive resources of our bodies for wisdom in moving toward an ecological age, we must also turn to revelatory stories in classical cultures, including revelatory stories from the Bible, to get a glimpse of how those themes might be distinctively amplified in human life. Certainly the stories of the classical traditions are not unambiguous in their revelatory value. Most of them are patriarchal, and all of them can be used for immensely destructive purposes. Still, images of *shalom* such as we find in the first creation story in Genesis *can* be helpful in guiding us toward becoming who we are called to become. The dreams of the Earth can rightly be supplemented by the dreams of the biblical authors.

A Second Reason for Affirming Fallenness in Creation

The second reason we might affirm the biblical intuition that the violence in creation is indicative of a fallenness, in addition to the fact that this violence falls short of divine aims for us, is that it falls short of revealing divine compassion for individual animals. As the fox chases the rabbit, the rabbit flees. The fox is hungry, and the rabbit is frightened. Ecologists may tell us that the situation is necessary to the health of the ecosystem, and no doubt the ecologist is right. Still, for the sake of honesty, we ought also imagine the situation from the rabbit's point of view. The rabbit is terrified; there is something wrong, something tragic, something "fallen" about what is happening. Her terror is a symptom that everything is not all right.

Is that terror shared by the Heart of the universe—by God? From a panentheistic point of view the anwer is yes. Holy Wisdom shares in the joys and sufferings of each living being, on its own terms and for its own sake. She shares in the rabbit's terror and, yes, the fox's hunger. This is the meaning of God's covenant with the animals. It means that God is "with" each of them, just as God is "with" each and every human being. As complex and awe-inspiring as they might be, the group dynamics of ecosystems do not reveal this individualized empathy, this "withness" of God. In this sense the planet falls short of complete revelation. The Earth does indeed reveal the glory of God, but it is Christ, and others like him, who reveal the tenderness.

The End of Creation

The notion of a God who is *with* all creatures to the end takes us to the final aspect of the biblical history of creation, the notion of the consummation of creation. No less than in speaking of creation as fallen, there is danger in speaking of creation as having an end. As Thomas Berry points out, the idea of an end to creation, when divorced from theistic roots, can easily give rise to the ideal of unlimited progress (1988, 204–6). Clearly, what much of the Earth needs is less emphasis on progress and more on communion with creation. If end-language contributes to the ongoing quest on the part of humans to conquer the planet, then such language is problematic. Still, Berry recognizes that creation is an adventure, and the question emerges, "adventure toward what?"

One option is to say that creation is an adventure toward the universe becoming conscious of itself in human existence. This is *not* an option panentheists endorse. From a panentheist point of view, each and every life is an end in itself toward which the adventure has moved. The divine Ocean has not lured the cosmos toward human life alone, but toward many forms of life, and many instances of life, each of which is an end in itself.

Another option is to say that creation is an adventure toward a distant Omega point, to use the language of Teilhard de Chardin, in which all things, particularly the violence in creation, is reconciled. The process panentheistic perspective is closer to this. Here it resembles the biblical image of an ultimate restoration of creation.

The major difference between panentheism and the Omega point discussed by Teilhard de Chardin is that, for the panentheist, the Omega point is not really distant at all. It is near at hand. It is the ongoing interiority of God.

Recall the panentheistic idea that the divine Ocean weaves the feelings and happenings of the living beings into as meaningful a pattern as possible, and that these feelings and happenings become part of an ongoing story which is a divine story, a story of God. This is to suggest that the universe is not only a community-of-subjects, each of which has its own interpretation of the meaning of the whole, but that it is also a community-within-a-Subject, whose own interpretation of the whole and each part within it is the most inclusive interpretation possible. Even when the music played by the orchestra is discordant, the conductor hears whatever beauty can be heard. There is a kind of harmony of the spheres, heard by the divine Life, that we do not hear with precision but can nevertheless sense, if we are open. The divine harmony can be part of our own inner harmony.

The purpose of sensing this harmony is not to become complacent with the features of our own lives that are unnecessarily violent. It is not to say that, after all, our own violence is of no consequence, because it will be harmonized in the music of the spheres. Rather, the purpose is to be energized by a recognition that, even when our own feeble attempts to reduce the amount of violence in our own lives seem to bear no fruit, they nevertheless contribute to a deeper harmony that is the final, ongoing story of the universe. Our efforts to live in *shalom* are woven into the Heart of the universe and thus stamped with ultimate meaning that may well elude our immediate vision. Here lies the wisdom of choosing to love and to care for the Earth, animals, and people—even when such love and care seem futile. Here lies the wisdom of serving the Earth, animals, and people, not only for their sake, but also for God's sake.

What is more, almost like a Buddhist doctrine of karma, it is possible that the *shalom*-bearing feelings and actions that we supply to the divine Life become part of a living reservoir of peace, which then feeds back into the universe in the form of possibilities for new life. It is possible that the fruits of the good karma we sow, though not seen by us, may be reaped by living beings who come after us.

At least this is what process panentheists suggest. They suggest that the love we contribute to "heaven," understood as the ongoing Life of the universe, floods back into the Earth. This means that the end of creation, Life itself, is a continuous source of new beginnings, and that we contribute to these new beginnings for life on Earth by contributing to the ongoing end. Such is the way in which tellers of the new story might appropriate the third part of the biblical story, the image of a new heaven and new Earth to come at the end of time.

One of the most important ecological theologians of our time, Rosemary Radford Ruether, makes the point tellingly. In *Sexism and God-Talk* Ruether closes with a discussion of the end of time, of eschatology. "But what of the meaning of our own lives?" she asks. "What of the good to be remembered and the evil redressed? Is this merely the disintegration of our organism into an 'impersonal' matrix of the all?" (1983, 258).

She suggests that it is not. "If the interiority of our organism is a personal center, how much more so is the great organism of the universe itself?" That great organism "is the Holy Being in which our achievements and failures are gathered up, assimilated into the fabric of being, and carried forward into new possibilities" (1983, 258). Perhaps one of our gifts to the Earth, Ruether suggests, is our contribution to this Holy Being, itself the very source of new possibilities for life on Earth. We might simply add, and Ruether would no doubt agree, that this Holy Being is itself a Holy Becoming. It is an End that is always a Beginning, an Omega that is always an Alpha. Such is the ever-continuing care of a "new heaven" that is always green, always fresh, and steadfast in its love of the Earth.

Chapter 6

After the Hunters and Gatherers

Christ-Centered Existence as a Response to Lost Innocence

The previous chapter presented the Christian story in broad strokes. Each generation will have its own ways of telling the story, and each will be shaped by its concerns and limitations. Mine is no exception. I am shaped by a need to affirm the whole of life, not human life alone, and by concerns that we learn to make peace with people, animals, and the Earth in an increasingly violent and unjust world. I tell the story as one of God's love affair with the planet, of God's willingness to forgive us even of our sins, and of God's hope that, awakened to divine Love, we might be peacemakers.

In truth, however, no generation's telling of the story is final or complete. First, insofar as the Christian story itself is a cosmic creation story, and insofar as creation itself is an ongoing, unfinished process, so the Christian story is an unfinished process. Everything that happens in the universe adds a chapter to the story, not entirely predictable on the basis of what came before. The Christian story changes with each swaying of the sycamore in the wind, with each chirp of the house sparrow, with each cry of the newborn child, with each laugh of the grandparent. With each happening there is something new in the history of the universe, and with this newness the story is altered.

Second, the tellers are limited in their capacities for storytelling. They must use language, with all its limitations. They must hope, almost against their own limitations, that somehow their words will evoke in the listeners a sensitivity not only to the changes that occur in the universe continuously, but also to the living Christ, to whose presence the story ultimately points. The purpose of telling the Christian story is to attune us to the living Christ, in whose very body the sycamore and sparrow and girl and grandfather live and move and have their being.

By the living Christ I mean the Christlike or Christic dimension of God, that dimension which draws us into the fullness of life relative to situations at hand, and which suffers with our sufferings and shares in our joys. There is more to God than this Christic dimension. God is like an Ocean, and we swim

in only a small part of it, surrounded by the rest which eludes our comprehen-
sion. The Christic dimension of God is that aspect of God which we partially
comprehend through Jesus and others who show the Way, and who inspire
trust and love. Christians believe that this Christic dimension is central to
God, that it represents the very Heart of the vast and mysterious Ocean. It is
as if all of the Ocean is permeated by a compassionate element, no matter
how strange and foreign it might seem. We believe that whatever else God
may be, God is Christlike.

The trustworthy and compassionate dimension of God was embodied but
not exhausted in Jesus of Nazareth. To say that it was embodied in Jesus is to
say that we learn about God from Jesus. To say that it was not exhausted by
Jesus is to say that there is more to the Christic dimension of God, more to the
living Christ, than we see in Jesus.

Of course, we must be careful with words like *Christ*. Sometimes the very
word *Christ* can function as an obstacle to tasting the healing waters of spirit,
chiefly because the word so often suggests exclusivism. People are understandably repelled by words like *Christ* and *Jesus* when they feel excluded by
them, or when they feel that assent to the meanings of such words forces
them to exclude others.

For this reason it is important to use other words to name Christ. In this
book I have used phrases such as Holy Wisdom, Divine Ocean, Sacred Whole,
and Mother of the Universe. All of these phrases can suggest a healing spirit
at work in our lives. But none ought be made absolute, because the words are
less important than the reality. The purpose of any talk about God, and of any
telling of the Christian story, is to orient us toward a healing Spirit at work in
our lives and the world, a Spirit whose aim for us is that we be whole in
community with others, and they with us. The purpose is to open us to life in
Christ.

One purpose of this chapter is to propose that the Christian life can itself
be understood as life in Christ. All of the themes introduced earlier—from
red grace to green grace, from peacemaking to earth-based spirituality—can
be understood as dimensions or aspects of a single life: life in Christ. Christianity is a Christ-centered way.

In this chapter I approach the theme of Christ-centeredness in a circuitous
fashion. In the first part of the chapter I will explain more about how Jesus
might be understood in the Christian story, and in the latter part I will offer an
ecological interpretation of three Christian themes: the Garden of Eden, the
Fall, and life in Christ. The treatment of life in Christ comes at the end, not
the beginning, as a way of bringing these ideas together.

In an earlier chapter I interpreted the Fall in two ways: 1) as a symbol of
the fact that we humans "fall short" of the aims of Holy Wisdom for us, and 2)
as a symbol that evolution itself "falls short" of revealing divine empathy for
individual creatures, particularly animals. In this chapter I offer a third, more
historical way of understanding the Fall: as a historical occurrence. It can be
understood as an event that occurred late in human history, when humans lost

the "ecological innocence" of living as hunters and gatherers, and "fell" into agriculture-based civilizations, amid which they gained new and dangerous powers over animals, the Earth, and one another.

The treatment of Jesus that I offer in this chapter is by no means complete. I do not offer a formal Christology, but rather a suggestion, a hint, as to how we might imagine Jesus in our time and our way, as others have in their times and their ways. In an earlier chapter I interpreted Jesus as a prophet who comforted the afflicted and afflicted the comfortable, such that peace on Earth might be enjoyed. Here I add to that view by interpreting Jesus as an enfleshment of Holy Wisdom herself, that is, as God incarnate.

To focus on Jesus as God incarnate is not to absolutize Jesus. Even Jesus made mistakes. Jesus has his purpose, not in pointing us to himself, but rather in pointing us beyond himself, to the living Christ whose spirit he so often embodied, and who is our salvation. Jesus was "the Way, the Truth, and the Life" (Jn 14:6), not because he wanted to be worshiped, but because in him we glimpse the Way that we ourselves can best live. This Way is filled with the Truth of the Christic dimension of God, and it is the Life by which our souls, and our relations with the surrounding world, can be enlivened into the fullness of life.

With these caveats, then, let us turn to a brief treatment of Jesus as God incarnate, and then to a contemporary understanding of the Garden of Eden, the Fall, and Life in Christ.

Jesus as the Dream Enfleshed

Recall the outline of the story told in the previous chapter. It is the story of a divine Wisdom at the heart of the cosmos, who inspired the universe to create itself galactically, geologically, and biologically, and who, in the process, fell in love with the planet Earth. Indeed, she loved the planet so much that, when it became possible for her, she called a young Jew to advance one of her deepest dreams: a kingdom of God on Earth or, to use less patriarchal terms, a community of *shalom* on Earth. The dream had already been revealed in many ways, not least through Jewish prophets that preceded the young Jew, and from whose wisdom he imbibed. But Holy Wisdom did not call him to *announce* the dream through teachings and proclamations, so much as to *become* the dream in feeling and action, in living flesh. With such an act, so she hoped, people would see the Way. They would learn to enact the dream of God "on earth as it is in heaven."

None of us really knows what happens "in heaven." We can only feel and speculate. In this book I propose that, in heaven, Holy Wisdom weaves a pattern of meaning from all that happens on Earth, whatever happens. It is as if all that we think, feel, and do are musical notes, and Wisdom creates a symphony from these notes such that the good that we do and feel, the suffering we undergo, and the joys we realize, are united with all other goods and sufferings and joys. A symphony is created, in which the meaning of each is nourished by and added to the meaning of all.

This symphony, I suggest, is "the end of time." It is "heaven," the inner life of God. Whether or not individual souls, human and nonhuman, live in heaven is best debated elsewhere.[1] The relevant point here is that, whether or not it includes living psyches, heaven is itself in process. The inner life of Holy Wisdom is continually being fed new notes by the world, such that the symphony in God's heart is changing at each moment. If the inner life of Holy Wisdom is a symphony, it is an unfinished one, new at every moment, fresh with every new note offered for its assimilation.

As new notes are added, new energies become available for Wisdom herself. The good news for us is that Holy Wisdom does not keep these energies to herself. She recycles them back to Earth in the form of fresh possibilities for wisdom and compassion, relative to what is possible in the situation at hand.

These possibilities are visitations from Wisdom herself. In times of fear they are possibilities for courage; in times of despair, they are for hope; in times of close-mindedness, they are for openness; in times of lukewarmness, they are for conviction. The love in heaven, the beauty of the unfinished symphony, is not static or self-enclosed. It floods back to Earth in the form of possibilities. At the Heart of the universe is an ongoing process of recycling; divine compassion is "recycled" in the form of terrestrial possibilities.

This does not mean that everything is getting better and better on Earth. It is not. There is much at work on Earth besides heavenly possibilities; human sin, for example, is quite destructive. We can and do fail to respond to our possibilities all the time. Witness the violence of our times, inflicted on other people, animals, and the Earth.

Still, there is hope for us and for life on Earth, because Holy Wisdom is forever recycling our energies back to us in the form of new and hopeful possibilities. Whatever devils we face, of our own production or foisted upon us, there are opportunities to make the best of the situation at hand.

In his own way, Jesus was presented to us in light of our devils. He was a fresh possibility, availed by God, presented to us, for the sake of hope. This does not mean that Jesus descended from the heavens, but rather that he was called by Holy Wisdom to reveal a unique truth, not by announcing it, but by becoming it, as best he could, in his own way and time.

Of course, Jesus was not the only person called by Holy Wisdom. Many have been called. Her healing spirit has spoken, and still speaks, through acts of kindness and charity, wisdom and courage, creativity and freedom, wherever they are found. It speaks through native peoples, who realize that openness to the numinous power of God's spirit requires openness to revelations from

---

1. With other process theologians, I believe that this a real possibility. In other works I have offered what I hope are plausible interpretations of both "heaven" and "hell," both understood in terms of the continued existence of the psyche after death (McDaniel 1990, 130–31).

plants, birds, hills, and trees; through Buddhists, who awaken to the deep interconnectedness of all things and invite us to do the same; through Muslims, who realize that religion must be a way of life and not just a set of beliefs; through Hindus, who insist that God has many names; and, of course, through Jews, who dwell in special covenant with God through grace-filled laws, through Torah. Not least, Holy Wisdom speaks through plants and animals, and through the universe itself, with its fifteen-billion-year process of unfolding. Holy Wisdom has many words to speak, many revelations to offer. The revelation that occurred in Jesus is one of many.

Still, like other revelations, his revelation was unique in form and substance. Most Jewish prophets before him recognized a difference between themselves and God. They may have heard a still, small voice within them, but they felt the voice to be one thing and themselves quite another. They felt called by this voice to speak the truth, but they did not say "I am the Voice."

There was something wise and humble in their insistence that they and God were different. Dangerous things happen when people claim they are God. One of the great strengths of the Jewish tradition, and of Islam as well, is that their adherents speak against any identification of self with God. The purpose of dis-identification with God is not only to highlight God but also to celebrate self. In Judaism and in Islam, people *like* not being God. It gives them space to be human.

Still, so the Christian tradition suggests, the young Jew risked identifying with God, because he felt deeply called by God to do so. He responded to Holy Wisdom's call that he become her Voice, her Dream. The Christian scriptures suggest that at times he so identified with her immanent energies that his self and her aims coalesced. When people saw him, they saw her; when he spoke, they felt she was speaking; when he forgave, they felt forgiven by her. He radiated a holy energy, a Buddha-field, and they responded. He was a spirit-filled charismatic, and his charisma revealed Holy Wisdom herself.

Of course, in speaking of the God of Jesus in feminine terms, I am taking poetic license. Most of us realize that the early followers of Jesus and his followers did not think of God as "she" but rather as "he." For them, the reality I am calling Holy Wisdom was God the Father. My point in using such imagery is to remind us that in our time we need to experiment with different images of the Divine, each of which can be beneficial in finding the Divine— and none of which should be made absolute. Feminine imagery is a corrective to the one-sidedness of so much masculine imagery, and it reveals truths about the Divine that masculine imagery often does not.

My guess is that this feminine imagery reveals a strength of connection, not separation, a power of relationality, not isolation. Jesus seems to have experienced God in this way; hence his endearing term *abba* for God. In our time, feminine imagery may well indicate *abba* better than masculine imagery. It gives us a relational image of the very Center of the cosmos, such that we realize that this Center, rather than self-enclosed, is an omni-empathetic, omni-adaptable Heart.

In any case, the followers of Jesus knew, as Jesus knew, that there was more to Holy Wisdom than was embodied in Jesus' own life. After all, Jesus prayed to God as a reality different from himself, and, at least at Gethsemane, he felt tempted to violate God's will. Still, he seems also to have identified with the energies of Holy Wisdom at various points in his life, such that he became, for others, her Spirit enfleshed. This enabled him to reveal things about her Spirit, her will and yearning, that have shaped Christian teachings ever since.

Among the most important things Jesus revealed was that God is not distant and removed, like a king lording over his realm, but rather tender and caring, like a shepherd tending sheep or a mother hen taking care of her chicks. Indeed, Jesus revealed that God has a special concern for the outcasts and despised of society, for the poor and powerless. Accordingly, he encouraged his followers to see her in the eyes of the broken-hearted, the tears of the sufferers, the fears of the powerless. He said that they served Holy Wisdom herself when they served "the least of these" (Mt 25:40).

It would have been tempting for Jesus to force his point like a king; that is, to marshall an army that would reverse the social and political order of his time. Instead, he chose to die as further revelation. Later generations would say, perhaps rightly, that when he died, God lost a piece of her very heart, that she died with Jesus.

A Christianity with roots and wings will affirm this fact. The point is not that, when God died with Jesus, God's own life ended. Rather, the point is that Jesus' death tells us something about what happens in the life of God all the time. It tells us that wherever there is suffering and death on Earth, there is suffering and death even in the Heart of the universe, even in the divine Mother. Insofar as the universe is the body of Holy Wisdom, then what happens to living beings on the planet happens in and to her. This means that God, that Holy Wisdom, knows what it is like even to die.

Sometimes the deaths of those we love are more painful than our own. If we are parents, we would rather die than see our children die; if we love others deeply, we would rather die than see our beloveds die. This was the case with the followers of Jesus. They thought that he would "succeed" in his mission to bring about the kingdom of God. Instead, he "succeeded" by identifying with the poor and powerless, even to the end. He died the death of a criminal. In many ways his mission was a failure.

Strangely, however, the failure became a success; his death became an occasion for grace. This is how Holy Wisdom works; she avails people of new possibilities for hope. Even after tragedies have occurred, she helps bring life from death. In the context of Jesus' death, she offered the followers of Jesus a fresh possibility. She invited them to experience the blood of Christ not as condemnation for human sinfulness, but as a medium for red grace. She seemed to say: "Let this cross be an occasion for you to recognize that you, my beloveds, are both the people who nailed Jesus to the cross and the Jesus who was thus nailed. His suffering is your suffering, and their violence your violence. Know that I love you amid it all. I share in your suffering, and I forgive even your violence." When they heard this word, they experienced red grace, as we can.

Still, red grace is not the end of the story, at least in the Christian vision. The end of the story is resurrection, not death. The heart of Christianity lies in the possibility of living a new life, daily and hourly, realizing that we must face crosses in the process, but that even as when we undergo crosses, new life is possible. This new life is called life in Christ.

The remainder of this chapter deals with life in Christ. My aim is to flesh out the Christian story by interpreting life in Christ and two associated symbols: the Garden of Eden and the Fall. As was the case with the previous two chapters, I will do so in an ecological way. My emphasis will be on the implications of life in Christ, not only for our own self-understanding and our relation to other people, but also for animals and the Earth.

Dominion

For obvious reasons, the biblical idea that humans are to have "dominion over the Earth" is not popular among environmentalists and animal rights activists. Too often *dominion* has meant domination rather than care; and too often the theme of dominion has lent itself to attitudes of separation from and superiority over the rest of creation. Attitudes of this sort are part of the problem, not part of the solution. For the sake of the Earth, it seems, we ought to reject the idea of dominion.

Obviously, dominion is not the best foundation for a comprehensive theology of ecology. In a Christian context there are many better models of human-Earth relations. In the following list, items 1, 2, 3, and 6 are Thomas Berry's; 4 and 5 are my own.

1. A Celtic model, developed by Irish saints in the early Middle Ages, in which a spirit world is associated with the natural world and in which nature is seen as a medium through which communion with spirit is possible.

2. A fertility model, embodied by Hildegard of Bingen and other nature-mystics of the Christian past, in which the Divine is seen in the fertility of earth processes.

3. A friendship model, embodied by Francis of Assisi and the desert Fathers, in which animals and the elements are befriended in a spirit of Christian compassion.

4. A covenantal model, first articulated in the biblical story of God entering into covenant with animals as well as humans, which emphasizes divine love for and fidelity to the whole of life.

5. A sacramental model, embodied by Orthodox traditions, emphasizing the sacramental dimension of the whole creation, and stressing that the whole creation, not humans alone, is involved in the redemptive process.

6. A history of creation (or evolutionary) model, exemplified early in Christian history by Irenacus and more recently by Teilhard de Chardin, Thomas Berry, and process theologians, in which Christianity is understood in an evolutionary context.[2]

These models can be combined in various ways. My own approach is to combine a history of creation model with a covenantal model, drawing upon other models to a lesser degree.[3] Using insights from process theology and Thomas Berry, I propose that the Earth is an ever-unfolding network of creative subjects, all of whom are imbued with their own interiority and intrinsic value. I suggest that these creatures are enfolded within and lured by an all-compassionate and all-faithful Life named God, whose nonviolent nature and dreams were disclosed uniquely but not exclusively in Jesus Christ.

Still, it would be quite dishonest for me, and for others as well, to reject the idea of dominion altogether. The fact is that humans *do* have dominion over the Earth, like it or not. It is not that we are *supposed* to have dominion, or that God *wants* us to have dominion, at least of the kind we exercise today. It is simply that for a long time dominion has been a historical fact.

By *dominion* I mean "rule" or "powerful influence." Most of us realize that such rule can be kindly or dominating or both. It is difficult to know what *dominion* in Genesis originally meant. Some biblical interpreters think *dominion* referred to a position of absolute command, to be maintained by force, analogous to the power of military subjugation; others believe it referred to a position of protection and care analogous to the love of God for humans (cf. Callicott 1991, 137).

My argument in this chapter does not concern what *dominion* meant for biblical authors, but rather what it can mean and ought to mean for Christians today. I suggest that it can mean and ought to mean kindly rather than dominating rule. As humans, our dominion over the Earth is our powerful influence over other creatures and their habitats both locally and globally. Because this dominion is now inescapable, as I will argue shortly, it is important that Christians, who now constitute roughly one-third of the world's population, learn to exercise dominion in ways that approximate the rule of Christ rather than the rule of a political dictator. The rule of Christ is one in which the first become last for the sake of others. It is the power of nonviolence, care, and service, as opposed to that of violence, indifference, and ego-centeredness.

---

2. I have obtained Berry's list from a videotape of a talk given at a meeting of the North American Conference on Christianity and Ecology held in 1989. The tape is distributed by Lou Niznik, 15726 Ash!and Ave., Laurel, Maryland. Berry also included a stewardship model, which I exclude here, because the dominion model I create in this chapter is a stewardship model of sorts.

3. Jay B. McDaniel, *Of God and Pelicans: A Theology of Reverence for Life* (Louisville: Westminster/John Knox Press, 1989). For my most sustained treatment of the implications of covenant thinking, see Jay B. McDaniel, "A God Who Loves Animals and a Church That Does the Same," in *Good News for Animals? Contemporary Approaches to Animal Well-Being*, ed. Jay B. McDaniel and Charles Pinches (Maryknoll, N.Y.: Orbis Books, 1993).

The Christian way of making this point requires a creative interpretation of three traditional symbols: the Garden of Eden, the Fall, and new life in Christ. In what follows I offer one such interpretation.

The Garden of Eden

Unfortunately for much of the Earth, human dominion is now inescapable. By United Nations estimates the global population will be around 6.3 billion by A.D. 2000 and 11 billion by the end of the next century (Fellmann, Getis, and Getis 1985, 96). It is technically impossible for 6.3 billion people to live on the planet without exercising inordinate rule over other creatures and their habitats, if only to meet basic needs. This is the case even if we learn to love the Earth deeply, respect other creatures, reduce our levels of consumption considerably, and stabilize our population growth to its present level. Even if we live up to the call of a just and sustainable future, we are doomed to dominion.

There is, of course, one tragic alternative. Through some combination of war, disease, starvation, and ecological collapse, the human population can be reduced to pre-dominion levels. At the very least this would be to reduce the population to pre-industrial levels, say to five hundred million. More likely, for reasons that should be clear shortly, it would be to reduce the population to pre-agricultural levels, say five to ten million (Fellmann, Getis, and Getis 1985, 97). In either case, more than 90 percent of the current human population would need to be eliminated.

The problem is that a violent diminution of the human population would involve unimaginable tragedy not only for most humans—whose lives, like those of other creatures, are precious—but also for members of other species, who would perish through habitat destruction and other forms of violence. For ecological as well as humane reasons, not many of us are willing to hope for such tragedy. Nor should we. Once endowed with sentience, all individual creatures have intrinsic value, humans included.

Our best option is to accept the ambiguity of such a high number of humans on the planet, stabilize that population as much as possible, and find ways of allowing 6 to 11 billion people to live on the planet in relatively sustainable but nevertheless dominion-oriented ways. These are ways that nurture the quality, not the quantity, of human life, with minimum impact on wildlife areas and with humane treatment of domesticated animals. This option means coming to grips with our dominion and learning to use it wisely and compassionately, in a Christlike manner.

The Long Age of the Hunters and Gatherers

Even as we acknowledge the inescapability of dominion, however, we must also recognize that dominion as we now exercise it is a latecomer in human history. For more than two-and-a-half million years human rule over other

creatures and their habitats was relatively minimal. During this period geneti-
cally modern humans and their hominid predecessors lived in families of
twenty to forty, foraging for food and hunting game. We were hunters and
gatherers. In truth they—we—exercised dominion over other creatures even
in these times, and some of it was destructive. In the Pleistocene overkill, for
example, species of large animals the world over were exterminated by unre-
stricted hunting. We have always been an assertive species.

Still, our dominion during the hunting-gathering times was quite limited.
Our powers of influence, and therefore our opportunities for destruction, were
restricted by our population, which was but five to ten million; by our tools,
which were limited to chopped rocks and sticks; and perhaps also by spiritual
sensibilities. If ever we lived in some degree of deep balance with the rest of
creation, as a species among species without inordinate rule, this was the
time. We were in the Garden of Eden.

Were we *happy* in the Garden? It is difficult to say. We can only speculate.
Archeological evidence shows that we lived well by foraging and hunting;
buried our ancestors in special ways; knew the plants and animals in their
immediate environments with intimacy; and, as cave paintings make clear,
had distinctive creative talents. At the very least our lives were not absolute
misery.

It is even possible—if contemporary hunting and gathering societies tell
us anything about our ancient history—that we did not work that hard in the
Garden. The San of South Africa work only two-and-a-half days a week, spending the rest of their time in storytelling, play, tool-making, and ritual. Perhaps
our ancient ancestors did the same.

We can also speculate concerning the spirituality of the hunters and gatherers. By *spirituality* I mean underlying, unobjectified attitudes and
feeling-tones, not formally articulated beliefs. Synthesizing data from contemporary anthropology and paleoanthropology, philosopher Max
Oelschlaeger identifies several feelings that, in his view, were part and parcel
of the ancient hunting-gathering mentality. According to Oelschlaeger our
ancient ancestors felt that 1) irrespective of place, nature was home, 2) nature
was alive, 3) the entire world of plants and animals, even the land itself, was
sacred, and 4) divinity could take many natural forms (1991, 12).

If Oelschlaeger is correct, then during our long period in the Garden
we felt no special separation from the rest of nature. We were in the web
of life, not apart from it. This does not mean that we lacked all tendencies
toward aggression and subjugation. Such tendencies were in us, just as
they were in our cousins the apes and chimpanzees. But it does mean
that we did not channel these tendencies in the destructive ways we now
channel them. There was no organized warfare, no class division, no racism
or sexism, no sense of ourselves as "lords" over nature or one another. Like
Adam and Eve before the Fall, we were relatively innocent. We did not know
we were naked.

The Fall

When did the Fall occur? When did our dominion increase and our potential for domination emerge? Some might point to the emergence of modern, industrial civilizations in the seventeenth and eighteenth centuries. Certainly human dominion increased rapidly during this period, often in destructive ways. But the better answer, I submit, is some twelve thousand years ago, with the dawn of plow agriculture. At least this is the suggestion of Christians such as Wes Jackson and John Cobb, and of environmental philosophers such as J. Baird Callicott (Cobb 1991a, 27–31; Callicott 1991, 107–40; Jackson 1987). Jackson, an agroecologist, puts it this way: "The Fall . . . can be understood in a modern sense as an event that moved us from our original hunting-gathering state, in which nature provided for us exclusively, to an agricultural state, in which we took a larger measure of control over food production, changing the face of the earth along the way. . . . I suspect that agriculture is at the core of the Fall" (quoted in Callicott 1991, 125).

Of course, the Fall did not occur all at once or in a single location. It occurred over many thousands of years in Egypt, Mesopotamia, the Nile River Valley, India, China, Africa, and the Americas. Still, when we take into account the long view of human history, we realize how sudden it was. As Richard Leakey writes: "For perhaps two million years human ancestors had practiced nomadic hunting and gathering, a way of life that was characterized by stability rather than change in its technology and culture. Then, over a period of a few thousand years, the ancient way of life was virtually abandoned" (1981, 200).

In history books we do not speak of the emergence of agriculture-based civilizations as a Fall. Rather we speak of it as an advance for the human species. We celebrate the tremendous creativity involved in spinning and weaving, brick-making and mortaring, mining and smelting, law and religion, in urban life itself. Sometimes, by contrast, we imagine the hunters and gatherers as "primitives," whom we have transcended.

I recommend instead that we recall them as our revered elders and as the first humans, like Adam and Eve. In truth there were many "Adams" and many "Eves," five to ten million of them at any given time in the hunting and gathering period, and their ways had a certain innocence that ours lack. To be sure, agricultural civilizations brought with them goods we rightly cherish. I, for one, would not give them up. But the Fall was also a decline, insofar as it brought with it many human evils unknown to the early foragers, including slavery, patriarchy, organized warfare, and, as I emphasize here, a loss of ecological innocence. As agriculture-based civilizations emerged, humans began to modify plant and animal species, breeding them for our own purposes; to manage soil, land, water, and mineral resources; and to utilize animal energy to supplement human energy. In many ways we became lords of the planet. We gained increased dominion over other animals and our bioregions.[4]

We ought not underestimate the destructive effects of this increased dominion on wild animals and their habitats. With the rise of farming, fields and settlements began to displace animal habitats at alarming rates. Moreover, as food sources became more stable, the human population began to increase dramatically, thus requiring still more habitat destruction. What seemed good news for some humans was in fact bad news for many wild animals. Wes Jackson's words ring true: "I suspect that agriculture is at the core of the Fall."

The Psychology of the Fall

Cobb and Callicott emphasize a more psychological dimension of the Fall into agriculture-based civilizations (Cobb 1991a, 27–31; Callicott 1991, 122–24). As they see it, the Fall involved the gradual emergence of a certain mode of consciousness that is both a blessing and a curse in human existence. The Bible speaks of it as "the knowledge of good and evil" (Gn 3:5).

Two aspects of this knowledge are worth noting. First, knowledge of good and evil involves a sense of self-awareness, such that we understand ourselves as separate from other creatures in certain ways and capable of exercising inordinate rule over them and, for that matter, over one another. We have choices to make in whether and how we will exercise our newfound power. We become aware that there are good ways to use power, and bad ways. We have the knowledge of good and evil.

Second, as Callicott emphasizes, the knowledge of good and evil involves a kind of ranking, or evaluating, of items in the world as good or evil relative to their human utility. Of course, hunters and gatherers partook of such ranking. They knew that some plants were edible and others not. But in the urban-agricultural civilizations, so Callicott suggests, this ranking was intensified. Some plants become good plants and others become weeds; some animals become good animals and others become varmints. With the Fall into agriculture, so Callicott suggests, anthropocentrism emerged in many cul-

---

4. I have already said that some dominion can be good for other animals and the Earth as well as for humans. In domesticating animals, for example, possibilities emerge, not only for an abuse of animals, which is now widespread, but also for intimate relations with these animals. Animals can become part of our communities and enjoy the benefits of our kindly treatment. Indeed, in its encouragement of warm relations with pets and other animals under human dominion, the contemporary animal welfare movement in the West is an extension of sensibilities that emerged after, not before, the Fall. These sensibilities were developed most extensively in Indian civilizations, with the doctrine of *ahimsa* or non-injury to animals. They have yet to be developed, and need to be developed, in Western civilizations as well. Still, the development of ideals such as non-injury is a late emergent in human history. It is only after animal domestication, not before it, that animals could be imagined as having rights to life and happiness, such that even killing them for food is seen as morally problematic. *Ahimsa* would have made no sense to early hunters.

tures. Anthropocentrism was itself a feature of the Original Sin that post-agricultural peoples have inherited ever since (Callicott 1991, 124).[5]

New Life in Christ

In light of this Original Sin, what are we to do? I have already said that we cannot return to the ways of the hunters and gatherers. Hunting and gathering societies require considerable territory to support a relatively small number of individuals (Fellmann, Getis, and Getis 1985, 36). The planet cannot hold six billion hunters and gatherers.

But we *can* learn from contemporary primal peoples. Following their guidance, we can learn to feel the Earth as alive, as our home, and as sacred revelation. Without such sensibilities, our dominion will indeed be domination.

Still, urban and industrial peoples cannot regain Paradise. After the Fall, we can only move forward into as yet uncharted but hopefully benign relations with the rest of creation. Callicott makes this point: "We can no more re-create the original Garden of Eden than we can recover our original unself-consciousness. But we can try to live harmoniously in and with nature . . . by employing all of our postindustrial ingenuity and ecological understanding to create an environmentally benign sustainable civilization" (Callicott 1991, 132).

If our civilizations are to be sustainable, two things are needed. First, at local, regional, and national levels, we need to develop forms of community that are humane in their treatment of animals, just in their relations between humans, and sustainable in their relations with bioregions. Toward this end, much creative thinking and social experimentation is necessary. Christians rightly understand creative thinking and experimentation as one way of responding to the Lure toward adventure within the cosmos itself, that is, to God.

Second, we need to become the kind of people, with the kinds of sensibilities, that can sustain such communities once they emerge. It is at this point, I believe, that the inner dimensions of the Christian life become relevant.

Christian spirituality does not offer a way of returning to the Garden of Eden, however understood. It does not promise a recovery of lost innocence or a return to original unself-consciousness. Instead it encourages us 1) to accept our lost innocence, 2) to trust that, despite the loss, we are embraced by an all-compassionate Mystery—a Christlike God—who seeks our own good

---

5. The kind of consciousness I have just described is something that many of us are socialized into as young children. Our parents and peers teach us to think of ourselves as "selves," to recognize our own capacities for good and evil, and to rank the world in terms of our own interests. Cobb and Callicott point out that this mode of consciousness was itself an emergent in human history. It brings with it much joy and suffering, much good and evil. Like everything else about the Fall, it was, and is, ambiguous.

and that of the whole creation, and 3) to open our hearts to the healing powers of this Mystery, so that we become vessels of the Mystery's own love. To the degree that we are open to these healing powers, the divine Mystery unfolds within us, as a self deeper than our own egos, who lives through us yet is more than us. As present within us, the Mystery of God is named the living Christ. To live from nourishment of the living Christ is to enjoy life in Christ. We are able to say, with Paul: "It is no longer I who live, but Christ in me" (Gal 2:20).

The living Christ is conceived in different ways by different Christians. Conservatives are inclined to conceive the living Christ as a divine reality who enters us after we have accepted our lost innocence and accepted God's grace. Accepting God's grace is itself tied to accepting Jesus as personal lord and savior. Thus, for conservatives, life in Christ is limited to born-again Christians.

More liberal Christians have an alternative view. They see the living Christ as a divine consciousness that is already within us at a deep level, even prior to our recognition of it, to which we awaken. Here Christ does not enter from afar; rather, Christ wells up from within, to the degree that we are in touch with the deepest center of our lives. I recommend this point of view.

This liberal approach opens up possibilities for interreligious dialogue that are not available to conservatives. Liberals can see the living Christ in all people, not just in Christians, and then recognize that people of other faiths may well be inspired by the living Christ in ways not present in historical Christianity. I often see the living Christ in people of other paths who are more centered in the Mystery than I, and whose compassion exceeds my own. I find myself grateful that Christ is not limited to Christianity.

In any case, for liberals and conservatives alike, the very heart of Christianity lies in living out of, and from, the indwelling Spirit of God, the living Christ. Christianity is not an abstract philosophy or even an application of such philosophy. It is a Spirit-inspired Way of living, a Christ-centered Way.

Awakening to the living Christ is itself an evolutionary possibility, the way for which was paved by billions of years of cosmic evolution and millions of years of biological evolution. Indeed, this possibility became available and relevant only after the Fall into agriculture. Our distant elders, the early foragers, had their own ways of dwelling in communion with God, relative to their time and situation, as do other animals. Life in Christ is for people who have lost their innocence.

This life can be conceived in two ways. On the one hand, it is a post-agricultural salvage operation, a way of making the best of a bad situation. Understood in this way, life in Christ is a way of enjoying redemption, that is, of enjoying divine forgiveness despite human sinfulness.

On the other hand, life in Christ can also be conceived as an advance in the history of life on Earth, at least if it is lived to its fullest. Understood in this way, it is more than a way of being saved from the consequences of the Fall.

It is a contribution to the very history of creation, without which creation would not be as rich.

To conceive of life in Christ as contributing to the history of creation, of course, is to believe that human history, and the universe itself, is an ongoing process capable of growth and change, and that new things can happen that lack precedence in the past. This is a traditional Christian view, rooted in the prophetic idea that God can offer new possibilities in new historical situations. As a process theologian, this is something I, too, believe. I believe that new possibilities emerge from the Life at the heart of the universe, which were not available or relevant beforehand, and that offer genuine possibilities for new life relative to the situations at hand. Life in Christ is one kind of new life, of which I am sure there are others, including Buddhist enlightenment, Hindu *moksha*, Taoist *wu wei*, and Muslim submission. Life in Christ is a Way among Ways. The degree to which these Ways overlap is difficult to decide in advance. At present, it is best to be pluralistic and thus to recognize that there are many valuable Ways—many post-agricultural salvage operations—toward which God has lured humans relative to their cultural situations. They may or may not resemble one another, but all have something to offer the whole.

Among Christians, what is sorely needed in our time is a spelling out of some of the implications of life in Christ for ecology. I conclude with some reflections on these implications.

Recall that life in Christ involves 1) an acceptance of lost innocence, 2) a recognition of the limitless love of God, and 3) an openness to the healing powers of God as they well up from within the very depths of our existence. To accept our lost innocence is to accept the fact that many of us in urban-industrial civilizations *do* feel separate from one another and the rest of creation, and that, in the latter regard, we *do* tend to evaluate other creatures in light of their usefulness to us. We must confess that we partake of what Callicott calls "anthropocentric consciousness." This is part of our sinful existence.

To recognize that we, and the whole of creation besides, are embraced by a Christlike Mystery is to understand that this "fallen consciousness" is not the ultimate perspective. It is to realize that the most inclusive perspective belongs not to us but to God, who loves each and every creature for its own sake—the amoeba no less than the chimpanzee, the mosquito no less than the human.

This does not mean that God loves all creatures equally or in the same way. There may be more to love in the chimpanzee than the amoeba, by virtue of the richness of the chimpanzee's sentience. The point is simply that each creature is loved by God on its own terms and for its own sake, however rich those terms might be. As theologian Schubert Ogden states: "Because God's love itself is subject to no bounds and excludes nothing from its embrace, there is no creature's interest that is not also God's interest and, therefore, necessarily included in the redeeming love of God" (Birch, Eakin, and McDaniel 1990, frontispiece).

To be healed by God is to allow our life, as best we can, to be a vessel for this limitless love. I have proposed that the limitless love wells up from within the depths of our existence as a living Christ, who is our deepest center. To the extent that we partake of this love, our own dominion will be tempered by a deeper recognition of the sheer goodness, the sheer lovability, of each and every living being whom we influence. We will have put on the mind of God.

Putting on the mind of God is no mean feat. It entails worship and prayer, study and service, community and contemplation, all of which are best understood as ways of cooperating with divine grace. Moreover, God-consciousness occurs in degrees. Few Christians have put on the mind of God fully. Not even Jesus did so completely, for he, like us, was fully human. Life in Christ is an ideal to be approximated by finite creatures. To the degree that Christians learn to feel the world as God feels it, with sensitivity to the intrinsic value of each and every life, and with delight in the sheer diversity of forms of life, we will approximate life in Christ. And to the degree that we approximate this life, we will be the kind of people the world sorely needs today.

Part 2

ADVENTURES IN DIALOGUE

Chapter 7

Many Paths and Many Truths

A Christian Approach to Other Religions

A rabbi at a Reform Jewish synagogue in Hot Springs, Arkansas, once invited me to attend Friday Evening Services. Her name was Angela Graboys. Rabbi Graboys knew that I was interested in Judaism, and she wanted me to experience Jewish worship firsthand. She told me in advance that she had a yardstick for measuring how successful the service ought to be. "If you feel at home in our service *as a Christian*," she said, "it will have been a successful service. If you feel as though you should convert to Judaism, it will have been unsuccessful."

Her point was that she hoped that I would hear nothing in the service that would make me feel excluded from God's grace. She wanted me to feel the presence of God in her Jewish congregation, but also to realize that, in Judaism as she understood it, it was all right for me not to be Jewish. The stakes were not heaven and hell.

I was grateful and surprised by her attitude. I knew that she, like I, had studied the history of Christian anti-Semitism. I learned about it in seminary. I knew that the author of the gospel of John identifies Jews with the devil because, so it seemed to him, they murdered the Son of God (Jn 8:43–44, 47). I knew that early church leaders—St. John Chrysostom of Antioch, for example, and St. Ambrose of Milan—had developed this theme of deicide in horrible ways, recommending persecution of Jews. I knew that in the Crusades Jews were either killed or given the choice of converting to Christianity by militant Christians. I learned how the Catholic church had issued various Jew-persecuting laws that were later used as precedent in the establishment of Nazi laws. And, in reading Martin Luther, I saw how, in a pamphlet published at the end of his life, *Concerning the Jews and Their Lies*, the founder of Protestantism identified eight actions to be taken against the Jews, including burning their synagogues, confiscating their holy books, and

131

expelling them from provinces where Christian live.[1] The seminary profes-
sors who taught me these things were Christian, but they were not defensive
about the dark side of their heritage, my heritage. Even as they spoke highly
of Jesus, they spoke in shame of the Christian persecution of Jews, Muslims,
and indigenous peoples, so often in Jesus' name. I left the seminary feeling
that we Christians have much to repent of.

Rabbi Graboys had learned about Christian anti-Semitism in yeshiva. She
too knew about pogroms and forced conversions, about persecutions and blood
libels. She knew that the Holocaust in the twentieth century was the result,
not only of economic and political factors, but also of a cultural climate—a
climate of hatred—promulgated by intolerant Christian majorities. Given her
knowledge of this fact, she had every reason to believe the Christian path
inherently evil, inherently flawed. Yet she chose to separate "Christianity"
from "Christian intolerance," believing that the former, if purged of the latter,
could be a good path.

As it turns out, I was unable to attend services at her synagogue. I had
other obligations. But some Christian students of mine did attend, and they
said that they felt welcome and included. Soon after our conversation, the
rabbi moved to California to attend graduate school in Jewish Studies.

I have always wished I could have attended her services. I have attended
many other Jewish services, and I have felt the kind of openness she described.
In Orthodox and Reform services alike, I have sensed the presence of God in
the chanting, in the reading of Torah, and in the laughter of the children as
they wandered about in the midst of the service. I have felt a sense of tradition, of sadness and joy, in the mood of the worshipers and in the rituals. My
deepest feeling in these services is described by the Jewish playwright Herman
Wouk. "Deep in the heart of both critical Christian and alienated Jew," he
says, "there is a—I cannot say that, a feeling, not even a feeling, a shadow of
a notion, nothing more substantial than the pointless but compelling impulse
to knock on wood when one talks of the health of children—something that
says there is more to the Jews than meets the eye. There is a mystery about the
Jews" (1987, 15). In Jewish worship, I have sensed this mystery.

Amid the mystery, however, I have heard little if anything that suggests I,
as a Christian, am doomed to perdition because I am not Jewish. Perhaps this
is because Judaism is not focused on questions of afterlife in the first place;
or because, in the case of the Orthodox, I could not understand all the Hebrew. But I suspect it is because, while Jews believe that their Way is quite
special, they do not believe it is the only path to God. I have left most Jewish
services that I've attended very glad that there are Jews in the world, somewhat envious that I am not Jewish because there is so much richness, and

---

1. This list of abuses against Jews, including the mention of Luther and his pamphlet, comes
from and is clarified by Prager and Telushkin in *Why the Jews: The Reason for Antisemitism*
(1983, 90–109). The book is an account of the history of anti-Semitism for the general reader. It
seems to me that it, or something like it, ought to be required reading for all Christians.

eager to recognize the Jewish roots of my own Christian faith, without denying the independent integrity of Judaism.

A Fantasy

After Rabbi Graboys moved away, I sometimes fantasized what it might
have been like to take her to a conservative Protestant worship service. My
guess is that she would have liked the gusto with which we sang and the
fervor with which some loved God. But some dimensions of our faith would
have troubled her. I imagined her listening to us singing hymns and reciting
creeds that proclaim Christ as the *only* way to God. I imagined her sensing
that there were some people who would wonder why she wasn't Christian,
given that Christianity is the only "true" way. In my fantasies, I felt embarrassed and apologetic about the exclusivism.

I imagined us leaving the service afterward. I would ask her what she thought.
She would be gentle, but honest. "I did not feel at home," she would say. "I felt
that the hymns and creeds were saying I had to be Christian in order to find God.
I felt that, from the point of view of Christianity, it is wrong for me to be Jewish.
I don't understand why Christians must exclude other faiths as ways to God." I
have had many Jewish friends utter these very words.

I utter them as well. I do not understand Christian exclusivism either. Like
many other Christians, my heart is not engaged when I sing "only Way" hymns.
I feel that we are vain, and I feel saddened by our arrogance. Surely there
must be a way in which Christians can recognize the value of Christianity,
while at the same time recognizing the value of other Ways too. Surely Christians can approach other religions with respect, recognizing that all religions
have significant truth, and that no religion has a monopoly on truth. Surely
Christians can be open to truth wherever it is found, trustful that it is of God
and from God, however named.

Perhaps we can speak of such openness as dialogue, but we must be clear
about what we mean. Usually the word *dialogue* suggests a two-way conversation, in which the parties understand one another and learn from one another.
Perhaps this is dialogue in its ideal form. However, given the legacy of Christian exclusivism, it is presumptuous for Christians to insist that others learn
from us as a precondition for us learning from them. There may well be others—Jews and Muslims, for example, or Native Americans and Native
Africans—whose ways have been so disrupted by Christians, and whose histories are so full of persecution, that they are not in a position to "learn from
Christianity." Sensitive to their points of view, Christians must be humble.
We need to learn from others, without pretending that we fully understand
their Ways, and without insisting that they learn from us. Such is the Way of
Christ, where the first become last.

As I use the word in most of what follows, then, *dialogue* refers, not necessarily to a two-way conversation, but rather an attitude, a stance, that

Christians can take in relation to other traditions. This is an attitude of willingness to hear others on their own terms and to learn from them, even if they are not willing or able to reciprocate. The dialogue occurs in our minds, heedful of what we have heard from our dialogue partners, even if it does not occur in the minds of our partners. The need in our time is for Christians to take this kind of dialogical stance toward other Ways, and in so doing bear witness to the living Christ by whom we feel called.

If we are to take such a stance, however, we must get our bearings. We must first have a general image—an overview—of the various world religions and their functions; we must have a general understanding of how we, as Christians, might approach them. Accordingly, the purpose of this chapter is twofold. First, I want to offer those unfamiliar with the world religions a visual image that might help in understanding their variety, unity, and function. Through this image I hope also to illustrate the current situation among religions, showing how, in principle, they can learn from one another about how to be more rooted in the Earth. Second, I want to offer some guidelines for entering into dialogue. The chapter is divided into two sections corresponding to these two aims. In the chapters that follow I will illustrate a Christian dialogue with Buddhism, Judaism, Hinduism, and Native American religion.

The World Religions

To gain an overview of the world religions, imagine a very wide and deep river on which there are many rafts.[2] Let the river represent the Earth itself, with its plants and animals, its soil and water, its elements and powers; and let each raft represent a world religion of one sort or another. One might be "the Christian raft" and another "the Buddhist raft" and another "the Muslim raft." Then let the "other shore" represent that *wholeness* or *happiness* or *peace of mind* or *contentment* for which the passengers on the rafts yearn, and to which they believe their rafts will take them. On the Christian raft, for example, the wholeness of the distant shore might be called salvation, while on the Buddhist raft it might be called nirvana, and on the Muslim raft it might be called paradise.

Many raft passengers envision the other shore as something to be fully enjoyed only after death. Still, for at least some passengers, the other shore of wholeness is actually this very world, rightly understood. Zen Buddhists, for example, speak of nirvana as the activity of the world itself, seen with enlightened eyes; and some Christians speak of salvation as the wholeness we experience in this life, when we have put on the mind of Christ. Thus the

---

2. This analogy comes from the Buddha, who once compared religions, including his own, to rafts whose purpose was to transport people to a state of fulfillment. His point was that, on arriving on the other shore, there is no need to carry the raft. Religions are tools, not idols.

other shore may not be distant at all. It may be right in front of our eyes—in the river itself, and in our journeying—if we have eyes to see.

However the other shore is understood, it is important that we recognize its multi-dimensionality. The more we study world religions, the more we realize that nirvana may be one form of wholeness, salvation still another, and paradise still another. This is not to say that nirvana and salvation and paradise have nothing in common. To the contrary, each seems to involve a gain in fulfillment, in what might be called self-realization, through a loss of ego-centeredness. In the words of Jesus, they involve finding the soul by losing the self.

Still, these forms of wholeness have different tonalities and ambiences. They sound different when their adherents describe them, which may well indicate that there are different types or styles of self-realized existence. To include this possibility in our analogy, we might imagine various vistas on the other shore. With its cool elimination of ego-centered desire, nirvana might be a sacred grove where people lie in the shade; with its various sensual pleasures, Muslim paradise might be a wide expanse of sand where people dance in the sun; and with its promise of reconciliation with enemies, Christian salvation may be a small inlet where former enemies unite in friendship. Of course, these are but visual images for psychospiritual realities. What is important is that we recognize that the other shore is itself multi-dimensional, and that different rafts may lead to different dimensions of self-realization.

Rafts, Canoes, Swimmers, and Drowning Ones

What, then, are the specific rafts and other water vessels in our world today? What are the spiritual traditions? What are the paths to wholeness?

Let us imagine three major fleets of rafts. One fleet consists of religions emerging from the ancient Near East: Judaism, Christianity, Islam, and, recently developed, Bahai. This is the Abrahamic fleet, since each religion in the fleet traces its roots to the biblical figure Abraham. This is the largest family of religions. The *Encyclopedia Britannica* estimates that Christians number about 33 percent of the world's population, Muslims approximately 20 percent, and Jews less than 1 percent, which means that, considered as a whole, the Abrahamic peoples consist of just over 50 percent of the world's population (cited in the *World Almanac* 1992, 724).

Another fleet consists of religions emerging from the Far East: Confucianism, Taoism, and Shintoism. This is the Sino-Japanese-Korean fleet. At one level, this is the least populous of the religious families. The *Encyclopedia Britannica* estimates that approximately 4 percent of the world's population consciously follows the way of Confucianism, with less than 1 percent being Taoist and Shinto. Still, it is arguable that this religious family is much larger, because the entire populations of China and the rest of East Asia are so deeply shaped by Confucian habits of thought. Thus we might say that the East Asian fleet includes approximately 25 percent of the world's population.

Still another fleet consists of the religions emerging from India: Hinduism, Buddhism, Jainism, and Sikhism. This is the South Asian fleet. The *Encyclopedia Britannica* estimates that approximately 13 percent of the world's population is Hindu, 6 percent Buddhist, and less than 1 percent Sikh and Jain. This means that approximately 20 percent of the world's population belongs to the South Asian fleet.

Of course, these fleets have now cross-fertilized. Buddhism, originating in South Asia, wandered into China to be influenced by Taoism, and into the United States to be influenced by Christianity. The image of fleets represents origins, but not current status.

Moreover, not all the passengers on the various paths to wholeness are serious about their journeys. Some are simply on for the ride, more deeply shaped by the religion of economics—which promises wholeness through material acquisition—than by the traditional paths. Arguably, the dominant path toward wholeness in our time is the religion of economic growth, the chief priests of whom are economists, and the sanctuary of which is the mall. In my analogy, however, only the traditional paths are included, not this new path.

In any case, these traditional fleets are the religions introduced to college undergraduates in a course in religious studies. They are the classical religions, not because they are better than others, but because each produced literature which has become a "classic" for the cultures in which they reside. With the exception of the new raft of economics, which in some ways permeates the entire river in its own invisible way, the classical rafts are the dominant religions in the world today.

Still, these rafts are not the only vessels on the river. We need also imagine some canoes: the indigenous traditions of the world. These include, for example, Native American religions, African primal religions, and Australian aboriginal religions. These too are paths to wholeness, though often the wholeness they offer is less individualized than in the classical traditions and perhaps more closely connected with community survival. I speak of them as canoes, not because they are less important than the rafts, but because today their numbers are fewer. Their peoples have been overwhelmed by the powers of colonialism, neo-colonialism, and missionary conversion. The *Encyclopedia Britannica* estimates that their peoples number approximately 2 percent of the world's population.

Despite their dwindling numbers, however, they represent the earliest and most enduring forms of religion on our planet. Long before there were rafts on the river, there were canoes. The first canoes belonged to the gatherers and hunters, some twenty-five thousand years ago. We now realize that many of them, and many of the early forms of religion in the early period of the Neolithic revolution, worshiped a female rather than a male deity. Many but not all indigenous traditions remind us of the one-sidedness, the patriarchal character, of the so-called classical religions.

Moreover, the indigenous traditions are the most ecologically sensitive of the religions. If we ask which religions have been best at promoting a sense of place with respect to local bioregions, the canoes win. They have evidenced an embeddedness in the land and a willingness to learn from nature rather than books that members of classical religions need to emulate.

Still, we cannot all be canoeists, and it is arrogant to pretend that we are part of a canoe culture if we are not. Furthermore, there are others in the river who do not identify with canoes or rafts at all. In order to take these additional people into account, let us imagine that, in addition to the rafts and canoes, there are swimmers.

Swimmers are the many people, mostly contemporary, now journeying toward wholeness without any affiliation to any of the world religions. They are people for whom reason and experience are much more authoritative than sacred teachings, who are "secular" from the vantage point of some raft travelers, but who may well have forms of spirituality that supersede those of the raft travelers themselves. Some swimmers may have been kicked off rafts, others may have jumped off of their own accord, and still others have never been part of a raft. A person does not have to be religious in order to be spiritual.

Finally, in addition to the swimmers, let us recognize the drowning ones. These are people who don't have the luxury of seeking spiritual wholeness, because they lack the basic goods of survival in the first place. They include the children who die every day of hunger, the victims of debilitating diseases, the people who die of gunshot wounds and torture. The wholeness they seek is simple survival, and they do not find it. If they were once on rafts or canoes, they have slipped through the cracks.

In our world there are far too many drowning ones and far too few raft passengers and swimmers willing to help them. One of the great challenges of religion in the present and future is to cast its lot in with the drowning ones: the hungry, the naked, the lonely, the forgotten. The raft on which I travel—the Christian raft—teaches that God is to be found in their suffering and that service to God requires service to them. Many other rafts emphasize the same. We must hear these teachings and follow them.

Four Correctives to the Analogy

The raft analogy is admittedly quite schematic and general. Before extending it a bit, let me acknowledge four deficiencies. In the process we may gain a still more accurate picture of the world religions.

First, it is important to acknowledge that I have presented religions only in the ideal, as paths to wholeness. In fact, religions also exist in the concrete, instantiated by particular people in particular social situations. The difference between the ideal and the real is often great. In practice, religions can be conduits for violence against women, people of color, freethinkers, animals, and the Earth. Christians only need to look within their local congregations to realize that the wholeness of salvation, and the compassion that is supposed to result from such salvation, is often preached but not practiced, discussed but not experienced. Jews, Muslims, Buddhists, Hindus, Native Americans can do the same. The dichotomy between ideal religion and real religion has led many a raft traveler to jump off the raft and become a swimmer. A balanced picture of religions must include not only what they aim at, namely wholeness of one sort or another, but also what they actually are.

Second, the analogy presents religions as somewhat static, consisting of solid objects that remain the same as passengers are ferried from one shore to the other. In fact, religions are not static at all. They evolve along with their passengers. They are modified and repaired even as they ferry their passengers. The Christian raft in the twentieth century is not the same as the Christian raft in the thirteenth, which is not the same as the Christian raft in the second century. Rafts and canoes are constantly changing, sometimes for good and sometimes for ill. At best their changes help them become even more serviceable.

Third, the analogy suggests homogeneity on the rafts, as if, for example, all the raft travelers are of the same mind. In fact, even in a given contemporary generation, there is much diversity on any given raft; some raft travelers might even deny the right of others to travel on the raft. In Islam we find differences between Sunni and Shia; in Judaism between Orthodox and Reform; in Christianity between Protestants and Catholics and Orthodox; in Buddhism between Mahayana and Theravada. Single rafts are actually many rafts tied loosely together, each with its own inhabitants.

Fourth, the analogy suggests that people are limited to one option. In fact, most of us are not like that. We may have some swimmer in us, some raft traveler, and perhaps some canoe-appreciation as well. Therefore, it is best to take the various options as realities in which we participate rather than as mutually exclusive alternatives. To the degree that we are shaped by the teachings of one of the great religions, and that we identify with these teachings, we travel on the raft; to the degree we find reason and experience, understood in isolation from those teachings, more significant to us than the teachings, we are swimmers.

Keeping in mind these correctives to the analogy, I now extend it a bit. In what follows I offer what I think the future holds, or ought to hold, for people on or influenced by the Christian raft, in their relations to other river travelers and in relation the river itself, which is the Earth.

The River as Context for Dialogue

Imagine that for a long time the people on the various rafts crossed the river in relative isolation from most of the other rafts. They thought that their raft was the only raft, or at least the best raft, given the few other rafts that happened to be in their vicinity. They developed strategies for dealing with these few neighboring rafts. Some said, "Ours is the only true raft"; others said, "There are many ways to get to the other shore, and ours is but one." But none of these strategies was designed with the knowledge that there were so many other passengers trying to cross the river, with so many different ideas concerning how wholeness might be found.

Then, one day, by virtue of developments in economics and advances in communications, all the rafts came into view of one another. It was as if a fog had lifted. The passengers on the individual rafts began to realize that there were more rafts than they had ever imagined, that their raft was but one among many. For a while, some passengers on some rafts felt the need to show that, despite the many rafts that have existed throughout history, their raft was the best for *all* people. "At least," they said, "ours is the best for people now." In their fear and insecurity, they insisted that those riding on other rafts ought to abandon them and jump on theirs, the "right" raft. This caused no small amount of tension on the river.

About the time these new tensions emerged, however, another problem emerged. They were having trouble finding clean water to drink. The river, the source of their water, had become polluted with their own garbage. The Christians could not find any clean water to baptize with, the Hindus clean water to bathe in, the Muslims clean water to wash their hands prior to daily prayer. There was talk that soon there might not be any clean water for any of them to drink. They realized that the drowning ones were already suffering from the situation, that the poor are the first to suffer from environmental degradation.

In truth, the rafters and swimmers and canoeists and drowning ones are themselves dimensions of the river Earth, as are the components of the their rafts. They—we—are earthlings; or, to adjust to this analogy, waterlings. But we are earthlings of a special sort, because, at least since the rise of agriculture, we have had a certain kind of control over the rest of the Earth and its creatures. Thus, we are earthlings who stand over the earth even as we emerge from it; riverlings who cross over the river even as we come from it. The river of Life represents both a reality from which we have emerged, and a reality which we control.

The Need for Dialogue

In light of their awareness of this control, the raft travelers decided to hold a conference—on a neutral raft—concerning actions they might take. "We must each look at our own ways," said one, "and see what ideas and aids we can find to help us stop polluting the river." "And we must learn from one another," said another. "Without abandoning our rafts, we might get some ideas from other rafts."[3]

---

3. Earlier in this chapter I suggested that, for Christians, dialogue can be a internal process in which the other participant is not required or expected to seek to learn from Christianity. However, when it comes to learning from one another about how to be more humble in our relations with the Earth, it seems to me that dialogue should indeed be two-way, with the Earth as reference point. The Earth is the responsibility of everyone, not just of Christians. On this I have learned from Paul Knitter, who proposes that the appropriate purpose of two-way dialogue is to promote justice between humans (Knitter 1987, 178–200). My suggestion is that, in addition, it is to promote sustainable and responsible relations with the Earth.

The raft travelers further realized that many of the canoes were much more sensitive to the water than the rafts; that is, the indigenous traditions of the world have been closer to nature and more attuned to its rhythms than have most of the rafts. They have stressed that wholeness comes through learning to live with nature and learning to be embedded in local places, themselves full of sacred ambiences. This is not to romanticize the canoeists and say that in all ways they are superior to the classical religions. Nonetheless, their Ways are immensely edifying in light of the fact that in our time the water of Life has become so polluted.

This led one traveler to say, "Maybe we've all been spending a little too much time worrying about getting to the other shore. Maybe we ought to become more aware of our immediate situation." Some people added, "Maybe we need to see ourselves and our rafts as parts of a larger pilgrimage, the river's pilgrimage. Maybe we need a common story, one about the river, that can help us respect and care for it."

They agreed to look within their own traditions and find what resources they could to help their people stop throwing garbage and they agreed to send emissaries to other rafts to gather new ideas for garbage-reduction. Their task was not simply to come up with techniques for pollution abatement; it was to come up with ideas that might make them better, more river-sensitive people.

A Christian Approach to Dialogue

Many people in different religions are realizing that the water is polluted, and that in order to cease polluting it, they need not only to dig within their heritages for help but also to learn from other religions. At least this is the situation in which many Christians now find themselves. I am among them.

In the next three chapters I will recommend specific insights we might gain from other religions, which might themselves enable us to be more open to the Earth. In the remainder of this chapter, I try to pave the way for such lessons by offering six reflections that we, as Christians, might keep in mind as we attempt to open ourselves to the truths of other religions. They are:

- That openness to other religions does not come easy, because exclusivism is part of our past.
- That despite our exclusivist legacy, there are resources within the Bible and the Christian past for overcoming exclusivism.
- That even as we engage in dialogue with other religions, we can recognize the uniqueness of Christianity in what it highlights—the Christlike nature of God—without being exclusive in its understanding of who benefits from that love.
- That even as we might affirm the uniqueness of Christianity, we rightly affirm the uniqueness of other religions too. They may well reveal insights unknown to historical Christianity.

- That a primary purpose of learning from other religions ought to be peace-making.
- That peacemaking is itself a cosmic vocation, which amplifies the tendencies toward communion, differentiation, and subjectivity inherent in the creative process from the beginning.

Let us turn, then, to the first reflection.

Reflection #1: Openness Does Not Come Easy

For many of us, openness to other religions does not come easy. We have been shaped by exclusivist habits of thought which suggest that revelation and salvation are to be found only in Christ, and that all other religions are false paths. Deep in our minds we fear that openness to other religions violates loyalty to Christ.

But openness to other religions does not violate loyalty to Christ, at least if by *Christ* we mean the living Christ, the aspect of God that shares in our joys and sufferings, seeks a liberation of the oppressed, and calls all living beings into wholeness. Openness to the Christic dimension of God naturally involves openness to the wisdom of other people whose religions differ from ours, including Jews and Muslims, Buddhists and Hindus, Taoists and Confucianists, Native Peoples and free spirits. It also involves openness to the wisdom of rabbits and redwoods, ferns and fossils, landscapes and lakes, seashores and stars.

Still, the legacy of exclusivism is strong in our consciousness, and it affects both our relations with people of other religions and our relations with the other 99 percent of creation. The heart of exclusivism is a mindset, an attitude, which says that loyalty to Christ or loyalty to God requires a turning away from other sources of wisdom, because they are impure or unholy.

For Christians, the roots reach back into Hebrew scriptures, where we find the assumption that Gentiles, or at least their rites and rituals, are impure. Of course many contemporary Jews, such as my friend, the rabbi from Hot Springs, reject this way of thinking. In general, Judaism has been much more accepting of "otherness" than has Christianity, often by necessity, since Jews themselves have so often been "other" and are therefore sensitive to what it means to be different. Nevertheless, the Jewish heritage includes exclusivist leanings. As Judith Plaskow, a Jewish theologian, puts it: "Thinking of itself as a 'kingdom of priests and a holy nation,' the Jewish people understood its own holiness partly in contradistinction to the beliefs and behavior of surrounding nations. Serving the Lord meant shunning and destroying foreign gods and morality, thus refusing the 'snare' of a different religious system (Ex 23:23–33)." Plaskow sees this tendency to shun foreign gods and morality as consummated in the notion of Jews as chosen people.

Plaskow recognizes that the idea of chosen people has had value at certain points in Jewish history: "The concept of chosenness has been an important solace to Jews in the face of anti-Jewish oppression, and it was often articulated more strongly where suffering was more severe." But she believes the concept problematic and recommends an alternative, from which Christians can well learn.

> What must replace chosenness, then, as the model for Jewish self-understanding is the far less dramatic distinctness. The Jewish community and the sub-communities within it, like all human communities, are distinct and distinctive. ... The term distinctness suggests ... that the relation between these various communities—Jewish to non-Jewish, Jewish to Jewish—should be understood not in terms of hierarchical differentiation but in terms of part and whole (1993, 102–3).

Thus Plaskow recommends what we might call a "distinctivist" understanding of Judaism, with Judaism being a distinct family of people in the world community and thus unique, but nevertheless part of a greater whole, which itself includes other families who are no less distinct.

I believe that a distinctivist approach is relevant to Christians too. It seems preferable to an inclusivist approach, which says that the truths of all other religions are somehow included within, or consummated by, Christian revelation. It is also preferable to a pluralist approach, which says that religions are indeed distinct, but that they have nothing in common, that they are not parts of a greater whole. Analogous to what Plaskow recommends for Jews, we Christians can understand ourselves as a family of people in the global community, with our unique heritages and insights—and also with our limitations—best complemented by other families. We too can see ourselves as parts of a greater whole rather than top rungs of a spiritual ladder.

Most of us realize how difficult it is to shift from a "top of the ladder" mentality to a "parts of a whole" mentality. Part of the problem lies in our own appropriation of a "chosen people" point of view. After all, we speak of ourselves as the new Israel. In ways much more destructive than the ways of Judaism, we have elevated our religion to an idol: proclaiming that other ways are unholy, because not "chosen" by God.

For us, however, the deeper problem lies in habits of thought found in the Christian scriptures, where we are told that Jesus is the "one mediator" between God and humanity (1 Tm 2:5); that there is "no other name" by which persons can be saved (Acts 4:12); that no one comes to God except through Jesus (Jn 14:6); that what took place in Jesus is "once and for all" (Heb 9–12). The implication is that Jesus is the one way to salvation and that other religions have nothing to offer in terms of revelation or salvation.

Many in the history of Christianity have accepted this implication at face value. They have believed, with those at the Council of Florence in the fifteenth century, that non-Christians "cannot become participants in eternal life, but will depart 'into the eternal fire prepared for the devil and his angels' (Mt 25:41), unless before the end of time" they become Christian (Cobb 1982, 9).

This is exclusivism in its most extreme form: the claim that neither revelation nor salvation can be found in any tradition other than Christianity. It is rooted in a fear of otherness, a fear that the Holy Wisdom at the heart of the universe may well love others in their distinctiveness, just as she loves us in ours.

To overcome the fear, it helps if we realize that exclusivist voices such as those of the Council of Florence are not the only voices in our past, and that they are not the only voices in the Bible. This takes us to the second reflection.

Reflection #2: There Are Antidotes to Exclusivism within the Bible and the Christian Heritage

In the Bible there are at least two ideas that can serve as antidotes to exclusivism. One is the simple idea that God is the God of all creation, not just Israel or the Christian church. In the Hebrew scriptures we read that God is the life of the world, in the sense that God energizes and preserves the whole creation; in both the Hebrew scriptures and in the gospel of John we read that God is the light of the world, in the sense that God has inspired many peoples, not just Jews and Christians, to wisdom; and in Johannine literature we read that God is the love of the world, in the sense that wherever there is love of neighbor, there is God. The idea that God is universal—and hence the life, light, and love of the entire world—is in tension with the view that God's saving and revealing love is found *only* in the Christian community. Indeed, it is a corrective to such arrogance. It enables us to say that wherever there is life, wisdom, and love, there is the saving presence of Holy Wisdom.

The second idea that can help us move beyond exclusivism concerns the "end of time." In Paul's writings we find the idea that the end of time has not yet arrived, and that, until it does, we "see through a glass darkly." Such an orientation invites both humility concerning what we now know and openness to what is yet to be revealed.

Much depends, naturally, on how we understand the end of time. I propose that the end of time is the interior life of God, understood as an ongoing symphony of meaning, created out of the notes that are given from the unfolding universe, as they are given. I suggest as well that this end of time may flood back into the Earth in the form of new and hopeful possibilities, themselves unrealized in the historical past.

If we take this idea seriously, it means that we never claim to have the whole truth, only partial truth, and that we hold ourselves ready to receive n⸍ w truth at any and all times. It means that we recognize that we "see through a glass darkly" and that we open ourselves to further revelations. Some of these revelations can come through other religions.

In short, there are at least two strands of thinking in the Bible that can help Christians: 1) the idea that God is the God of all creation, found wherever there is life, wisdom, and love, and 2) the idea that there is always more life, wisdom, and love to be known than we ourselves know. In addition to these biblical themes, of course, there are also ideas in historical Christianity that can help us move beyond exclusivism.[4] These include the idea that God's Logos has been present throughout world history and that in the depths of mystical prayer all religions are the same. John B. Cobb, Jr., points out that, whatever their limitations, all of these points of view are alternatives to exclusivism, at least if exclusivism means that people outside Christianity are "excluded" from salvation. As Cobb sees it, and as I see it, none of the patterns is quite adequate to our time. We need new approaches, many of which are being proposed. In what follows I offer my own approach, which, as noted above, I call distinctivism.

Reflection #3: Christians Can Affirm the Uniqueness of Christianity Yet Reject the Arrogance of Exclusivism

A distinctivist approach tries to affirm what is true about exclusivism, or at least about some of the insights that gave rise to its formulation. At the same time, a distinctivist approach rejects the arrogance of exclusivism. The truth of exclusivism lies not in the claim that the revelation of God in Jesus is final, or in the claim that this revelation excludes other revelations, but rather in the claim that it is unique or distinct. This claim stems from historical honesty. As a movement in history, Christianity *is* distinct, with its own forms of thought and feeling, just like any other living tradition. The task is to learn to affirm the distinctiveness of Christian insight without denying the distinctiveness of other revelations as well.

---

4. John B. Cobb, Jr., identifies five approaches to other religions that have emerged in Christian history (1982, 1-15):

Logos Christology: The Logos is understood to be the creative voice of God present in the history of creation and also in various strands of human history, offering wisdom and guidance. Jesus enfleshed the Logos and revealed it in a distinctive way, but the Logos was also present in human history prior to Jesus as a guiding and enspiriting power.

Universal History: Nineteenth-century philosopher Hegel viewed the whole of human history as aiming toward consummation in God, and he viewed the various religions as positive contributions toward this end. Thus all religions play a constructive role in fulfilling the aims and evolution of God.

Religious Essentialism: There is a religious essence to life of which all partake; its supreme expression is in Christianity. Christians can recognize and affirm the religious essence in all people, and yet also believe that that essence finds its fulfillment in Christianity.

Dogmatic Confessionalism: Modeled by Karl Barth, this view holds not so much that Christianity is a better religion than other religions, as that Christianity is not a religion at all. At least, the revelation at its core is not part of religion, but rather, God's entrance into human history in the form of Christ. Yet Barth also believed that the salvific act, accomplished and revealed in Christ, accrues to all peoples, whatever their religion.

Pluralistic Confessionalism. This is exemplified in H. Richard Neibuhr's *The Meaning of Revelation*. Christians can and should learn to live out of their memories and histories, confessing the truths found therein, but also will find value in listening to others. There can be no objective vantage point by which to adjudicate or evaluate diverse confessions.

As I see it, the distinct or unique truth revealed in Christianity is that the Heart of the universe resembles the compassion of Jesus, magnified by infinity. It is that God is Christlike, plus more. This is not to say that the idea of a loving God is absent from all religions save Christianity. On the contrary, the idea is found in various other traditions, including Judaism, Islam, certain forms of bhakti Hinduism, and Pure Land Buddhism. However, the idea of an all-loving Heart at the center of the cosmos is intensified and given concrete content by the claim that God's love was revealed in Jesus. To say that God's love was revealed in Jesus, and hence that God is Jesus-like, is to particularize the universal and show the finitude of God. It is to say that God has a special concern for the poor and powerless, such that God's own well-being is partly dependent on their well-being; that God is nonviolent, even to the point of suffering violence without responding in turn; that God is vulnerable, even to the point of dying with us on a cross; that God is forgiving, even to the point of forgiving our most heinous of crimes against one another and the Earth; and that God is healing, even to the point of offering possibilities for hope amid the most deadly of despairs. The truth of Christianity is not an abstract idea. It is the living reality of this all-adaptive, all-suffering, all-forgiving, all-embracing God, whose nature was revealed in the life, death, and resurrection of a carpenter from Galilee. Christianity begins and ends with this insight.

This does not mean that only Christians partake of, or benefit from, divine love. With its recognition that God is Jesus-like, Christianity may be unique in the way it points to the love of Holy Wisdom, but Christians are not the unique beneficiaries of this love. The God who is Jesus-like loves all people for their own sakes and, as much as possible, on their own terms. God may not love the Nazi on Nazi terms or the racist on racist terms, but I suggest that God does indeed love the Buddhist as Buddhist, the Jew as Jew, the Hindu as Hindu, the free spirit as free spirit. No less than Christians, they are forgiven their sins; no less than Christians, they are called into wholeness. They do not have to "believe in Jesus" in order to find God or to be peacemakers.

Still, some people might benefit from believing in Jesus, if such belief offers a way of centering their lives around the God of limitless compassion. Christian evangelists ought not assume in advance that all can benefit in this way, but they can be open to the possibility that, for some, belief in Jesus may be precisely the way in which personal transformation into a Christ-centered life can occur. There is room in distinctivism for evangelism and for invitations to conversion.

There is also room for being converted. Holy Wisdom may well call some people to leave Christianity and embrace other paths, either because they have been socialized into forms of Christianity that are destructive and therefore need escape, or because their hearts and personality types are more attuned to other ways than to Christianity. In some ways religions are like medicines as well as like rafts. Their purpose is to promote healing, but the healing at issue depends on the diseases from which people suffer and the people themselves.

Different people need different medicines, relative not only to the diseases they suffer, but also to their constitutions. In the divine economy it is good that there are many religions, not just one.

For Christians open to this divine economy, yet nourished by Christianity itself, the possibility of being converted remains yet open. We may be converted into the truths of other ways, even as we enter more deeply into the truths of the Christian path, and in so doing, we may be nourished more deeply by the living waters of God. If our Christianity has roots and wings, our primary roots may be in the Christian heritage, and yet we may have secondary roots in other traditions. Hopefully our multiple roots make us better Christians, just as the multiple roots of trees make them stronger.

Whether it is helpful or unhelpful for Christians to learn from other religions will depend on the Christians at issue. Often, for Christians new in the Christian path, learning from other religions is not, and need not be, a priority. Their task is to explore the territory of Christianity itself, to sink their primary roots as deeply and yet as creatively as they can, so that they also have wings to fly. Furthermore, for the many Christians who are simply struggling to survive in difficult circumstances, concern for other religions can be an unnecessary distraction. Dialogue is not for everybody.

Reflection #4: Other Religions Are Also Unique

As indicated by the raft analogy, dialogue with others need not presuppose that all religions offer the same wisdom. What Buddhists mean by nirvana may be different from what Christians mean by the kingdom of God, and both may be true.

In order to make this point, I offer another analogy. We might imagine the religions of the world as a grove of trees. There would be a pear tree, an apricot tree, an apple tree, a lemon tree, a fig tree, and so on—and each tree would be a religion.

From a distance these trees look the same. They are "trees," that is, religions. But the more we get to know them, the closer we are to them, we realize that they are different. They bear different fruits.

The "fruits" of a given religion are the forms of life, light, and love that they offer to their participants and others. One fruit of Buddhism, for example, is its realization that all things are deeply interconnected, such that if one is affected all are affected, and that human wholeness lies in awakening to this interconnectedness. A fruit of Islam is its realization that the whole of life—inner as well as outer, social as well as individual—is best oriented toward the ungraspable Mystery at the Heart of the universe, namely Allah. A fruit of many native traditions is their realization that the whole of life is a life community, and that the Earth is a primary mode of experiencing the Divine. A fruit of Christianity is its realization that the Mystery of the universe is revealed through the Earth and also in a man, himself a dimension of the Earth, who dies on a cross to show the compassion and forgiveness of the Mystery itself.

Christians influenced by the image of God as the God of all creation, and also by the Logos Christologies of the early church, can affirm that the various fruits are themselves nourished by the same underground water supply: Holy Wisdom, who bubbles up from underground to offer life-nourishing sustenance. Indeed, they can see the wisdoms of different religions as responses to the Christic dimension of Holy Wisdom, responses to the living Christ. Understood in this way, the living Christ is not reducible to any of the trees, though present in all. She is the Mystery itself, in its compassionate aspect, as it influences all in its guiding presence.

If *salvation* means not the uniquely Christian form of salvation, but rather wholeness as such, then all of these fruits can be dimensions of salvation. Each religion has its strength, its distinctive insights, that help humans to become whole. This means that, as Christians, we can recognize that Christianity itself has unique fruits to share with the rest of the world, even as other religions have fruits to share with us.

But we must also recognize that our fruits are not exclusive or final; they do not exclude other fruits from other trees, that is, other truths from other religions. They are not final because there is always more to God than is ever seen in any of the truths of any of the religions.

Reflection #5: A Central Purpose of Dialogue Is Peacemaking

The fifth point to keep in mind as we learn from other religions is that such learning must bear fruit in action. Recall the proposal of Chapter 3; namely, that Christianity is a Way of living, the social dimension of which is to be midwives to peace in communities both local and global. As we learn from other religions, our aim as individuals cannot simply be to become inwardly whole, important as that is. It must also be to become more competent in the arts of peacemaking.

For example, if we learn from Buddhism of the interconnectedness of all things, then we must use this lesson to enrich—to make more just and sustainable—the connections people have with one another, with animals, and with the Earth. If we learn from Islam the importance of daily prayer five times a day, then our daily prayers must be for the poor and powerless, for animals, and for the Earth, and they must empower us to be more sensitive to their needs. If we learn from Hinduism the importance of recognizing many names for the Divine, then we must use this knowledge to help us appreciate those cultural minorities whose "names" for the Divine, and for themselves, are so often neglected by dominant classes. We are responsible to Holy Wisdom, and to the Earth itself, not to use our knowledge from other religions for purely self-centered reasons. Even as we gain from others in our own journeys toward wholeness, we best serve others in their journeys as well.

Interreligious dialogue is validated by the degree to which it results in such service.

Reflection #6: Peacemaking Is a Cosmic Vocation

The final reflection involves the place of interreligious dialogue in the Christian story and in the cosmic story. One thesis of this book is that the Christian story is a cosmic story. It is the story of a God who beckoned the universe into existence some fifteen billion years ago and who beckons it still today. We learn about this God from Jesus and from other religious guides, but we also learn about God from the starry heavens above and from the soil beneath our feet. We realize that Jesus and others are themselves dimensions of the Earth, even as they extend its evolution in various ways by offering us possibilities for wholeness.

This cosmic story, interpreted through Christian eyes, contains three tendencies that pertain to dialogue.

First, there is the tendency toward communion, as when protons and electrons gather together to form atoms, or when atoms bond together to form molecules, or when molecules bond together to form living cells, or when living cells bond together to form animal bodies, or when animal bodies bond together to form herds, and so forth. Jesus himself expressed and amplified this tendency by calling people to enter into a new form of communion with one another, one characterized by love and forgiveness rather than tribal allegiance. The early church was an experiment in communion and thus an experiment in the history of creation.

Second, there is the tendency toward differentiation, as when protons and electrons are differentiated in the history of creation, or when different kinds of atoms emerge, or when different kinds of molecules appear, or when different kinds of cells emerge, or when different kinds of animals and people emerge. The early church was an experiment in differentiation as well as communion. Its aim was to bring together different kinds of people in ways that celebrated rather than masked their differences. The people were said to be different parts of the same body, each playing a distinctive role.

Third, there is the tendency toward ever-richer forms of interiority or subjective aliveness. Such aliveness is exemplified with the emergence of protons and electrons, which have their own forms of subjectivity; and with living cells, which have still greater subjectivity than their elements; and then with different forms of animal and plant bodies, which made possible still richer forms of interiority or awareness, including conscious interiority, itself an evolutionary development from preconscious forms of interiority. The early church was an experiment in a rich form of subjectivity; namely, that of love and forgiveness, of that wholeness which comes from ego-relinquishment rather than ego-enslavement.

In our way and our time, dialogue with other religions can be understood as an extension of these three principles and thus as an extension of tendencies within the early church. As we learn from people of other faiths, we extend and amplify the tendency toward communion by learning to commune with Buddhists and Hindus, Muslims and Jews, Native Peoples and free spirits. Our communion takes the form of entering into their points of view as best we can, recognizing the unique gifts they offer to the world and to us. The bonds of jealousy and resentment are broken, at least from our end, so that we can accept them as our teachers.

Still, communion is not enough. Some forms of communion are suffocating or imperialistic, as when we "commune" with others at the expense of recognizing their integrity, their otherness. The communion relevant to dialogue is one that respects differences even as it tries to overcome divisions. When we learn from the Jew, for example, we simultaneously realize that we will never be, and need not be, Jewish in the way he or she is Jewish; to some extent we will always be outsiders to that Way. We realize that we are parts of a greater whole, rightly complemented by other parts that are different from us. We honor the spirit of differentiation, without letting it divide us into "chosen" and "unchosen."

In honoring both the spirit of differentiation and that of communion, we enter into the third great theme in the cosmic story, namely subjectivity. The wholeness we seek occurs when we are able to shift the center of gravity of our own personalities to something beyond ourselves, to shift from "the ego" to something greater or deeper than ourselves. That something may lie within us, as the Self of our selves, or beyond us, as the God of the universe, or both. In any event, it is the Life of the universe, understood as a subjectivity deeper than all subjectivities.

When we enter into dialogue with people of other religions, learning from them in ways that enrich our own subjectivity and that draw us into deeper forms of wholeness, we add to the Subjectivity of the universe itself. We contribute to the living Christ, to Holy Wisdom, to God. Hopefully we contribute to others, as well, by honoring them, by recognizing their wisdom, by humbling ourselves such that they become our teachers. Inasmuch as they are so honored, we contribute still further to the Life of the Divine. For that Life is inseparable from their lives and from our lives. It is the adventure of the universe as One.

Chapter 8

Communion with Trees and Sea Pirates

Selected Lessons from Judaism and Buddhism
for Living in Community

According to John Cobb, the dominant religion of most industrial societies is not Christianity or Islam or even secular humanism. Rather, it is "Economism" (1991b). The god of this religion is endless economic growth; its priests are economists; its evangelists are advertisers; its laity are consumers; and its church is the mall. In Economism, virtue is called competition and vice is called inefficiency. Salvation comes through shopping alone.

To say that Economism is a religion is to say that it is the central organizing principle of industrial societies. Even churches now serve this religion. More than a few churches measure their well-being by the size of their buildings, budgets, and numerical growth of their congregations. The assumptions that growth is good and bigger is better are part of the very fabric of much modern life.

Economism is the religion of consumer culture. Today many of us are tempted by the two undesirable alternatives discussed earlier: rootless consumerism, which tells us that true happiness comes through prestige, wealth, power, and physical attractiveness; and wingless fundamentalism, which tells us that happiness comes through blind obedience to religious authority and that we—and we alone—have truth worthy of salvation. Sometimes the two go together. More than a few Christians are blindly obedient to the Bible understood as an inerrant authority, and yet unwittingly committed to salvation through shopping. It is possible to have inflexible roots *and* superficial wings, all at once.

In the previous chapter my emphasis was on avoiding fundamentalism, particularly as it is associated with exclusivism. I suggested that Christians can recognize the uniqueness of Christianity even as we recognize the uniqueness of all other religions; and that, in so doing, we learn to see the Wisdom of God in the unique wisdom of other religions. I recommended distinctivism over exclusivism.

150

In this chapter my focus is on avoiding consumerism and its attendant religion, Economism. My argument is that Judaism in one way, and Buddhism in another, offer us insights that can help us live in community with people, animals, and the Earth, cognizant that we and they are members of a single family, a life community.

The chapter is divided into three sections. The first offers further observations about Economism and its effects on self-understanding and community life. I augment proposals made earlier about the importance of community, and, in the process, try to advance this book's discussions of sin and grace. The second section shows how, with help from Judaism, we might respect the "otherness" of fellow members of the life community, with trees as a case in point. The third section shows how, with the help of Buddhism, we might recognize that others—even those we find morally reprehensible, such as sea pirates who rape innocent girls—are parts of our true selves.

Sin, Grace, and Community

Despite its power, Economism is a relatively new religion. In earlier societies the central organizing principle was not endless economic growth, but rather spiritual well-being or ethnic survival or harmony with nature or military conquest. Economism entered the world with the industrial revolution, as a modification of millennial dreams from the Bible (Thomas Berry 1988, 114–15). Just as the Bible promised a "new heaven and new earth" made possible by God, so Economism promises a "new heaven and new earth" made possible by free-market economies and international trade. Economism is a religion—a false god—whose roots lie in the future-driven spirituality of Western religion itself.

In Chapter 3 I drew from the work of Herman Daly and John Cobb to suggest that, whatever the benefits of Economism in the past, its costs now outweigh its benefits. Under the sway of the god of growth, it seems, nations battle each other for scarce resources, teenagers kill each other for tennis shoes, local communities are destroyed through the movement of capital, animals are reduced to commodities on the stock exchange, and the Earth itself becomes a stockpile for toxic wastes. The world cannot long endure an unfettered devotion to growth.

The need, however, is not for an end to economics or economists. Rather, it is for economic theories, policies, and institutions that take as their aim the promotion of human community in an ecologically responsible context—an economics for community rather than an economics for growth.

Nevertheless, shifts in economic policy alone will not suffice. Even as we urge changes in public policy, we need also urge changes at local levels, beginning with ourselves. Prompted by hopes for a greener peace, Christians and others need to embark on experiments in community development. We need to identify the pockets of community that exist in our world, and then work with them and in them to create local communities that exemplify the values identified in Chapter 3: respect for diversity, grass-roots democracy, political decentralization, economic self-reliance, nonviolence, post-patriarchal values, personal and social responsibility, global responsibility, future focus, and ecological wisdom.[1]

For some of us, the relevant communities will be the towns and villages in which we live, with their lovable and unlovable features. The idea that we should always move to "desirable" places, rather than sinking roots in a local place, is itself a feature of Economism. Economism tells us always to move on to desirable pastures, with "desirability" defined as "that which satisfies the ego." A more Christian option is to develop a sense of place for where we already are, and then to learn to love what we find there. It is to celebrate the ordinary yet lovable dimensions of our immediate surroundings: the plants and animals, the children and old people, the neighborhood and landscapes, the memories and the hopes of local culture. And it is to bemoan but help heal rather than abandon the unlovable dimensions: the violence of our city streets, the sadness of dying towns, the tragedy of broken lives, the horror of abused children. Healthy communities do not emerge out of nothing. They are built out of previously planted seeds, some good and some bad, to which we add love, hope, and courage.

If such communities are to survive, however, still more is needed. Transformations of inner character and spirituality are required. We must become the kinds of people, with the kinds of inner attitudes, that allow ecocommunities— "green communities" if you will—to flourish. The need today is not only for sustainable economics and sustainable communities, it is also for sustainable people.

And this is a problem. Most of us who live under the influence of Economism are not the kinds of people with the kinds of attitudes that can help sustain green communities. Influenced by images of upward mobility, we do not know how to live in community. We do not live in fidelity to the local regions in which we live; we are not responsible to the people and animals of our bioregion; we are not wedded to the land or to the human community around us. We are an individualistic and alienated people.

Sin and Grace

Conservative Christians tell us that part of our problem is sin. And, of course, they are right. Here *sin* means "missing the mark" of responding to the lure of Holy Wisdom, of the inner Christ, of the Sacred Whole, of God. This lure is toward abundant living in community with others. It is toward concrete acts of love for the people and animals of our local bioregions; toward the pursuit of wisdom for its own sake and for the planet's sake; toward

---

1. These are the values of the Green Party of the United States, as identified by Spretnak (1991, 262).

a realization of our own deepest potentials for creativity and compassion. We sin when we fail to perform such acts, seek such wisdom, and realize our potential.

Most of us sin all the time. Paul knew the experience well: "That which we want to do, we do not, and that which we do not want to do, we do" (Rom 7:14–25, paraphrase). We hear the call to love, itself part of our own deepest desire, and yet we fail to respond. We live, not from the inner Christ, but rather from the "I" of our own egos.

We are tempted to want to solve the problem by "doing something." There is truth in this solution, insofar as an exercise of the will can be effective in altering unhealthy forms of behavior. If our sin is gluttony, for example, it can help to exercise will-power and not pick up the fork; if our sin is sloth, it helps to get off our rear ends and do something for somebody.

Still, there is deception in "doing something" if it emanates from the ego. The ultimate solution to sin is not a further exercise of the ego-based will, but rather a surrender to the healing presence of God within us and outside us. When our acts of the will emerge from the living waters of Spirit, they are healthy; when they are in service to our egos, they are not.[2] In Christianity, part of the task of life is to learn to discern the promptings of grace in our lives, distinguishing them from the promptings of our egos and those of society. Discernment of this sort is by all means an art not a science, best facilitated by prayer.[3]

Even as sin is part of the problem behind Economism and prayer part of the solution, so Economism itself is part of the problem. As a mindset or way of thinking, Economism encourages rather than discourages ego-based living. It teaches us that "looking out for number one" is a virtue rather than a vice, because the market depends on our selfishness.

Let us be clear. The problem is not having an ego, defined here as "a sense of individual selfhood." All of us need such a sense, and without it we are lost. If we have children, we rightly rear them to have a healthy sense of self, to have positive self-regard. After all, they, like we, are made in God's image.

Rather, the problem is being *centered* in this sense of selfhood, as if the ego were the center of the universe. In fact, the individual ego is but one of many centers. Other people are also centers, as are squirrels, ferns, centipedes, and stars. All are embraced by a still deeper Center, who is in, but not exhausted by, all centers.

It is common to think of ego-centeredness as primarily aggressive or self-elevating. In truth, it can take the very opposite form. As feminist theologian Sue Dunfee points out, some of us commit the "sin" of ego-based existence, not by asserting ourselves over others, but by "hiding" from our own capaci-

---

2. A helpful distinction is drawn by Gerald May between willfulness, which is ego-based, and willingness, which is surrender to grace (1982, 6; 1988).

3. The theme of discernment is particularly pronounced in the Ignatian tradition of spiritual direction. For a good book on discernment in the Ignatian tradition, see Green 1987. For a discussion of prayer as it fits into a religious life with roots and wings, see Conclusion below.

ties for self-assertion and empowerment under socially-defined roles (1982). In short, ego-centeredness can take the form of ego-deflation as well as ego-inflation.

In ego-inflation we think too highly of ourselves, allowing our egos to become a center, a frame of reference, around which all things are understood and evaluated. Trapped in such inflation, we fail to realize that we are but one of many, all of whom are of equal value in the eyes of Holy Wisdom. Thus we cannot join the communion which is life itself.

In ego-deflation, we think too little of ourselves; we see ourselves as not one among many, but one *below* many. When we fall into this trap, we easily become preoccupied with our unworthiness at the expense of being honest about our gifts and open to possibilities for utilizing them to the service of others. We are self-preoccupied, and our lowly status becomes a frame of reference, a center, in terms of which we evaluate all other things, which seem superior to us. We forget the image of God within ourselves.

The preferable option is to recognize ourselves as one among many, neither above nor below others. We are valuable in our own right, made in the very image of God, and yet we are not the center of the universe. When we enter into this strong yet honest mode of existence, we have what Buddhist writer Rita Gross calls "a healthy functioning sense of self": a sense of self that allows for calmness, equanimity, and energy, but that is not fixated upon preoccupations of being "above" or "below" others (1993, 162). From a Christian perspective, this sense of self emerges as we awaken to grace, recognizing ourselves as beloved persons in community with the entire creation and in community with God.

Economism actively *discourages* a healthy sense of self. It is an assault on grace. It tells us constantly to compare ourselves to others, deeming ourselves either "on top" because we have more money or are more attractive, or "underneath" because we have less money or are less attractive. Economism follows a patriarchal way of thinking; when faced with diversity, it seeks to establish a hierarchy.[4] As an alternative to this tendency to rank, we need a healthy sense of self that is neither "above" nor "below" others, such that we

---

4. For some, being "underneath" may sound Christian. After all, Christianity encourages humility. But the underneath-ness of Economism is anything but humble. It is the flip side of a kind of arrogance that demands perfection through performance. As evangelical theologian David Seamands explains, consumer society teaches us that we must "perform" our way into heaven, either by working hard so that we can buy material goods, or by being as beautiful as the models, or by being as prestigious as the actors and actresses we admire. This performance-based orientation of consumer society is the very opposite of grace-filled life, which involves a healthy sense of our significance to God and to other people. By contrast, the performance-based life induces a sense of self-belittlement, which belies an inner addiction to a personal perfection that is never quite realizable. The assumption is that being the perfectly efficient businessman or the perfectly beautiful coed or the perfectly loving saint will merit God's grace. "Let's face it," says Seamands, "performance-oriented Christians are hard to live with. They are hard on themselves, hard on their spouses, and hard on their kids" (1989, 19). And so, we might add, hard on the Earth.

are capable of living in community with the people, animals, and plants around us. In what follows, I show how selected lessons from Judaism and Buddhism might enrich our capacities to live in community.

Communion with Trees

In approaching other beings as centers, we recognize that they have value or importance that is not reducible to their usefulness to us. Economism often blocks this recognition. Under its sway, we too often reduce things to their "worth" on the stock exchange. Thus trees are reduced to timber, people to consumers, animals to commodities, and land to real estate. Of course, there is nothing wrong with some degree of objectification; we cannot avoid using things. The problem comes when we fail to recognize that they are always *more* than their usefulness.

In our time, one of the most perceptive commentators on the problem of objectification is Martin Buber, a Hasidic Jew. Perhaps he understands objectification so well because his people so often have been objectified. Jews know what it is like to be a minority in the world. They know what it is like to be "other."

In *I and Thou* Buber draws upon the depths of Jewish personalism to distinguish two ways of being related to others. In the first place, says Buber, we can be related to others as "its," in which case we approach others as objects of use and manipulation. In the second place, we can be related to them as "thous," in which case we approach them as subjects with value in their own right. Only in the later instance, says Buber, are we truly connected with others.

Most of us know the reality of I-It relations. We have been objectified into an "it" by others, and we have objectified others into "its." Such objectification is the root cause of much racism, sexism, classism, and homophobia. It is also a root cause of broken friendships. When we reduce other people to stereotypes or to instruments for our well-being, we treat them as "its." They have become objects in our minds, rather than subjects in their own right.

A Christianity with roots and wings, like any other healthy spiritual path, will try to minimize such objectification. In solidarity with the mystery of human personhood, it will recognize that people cannot be reduced to our stereotypes of them, because all are more, infinitely more, than can ever be comprehended by our minds. In their subjectivity and mystery, they are souls. Part of dwelling in solidarity with God is learning to see others as God sees them, as souls to be appreciated not owned.

Animals too are souls. In ways different from humans, but not necessarily less valuable, animals are subjects of their lives and not simply objects in our minds. They have aims and feelings of their own. But where does "thou-ness" stop? Must a creature have eyes in order to be a thou? Or does thou-ness extend to the whole of life? Here Buber is instructive.

Buber thinks thou-ness extends at least to members of the plant community. To be sure, Buber's focus is on the thou-ness of fellow humans. He stands in the humanistic ethos of Abrahamic faiths, where human-human interactions take first place in the scheme of values; human relations with animals and the Earth take second place. Still, for Buber, second place is not no place. Just as, for many a psalmist, nonhuman creatures are regarded as alive with some capacity to praise and be related to God, so in Buber nonhuman nature is so regarded. Not only does he tell his reader that his own cat is a thou, he tells his reader that a *tree* is a thou. A tree has no eyes, at least of the sort that we have. But from Buber's point of view, it does indeed have thou-ness.

This recognition of the aliveness of cats and plants is in keeping with the general perspective of the Hebrew scriptures. The idea that animals and plants are mere machines, understandable according to the laws of chemistry, is a modern one. Biblical points of view recognize the aliveness of other living beings and also the aliveness of the rivers and mountains. As H. Wheeler Robinson explains in his study of nature in Hebrew scriptures: "Earth itself is alive. . . . The Earth has its nature which makes itself felt and demands respect." Indeed, "nature is alive through and through, and therefore the more capable of sympathy with [humanity], and of response to the rule of its Creator and Upholder" (1946, 13). In celebrating the thou-ness of cats and trees, Buber is being true to his biblical heritage.

Buber begins his section on trees with a description of various I-It approaches. In approaching a tree with an eye to its objective properties, he says:

> I can accept it as a picture: a rigid pillar in a flood of light, or splashes of green traversed by the gentleness of the blue silver ground.
>
> I can feel it as a movement: the flowing veins around the sturdy, striving core, the sucking of the roots, the breathing of the leaves, the infinite commerce with earth and air—and growing itself in its darkness.
>
> I can assign it to a species and observe it as an instance, with an eye to its construction and its way of life.
>
> I can overcome its uniqueness and form so rigorously that I recognize it only as an expression of [laws of nature].
>
> I can dissolve it into a number, into a pure relations with numbers, and eternalize it (1958, 57).

In short, Buber notes that he, and by implication we, can approach trees aesthetically, biologically, and mathematically. These are perhaps the dominant ways of approaching trees in Western scientific culture. In each case trees are objectified. They are objects of contemplation, not subjects with whom we are related.

Buber then proceeds to say that, "if will and grace are joined," we can also sense a tree as a thou. When we see a tree as a thou, it does not cease to be an

object, but it becomes an object that is also a subject. Our objective knowledge of the tree then contributes to our understanding of the tree's thou-ness:

> But it can also happen, if will and grace are joined, that as I contemplate
> the tree I am drawn into a relation and the tree ceases to be an It.
>
> This does not require me to forego any of the modes of contempla-
> tion. There is nothing that I must not see in order to see, and there is no
> knowledge that I must forget.
>
> Whatever belongs to the tree is included: its form and its mechanics,
> its colors and its chemistry, its conversation with the elements and its
> conversation with the stars—all this in its entirety (1958, 58–59).

In indicating the thou-ness of a tree, Buber wants to avoid both human projection and supernaturalism. His claim is not that a given tree has consciousness
"similar to our own," and it is not that the tree is really a "spirit" inhabiting a
tree. Rather his claim is that the tree is an "other," with integrity and presence
of its own, which is unlike human presence but nevertheless real and worthy
of our respect. The tree "is no impression, no play of my imagination, no
aspect of mood; it confronts me bodily and has to deal with me as I must deal
with it—only differently" (1958, 57–59).

The Significance of Buber's Insight into Trees
for Dwelling in Community

Buber's insight into trees has implications for our relations with people as
well. In dealing with people, we want to avoid projection and supernaturalism. We want to recognize that they are not gods; that they are fellow members
of the human family, with wants and needs much like our own; and yet also
that they may well be different from us in important ways. We want to honor
them in their differences as well as their similarities.

At least two things often block us from recognizing people in their differences. In the first place, we often assume that our own experience of being a
human is revelatory of all experiences of being human. If we are white-male-
Americans, for example, we assume that what we experience is what everybody
experiences. We forget that our experiences have been shaped by the privi-
leges and limitations of being white and being male in American society. The
experiences of people who are not white, or not male, or not American may
be very different from our own.

In the second place, we are blocked from recognizing people in their differences by feeling their presence through the lens of subjective, ego-based
needs. Consider people who go through life with a deep need to be needed. If
we are among these people, we tend to perceive others as candidates for our
service. We see them as needing us. Sometimes this is good. We help people
who do indeed need us. But sometimes it is bad. We project onto others a

neediness that is not actually part of their identity. Our need to be needed prevents us from seeing them as they are: independent subjects with unique value of their own.

Or consider people who go through life with a deep need to be approved. If we are among these people, we tend to perceive others as candidates for flattery. We are in a perpetual quest for applause, and we see others as people who, if we are wise or clever or efficient enough, will like and praise us. Sometimes, of course, this too is good. All of us want to be liked and praised at times. We feel fully alive when we are recognized and appreciated by others. Still, if we are obsessive in our need to be liked and praised, we cannot see others in their integrity. If they do not like or praise us, we have a hard time seeing them as they are: kindred subjects with value in their own right.

In short, our capacities to approach others as thous are often clouded by unwarranted assumptions that all humans are like us, or by unwarranted desires to being needed or liked. We may feel bonded with them, but we do not appreciate them in their otherness.

The wisdom of Buber, as illustrated in his treatment of trees, lies in his recognition that bondedness *and* a sense of otherness are required for authentic I-Thou relations. It is not enough to feel "at one" with others. We must also feel "at two" with them.

Elie Wiesel

Elie Wiesel, survivor of the concentration camps and winner of the Nobel Peace Prize, underscores this point, showing its connection to Judaism. In general, says Wiesel, "Judaism insists on every person's right to be different," because Jews themselves know what it is like to be strangers.

Having been a stranger in Pharaoh's Egypt, one is therefore compelled to respect all strangers for what they are. One must not seek to change their ways or views: One must not try to make them resemble oneself. Very human being reflects the image of God, who has no image: mine is neither purer nor holier than yours. Truth is one, but the paths leading to it are many.

In Judaism "it is the freedom of the stranger—his right to self-definition—that must be respected. It is because the 'Other' is other, because he or she is not I, that I am to consider him or her both sovereign and instrument used by God to act upon history and justify his faith in His creation" (1993, 54–55).

Wiesel's language concerning God may seem quite dissimilar to the language of this book. He speaks of God as acting *upon* history, whereas this book speaks of God as acting *within* history; he speaks of God as using people as instruments, whereas this book speaks of God as calling people to service.

One can sense that in Wiesel, as in much Judaism, God is "Other" to creation in a way not characteristic of Holy Wisdom as described in this work.

Whatever the differences, it is also the case that the image of God offered in this book has deep resemblances to some images that come from Judaism. The God of panentheism, like the God of the Bible, loves the whole of creation and calls humans to special responsibilities within creation. More important, God calls humans to respect one another in their differences, in their respective self-definitions, and, I might add, to respect other forms of life in their differences. Perhaps Jews, more than any, can help Christians remember that a failure to respect strangers is a failure to respect God.

The lesson is particularly important for Christians who have been tempted over many generations either to resent Judaism for its adherence to customs and traditions that seem "odd" by Christian standards, or to reduce Judaism to a mere antecedent to Christianity, a Christianity without Jesus. The truth is much richer. Judaism has integrity of its own, different from Christianity, with insights Christianity lacks, even as Christianity has insights Judaism may lack. One insight Christianity can well learn from Judaism is that people who are different from us are loved by God on their own terms and for their own sake. Wiesel reminds us to respect the freedom of other *people* to be different from us, to have their own self-definitions. Buber reminds us to do the same with *trees*.

Mindfulness of Trees

It is one thing to know that we ought not impose our projections and stereotypes on others, and quite another not to do it. We need specific practices to help us become less projective. Here, forms of Buddhist meditation can be helpful, particularly those that emphasize calming the mind so as to be "restful" in the sheer presence of others. In order not to limit ourselves to human concerns alone, let us consider the matter through the theme of trees.

One of the most interesting interpreters of Martin Buber's insights concerning trees is Buddhist writer Stephanie Kaza (1985). Kaza is a practicing Zen Buddhist, a social activist, and a conservation biologist by training. She is a board member of the Buddhist Fellowship for Peace, a community of North American Buddhists active in promoting social justice and ecological sustainability throughout the world.

Kaza grew up in Oregon and spent much of her early life in central California, wandering in the forests. Years ago, while reading Buber, it occurred to her that trees might in their own way be thous, even as animals and people are thous. She knew that thou-ness of trees was not a principle of science, but she also felt that people could know such thou-ness through other means, such as touch and sight and smell and what she called "the attentive heart." She began writing about trees and about human-tree relations as a spiritual experiment while at Starr King School of Ministry in Berkeley, California.

Years later, the experiment turned into a book that is now a classic in human-tree relations and, by implication, human-Earth relations. It is called *The Attentive Heart: Conversations with Trees* (1993b).

True to her roots in Zen Buddhism, Kaza does not approach real trees as symbols. She recognizes that trees have represented many things throughout human history—The Tree of Life, the Axis of the Earth, the home of spirits. However, her own Zen approach does not focus on trees as symbols, but rather on trees as trees:

> I am more interested in one-to-one dynamic relationship with trees than in cultural construction of trees or anthropomorphic projections. I am certain that I lapse into psychological projection in places, but my primary motivation is the desire for genuine contact at a core level. I have attempted to watch for the habits of language and mind that block the flow of communication between person and tree. These include stereotyping, objectifying, idealizing, and oversimplifying—all of which make a tree more or less than what it actually is.

Her aim, she says, is to ask: "What does it actually mean to be in relation with a tree" (1993b, 9–10).

To enter into such a relationship, says Kaza, it is important to have an attentive heart. An attentive heart is a quiet and focused heart, one that is able to see and feel trees—and by implication all other beings—on their own terms and for their own sakes. Such "seeing" is itself one form of "hearing into speech," which I described in Chapter 2. It is a seeing that is other-centered in its orientation, so much so that a sense of "I" sometimes disappears.

Meditation

In a Zen context, such ego-less seeing best arises through the practice of meditation. We learn to see by first learning to feel the sensations of our own body, such as breathing, ego-lessly. In *zazen* the aim is not to contemplate philosophical truths or even to attend to the splendor of internal visions. Rather, it is to attend, carefully and directly, to the movements of our own breathing, to be present to the breathing until, in a sustained way, there is just the breathing.

At first such attention is quite difficult. If, as beginners in the art of meditation, we try to focus on breathing by counting breaths, we quickly discover that we cannot do so. We may attend to the first breath, but soon our mind strays, and we begin to think about other things. For beginners, it is even impossible to count ten breaths without losing count somewhere along the way, so rambunctious is the "monkey mind" of fleeting thoughts and fantasies.

Gradually, however, we learn to stay with the breathing, to follow the inhalations and exhalations as if each were unique, existing only for the moment.

And of course this is true. No breath lasts forever, and each one is unique. Zen attention is attention to the unique and unrepeatable. It is attention to life.

Kaza shows how such attention can be directed not only to breathing, but also to trees and other living beings. When our consciousness becomes directed in this way, our heart is transformed. We become an "attentive heart," which learns to see trees and other living beings on their own terms and for their own sakes. We become present to them, and they become present to us. Our needs to be needed, or to be right, or to be in control, fall away. There is just the object.

Perhaps an illustration is in order. Consider Kaza's feeling for an alder, which is a hardwood, deciduous tree found on the Pacific coast:

> I have barely entered the forest when I see the alders across the pond. The invitation to stop fills my attention; I am riveted by their graceful beauty and still reflection. Alders, I see you from this open spot by the tall Douglas fir. You are quiet this morning. The light touch of the breeze tickles the pond's surface, rippling the reflection of your white trunks and open branches. Early April is such a tender time for you—all your fresh leaves just out, catching their first taste of sunlight. . . . Your gray-white dappled trunks are tall and smooth, as if you shot up fast before any injurious forces could do you harm. Your trunks are barely scarred except for the knots from past years' branches. I extend a shy hand, meeting your body, firm and cool against my skin (1993b, 26).

Kaza makes clear that the alders' mind and voice is different from her own. She realizes that it does not feel her presence the way she feels its presence. Yet she feels the presence of the alder as the presence of a thou, not an it. She knows that in touching the alder she is touching another being with a life of its own.

Stereotypes, Dualisms, and Projections

Kaza points out that Buddhist mindfulness practices can help us better relate not only to alders but also to other people, to animals, and to land. In an essay on Buddhism and ecology she points out that three prevalent patterns often block our ability to commune: stereotyping, dualistic thinking, and projection (1993a). All three are obstacles to the kinds of communing and community we need in our time.

With stereotyping, says Kaza, people "tend to lump the few characteristics they know of an organism or plant community into a generic representative that does not accurately reflect reality." They create "generic whales" that are playful, altruistic, intelligent, large, and gentle—"each characteristic fitting one species or another, but not existing anywhere in this combination in a real whale." Deserts "are viewed as wastelands, and all forests are seen as cool, dark places, despite the many differences in topography, climate, plant and animal inhabitants, and human history" (1993a, 55). Mindfulness helps people move beyond such stereotyping and pay attention to the particular on its own terms.

Dualistic thinking, says Kaza, leads people to view the world in terms of oppositions of one sort or another: reason versus feeling, soul versus matter, right versus wrong, light versus dark, human versus Earth. For Kaza, the basic opposition is "self" over "other." "Self-other opposition forms the mental basis for anthropocentric relationships with plants and animals, as well as prejudice and racism. . . . The mind separates and distances one side of the polarity from the other, rather than seeing the opposites as complementary and inclusive, each arising in the context of the other." This "self-other opposition" is not true to reality. In truth, our selves are complementary to the world around us, arising in the context of that world and including that world, even as the world is more than us. Mindfulness can help us move beyond oppositional thinking to relational perceiving. It can help us be mindful of the myriad ways in which, to quote the Zen Master Dogen, the world "authenticates" our very existence (Kasulis 1980, 89).

With projection, says Kaza, "the mind projects internalized ideas onto favored and unfavored elements of the environment." In relation to the natural world, for example, "cute" and "nice" animals, such as deer, rabbits, and songbirds, "elicit more sympathetic responses" than "mean" animals, such as coyotes, spiders, and bats. Likewise "good" land is "land that can be farmed or developed"; "bad" land is "what is too steep, dry, or impenetrable" (1993a, 56). Kaza shows how mindfulness can free our minds from internalized ideas and judgments, so that we can see animals and land and people in their unique integrity.

Of course, we must judge things. One way or another, we will judge some land as better for farming than other land, and we will judge some people as more to our liking than others. Certainly we will judge some actions as preferable to others. The value of Buddhist mindfulness is not that it excuses us from ethical discrimination and naming. Rather, it is that it allows us to realize amid our judgments that other living beings are not *reducible* to our thoughts and judgment. There is always something more to a tree, an animal, or a person, than is captured in our ideas about them. Buddhist mindfulness helps us to attend to this otherness. It helps us to see that trees are more than oxygen makers and, as we shall see shortly, that sea pirates are more than rapists.

Communion with Sea Pirates

So far I have emphasized that communion involves attention to otherness. I turn now to how this respect for otherness is best complemented by a recognition of identity, even with those we find morally reprehensible. We need to say to those we are tempted to hate, "I am you, too."

It may seem contradictory to say "I am you, but you are not me." Indeed, if we imagine the "I" as a self-enclosed atom and the "you" as another self-enclosed atom, it is indeed ridiculous. "You are not me" makes sense; "I am you" does not.

Still, the very idea that "I am you" can be understood in various ways. In what follows I will offer a Zen way of understanding it, which might be called "identity-in-difference" as opposed to "fusion." Fusion implies that as two people become one their two-ness is lost. From the vantage point of this work, nothing is fused in this way. God is not fused with the world, nor are creatures fused with one another. By contrast, "identity-in-difference" means that, at least from the point of the one who feels the identity, the "other" is felt as "part of who and what I am," even as he or she is also "more than who and what I am." Many of us feel identity-in-difference in relation to our family members and loved ones. I suggest that Buddhism can help us feel it in relation to the rest of the world.

Thich Nhat Hanh

In Thich Nhat Hanh's poem "Please Call Me by My True Names," which was quoted in the Introduction, Hanh describes his many identities, his many true names, and then writes:

> I am the twelve-year-old-girl, refugee on a
> > small boat
> who throws herself into the ocean after being
> > raped by a sea pirate
> and I am the pirate, my heart not yet capable
> > of seeing and loving.

What can he mean when he says "I am the pirate"? I will begin by trying to describe what it means to say "I am you" to anything at all. Then I will turn to the particular implications of saying "I am you" to sea pirates.

"I Am You and You Are Me"[5]

Many years ago, when I was a graduate student, I had the privilege of serving as an English teacher for a young Zen monk coming to the United States from Japan. At the time I had been reading much about Buddhism, and I had heard of the well-known *satori* or enlightenment experience in which, so I understood, Zen Buddhists awaken to the true nature of reality. I knew that I had never had such an experience, and I was sure that most Christians I knew had not either. So, with fear and trepidation, I went to meet the monk.

---

5. I realize that, grammatically, my newfound student should have said "you are I." But this was our first meeting, and I was not a very good English teacher anyway.

As we sat down to have our first visit, I was extremely nervous. I tried to make conversation, but I failed, because I really wanted to know what he "knew." So, instead of being polite, I simply blurted out the question, after having known him for about five minutes. "Tell me," I asked, "what do you know that I don't?"

Without any hesitation he answered: "I know that I am you. And you are me, too. But you don't know that." As he looked me in the eye, I knew that he was telling me the truth. Had I been a sea pirate, he would have said the same thing. Twenty years later my friend the Zen monk is now a Zen Master: Roshi Keido Fukushima from Kyoto, Japan. He is now my Zen teacher, and I have been thinking about what he said at our first meeting for many years now.

Zen and the Self

Part of what he was saying to me, and part of what Thich Nhat Hanh is saying, is quite simple. The objects of our awareness—trees or sea pirates—are part of our awareness, and this awareness is constitutive of our very existence.

This contravenes our customary habits of thought. Often we think of our self as one thing, and our awareness as another. We say "I am aware of the tree," and we think that the "I" is one reality and the awareness of the tree another. We presume further that the "I" is a real entity that stays the same amid different experiences. We say "I was looking at the tree and then I noticed that a man was standing behind it." We assume that the "I" who looked at the tree and the "I" who noticed the man are one and the same.

The Zen outlook suggests the contrary. It suggests that the "I" is actually a mental construct, and that our true selves are not different from the flow of experience, but rather the flow itself, as lived from the inside, moment to moment. Every moment, so Zen says, is a living and a dying, a death and a resurrection. We *are* the moments of our lives. We *are* the impermanence of our experience.

We might imagine what the Zen Buddhist is saying through the image of a woman swimming the length of a pool (McDaniel 1980). Each stroke is an "experience" of one sort or another, and she is the series of strokes, extending from one end (representing the beginning of her life) to another (representing the end of her life). Her true self is one stroke as it occurs, and then the next, and then the next, until she reaches the end.

But Zen is not content with this external perspective. It demands that we jump into the pool and experience the swimming from the inside, stroke by stroke. From the inside we are not a "series of experiences" stretched across the mind's eye, but rather the immediacy of experience itself, which is always present, and yet different at each moment. What is this immediacy like at its deepest level?

Zen answers that at its most profound level the immediacy of experience is 1) deep and wide, like a vast field of awareness that extends out beyond the body to include the entire universe, and 2) that it is immensely creative, such that, in the moment at hand, it can respond to what it includes with freedom and freshness.

Imagine, for example, a man walking out of doors on a starry night, gazing at a star. His act of gazing is analogous to a stroke in our swimmer's life. From an external perspective, the star is outside his body, hundreds of thousands of miles away. But from an internal perspective, that is, from the vantage point of his own experiential immediacy, the star is within his experience, as close to him as the glasses on his nose, or still closer. What is outside his body is within his experience, and he is his experience. Insofar as the star fills his field of awareness, he is the star.

This does not mean that the man creates the star. The star is given to his experience, as other people and plants and animals are given to his experience. The creativity of his true self does not lie in generating the objects that fill his awareness, but rather in the spontaneity of his own response to those objects. "That is a beautiful star" is one form of creative response. But "that is not a star at all" is another. The creativity of experience is neither true nor false, good nor evil. It simply is.

The Zen perspective bears remarkable resemblance to the perspective of process theology. From the vantage point of process theologians, the entire universe is gathered into the unity of each and every "actual occasion of experience" that constitutes a person's life. Each moment is a creative concrescence of the universe. In the immediacy of our experience the many become one.

Our creativity lies in *how* we allow many to become one. One way is through the lens of ego-centeredness. Earlier I defined *ego* as "a sense of self," and I spoke of two forms of ego-centeredness: ego-inflation and ego-deflation. Here a more precise definition of *ego* is in order. Tilden Edwards, an Episcopal priest and spiritual writer, offers the following:

> Ego is a self-construct that provides functional secondary control of the mind. It is an extra layer of willfulness, centered on a constructed self-image that seeks to protect a particular sense of territory, by manipulating whatever is not included in this self-image territory (1980, 233).

An operative phrase here is "self-image." When we approach the many of our world through ego-centeredness, we approach them through "a constructed self-image that seeks to protect a particular sense of territory." If, for example, I see myself as a helper, I approach others as needy subjects who need my aid; if I see myself as a perceptive person, I approach them as interesting objects to understand; and if I view myself as a needy person, I approach them as powerful figures to meet my needs.

All of us do this to some extent. The problem does not lie in the self-images themselves; sometimes they are truthful, and oftentimes they are necessary. Rather, the problem lies in *clinging* to these self-images at the expense of being open to others on their own terms. Our self-images become graven images in our imaginations, internal idols that prevent us from being open to others and to God. For example, even if we are helpers, some people may not need us, and we do them a disservice to think otherwise; even if we are perceptive, most people are more than we can ever understand, and we do them an injustice if we think we have them pegged; even if we are needy, some people may be more than servants to our needs, and we ourselves may be more than we realize. If we are to be open to "the many" of our experience in a wise and compassionate way, we need to be ego-endowed, but not ego-possessed; we need to be ego-aware, but not ego-enslaved. We need to see things as they are, not as our egos would like them to be.

The Zen preference is for seeing things as they are. Indeed, in Zen, "things as they are" are "the absolute." As Buddhist writer Charlotte Joko Beck puts it: "The 'absolute' is simply everything in our world, emptied of personal emotional content" (Beck 1993, 171). In my own writings I distinguish the absolute of Buddhism from the God of Christianity and other Abrahamic faiths (cf. 1989, 93–110); my distinction parallels Whitehead's distinction between God and Creativity. As I understand it, Whitehead uses the word *Creativity* to name the sheer "is-ness" of what is, as it is, in its relation to everything else that is. It is analogous to what some Buddhist philosophers mean by "suchness," and what Beck means by "the absolute." Understood in this way, the absolute is neither good nor evil, and it is unquantifiable. There is as much of the absolute in Hitler massacring Jews as there is in Francis of Assisi feeding birds. Still, there is also a dimension of reality that beckons us to be more like Francis and less like Hitler. This is what Whitehead means by God. It is the lure toward wholeness in each and every life. My proposal is that both the Lure and the absolute are real, but that they are different. "God" names a healing presence within reality, who beckons each and all to find fullness of life relative to circumstances at hand; "the absolute" names the circumstances themselves, including the world and God's presence within them. One of the beauties of Zen is that it reminds us to be present to, and mindful of, the circumstances themselves, God or no God. It is a way of living in which, at best, a person responds to each situation on its own terms, freely and creatively, yet also compassionately.

Part of the compassion of Zen lies in honoring the "other" as other. This is similar to Judaism. And yet part of the compassion lies also in recognizing that this "other" is also part of our own true self, which is different from the ego. The true self is the immediacy of experience here-and-now, in its depth and width. In Zen we love our neighbors as ourselves, because we realize that at a deep level our neighbors *are* ourselves.

I Am the Sea Pirate

But what if our neighbors are sea pirates? What if they are persons we find morally reprehensible, or at the very least, unpleasant and irritating? Here Thich Nhat Hanh offers advice. When he says "I am the pirate, my heart not yet capable of seeing and loving," we see both a recognition that the pirate is part of his true self and also a creative response to that pirate in an act of forgiveness and understanding.

Hanh's forgiveness of the sea pirate does not absolve the pirate of responsibility. He ought to be punished for his wrongdoing. Nor does it imply that all moral standards of right and wrong, of good and evil, are relative to the eye of the beholder. There may well be universal standards of compassion—obligatory to us all—which are violated in the pirate's violence, and in our own.

Still, we see in Hanh a freedom from resentment and self-delusion that is essential to human wholeness and to life in community.

Freedom from Resentment

Resentment is more than mere anger. It is anger clung to, when, without clinging, it would have run its course. Anger can be a constructive emotion. It brings energy and clarity which, if channeled in compassionate directions, can be conducive to community well-being. Communities need anger.

But they do not need resentment. Many people throughout the world are riddled with resentments that block their creativity and prevent them from dwelling in community with others.

The Buddhist antidote to resentment is mindfulness. When we become mindful of our anger, we allow it to be felt and then to pass, as it always will. We realize that internal anger is one of myriad emotional states that characterize the good life. But we also realize that it, like all emotional states, is impermanent. We feel it, but we do not cling to it. We let it go.

The Christian antidote to resentment is forgiveness. Forgiveness is a form of green grace: a healing of broken relations through the restoration of meaningful connections. Traditional Christian teaching is that we are able to forgive others because we recognize that we ourselves are forgiven by God. This is indeed true. The Holy Wisdom at the heart of the universe is deeply connected to all—people and penguins alike. In relation to people, we learn from Jesus that forgiveness is one of Holy Wisdom's primary modes of communion. She may feel angry at our sins, and indeed she may grieve. But like a Buddhist boddhisattva, she does not hold on. Her patience is infinite. Despite our failings, she keeps on trying to save us.

Many Christians, however, are better at talking about forgiveness than actually forgiving. We hold on to our anger as "righteous indignation" at having been wronged, feeling "justified" in it. Instead of saying, with Jesus, "Father forgive them, for they know not what they do," we say inwardly, "Father condemn them, for they know exactly what they do." Clinging to our anger, we seek destruction of our "enemies."

Buddhism's emphasis on mindfulness practices can help free us from the tendency to chase our thoughts and cling to our anger, so that we can let go. In addition, it can help us realize that, at some deep level, we are identified with those we are tempted to resent. If, as Thomas Berry says, the universe is a communion of subjects, then those "others" whom we are tempted to resent are parts of our true self, just as they are parts of Holy Wisdom's self.

The best way to taste our true self is to enter into a daily practice where we are released from ego-based clingings, which are rooted in ego-inflation or ego-deflation. If we are tempted to think of ourself as either "one above many" or "one below many," we easily become obsessed with rectifying the situation. The "many" who are above us or below us become objects of our jealousy or contempt. In some oppressive situations, of course, we are rightly angry—though not resentful—of injustices done to us. But in other less pernicious situations we are unable to live with the natural, non-oppressive, fluctuating hierarchies—such as parent-child relations, or teacher-learner relations—that are part of ordinary life. A daily practice such as Zen meditation, in which we taste the reality of our pre-ego state of existence, can remind us that we are not precisely identified with our own ego-image. It can help us find a balance, so that we can approach others as sisters and brothers in God, neither above nor below us, but rather with us.

Meditation cannot solve all ills. Learning to commune involves more than a daily practice; it also involves worship and prayer, service and learning to be served, struggle and sacrifice. In the Introduction I proposed that we might sink our roots in four sources of inspiration in order to become healers in a broken world: relations with other people, including relations of service; the wisdom of world religions, including, for the Christian, the wisdom of Christianity; a daily practice of prayer and meditation; and the Earth itself. Mindfulness practice of the sort recommended by Stephanie Kaza is but one dimension of a daily practice. This one dimension, however, can be part of the overall mix of practices that can help free us from resentment.

Freedom from Self-Delusion

We must also be mindful of our own inner idols, those ego-images that lead us to delude ourselves concerning our motives. Thich Nhat Hanh says that the sea pirate's heart is "not yet capable of seeing and loving." From the vantage point of a Christianity with roots and wings, that part of us which is capable of seeing and loving is the image of God within us. We are called to be wise and compassionate, to be seers and lovers; this call is within us as our own innermost possibility. It is one way in which Holy Wisdom is present in us, even as she is beyond us.

Yet few of us live up to the possibility of our divine image. The image of God in us is often replaced by an ego-image to which we are deeply attached, both consciously and unconsciously. For those who suffer from ego-inflation, the ego-image may well be "I am a nice person, incapable of the heinous crimes that others commit." For those who suffer from ego-deflation, it may well be "I am a rotten person, all too capable of such crimes."

Those who suffer from ego-deflation are sometimes closer to the truth. Aware that they are capable of the very worst, they find in their heart the sympathy to approach others as kindred children of God. They can love and forgive others, because they know that they are no better than those they might otherwise condemn. In this love and forgiveness they begin to taste the image of God within themselves, and to find personal power in the process. Their ego-deflation begins to evaporate, but it is not replaced by ego-inflation. Rather, it is replaced by honesty. They begin to see all people—themselves included—as on the same plane, all with gifts and sins. In learning to see themselves in this way, they put on the mind of the One who loves all people in a similar way. They put on the mind of Holy Wisdom.

On the other hand, those of us who suffer from ego-inflation are sometimes in deeper trouble. We live under the illusion that we possess no capacity for evil within, and hence no need for additional seeing and loving. We do not feel that we need to grow in wisdom and compassion, because we have already arrived.

Hanh's poem offers a special word to us. It reminds us that we are "sea pirates," too. We resist recognizing this because we like to think of ourselves as better than the rest. Our resistance is a form of self-deception. More often than not, the very things we detest in others are things of which we ourselves are capable. We project onto them evils, or at least potentials for evil, that lie within us. We hide from our own humanity, including our sinfulness.

Hanh invites us to become more Buddhist in orientation, and indeed more Jewish. In Judaism humans are understood to be a little lower than the angels and yet capable of much sin. They—we—are neither totally depraved nor totally compassionate, but both. There is a little Mother Teresa, and a little sea pirate, in all of us.

Usually, if we are ego-inflated, we have to face some crisis in which our own inflated self-image shatters before we can accept our humanity. If we think of ourselves as more helpful than others, our crisis may be a circumstance in which we recognize, somewhat painfully, that some of our "help" actually has been a way of enlarging ourselves by interfering in people's lives; if we think of ourselves as more successful than others, our crisis may be a circumstance in which, despite our best efforts, we fail miserably and are embarrassed in the process; if we think of ourselves as more powerful than others, our crisis may be a situation in which we become vulnerable to circumstances far beyond our control, in which we become totally dependent on others. We need not think that Holy Wisdom places these situations in our lives. She is no puppeteer. But we can recognize that, out of such situations, good can come, which is partly inspired by Wisdom's lures in our lives. One way or another we will need to encounter situations that "bring us down a notch" in order to arrive at honest self-understanding.

Can we be honest about ourselves? The proposal of this chapter has been that such honesty is both desirable and necessary, if we are to be the kinds of people who can help heal a broken world. The world needs people who can live in community with one another, with plants and animals, with the Earth. It needs people who accept the finitude of others in a spirit of love, and who accept their own finitude in a similar spirit. If we become honest about who we truly are—half broken and half whole, half sinner and half saint—we become a people of forgiveness and creativity, of wisdom and love. We learn to love our neighbors as ourselves, including sea pirates and trees, not because we feel obliged to love them, but because we want to love them. We know that they are us and we are they, even as each is more than the other.

Chapter 9

Communion with Goddesses and Rivers

Selected Lessons from Hinduism for Finding God in Earth and Imagination

In Hinduism there is a legend about the goddess who so loved the world that she became a river, that all who bathe in her might be elevated to divinity. The goddess is Ganga, and the river is the Ganges. On any given day, and especially at festival times, millions upon millions of Indians bathe in the waters of the Ganges, feeling her presence in the warm flow of the Ganges currents. They experience the waters of the Ganges as Shakti, a word which literally means "energy" or "power," and which refers to the female energy of God. The Ganges, they say, is liquid Shakti.

This Hindu legend and practice reminds us of John 3:16: "And God so loved the world that he gave his only Son, so that everyone who believes in him may not perish but have eternal life." In one case the Divine becomes en-fleshed, in another it becomes en-rivered; in one the Divine is a God, and in the other a Goddess. Still, the principle is similar. A generous divine power reaches out to help lost souls, so that they might participate in eternal life. We can almost imagine a Hindu addendum to the Johannine passage: "Yes, God may well have sent a son to help save the world. But God also sends rivers. And God is also a Goddess. The Word that became flesh has many faces."

In this chapter I want to affirm this addendum. I want to suggest that even as Christians recognize God in the face of Jesus, we might also recognize God in the face of living rivers and living goddesses.

For many Christians this proposal is controversial. Neither goddesses nor rivers are ordinarily admitted into the Christian pantheon. Our tradition permits attachment to the verbal icons of God-the-Father and God-the-Son, both of which so often evoke images of God as male presence. And yet it seems to forbid openness to God-the-Mother and God-the-River. For many, the Christian tradition has been one-sidedly male and anthropocentric.

When tradition functions in this way, it is an idol. It is not a nourishing soil in which we can sink our roots, but rather a polluted soil that stifles growth.

171

Functioning as a false god in our own imaginations, such tradition violates the Spirit's freedom to appear to us in fresh ways, adaptive to our authentic needs for love and wisdom. When we find ourselves trapped by tradition in this way, our imaginations need stretching.

I think that Jesus would approve. He was open to fresh images; his teachings and parables embody a creativity that destabilized any addiction to ordinary and even orthodox ways of looking at things. Contrary to the orthodoxies of his day, he told his followers, and tells us, that outcasts and prostitutes are the first to enter the kingdom of heaven; that enemies are to be loved not hated; that we can live only if first we die; that there is wisdom in insecurity; and that, in their freedom from concern for the morrow, even birds and flowers can be spiritual guides. He advises us that God's love is like that of a mother hen, a shepherd, an aged woman who has lost a coin. He opens himself to the healing influences of women in his life, whose faith helps make him more whole. One can almost imagine Jesus, two thousand years later, recommending that we find God in goddesses and rivers, not only because the recommendation is valid, but also because it is shocking. In any case, our task is to imitate Jesus, not by reducing him to an abstraction in our minds, but by being open to the God of Freshness in our way and our time, as he was in his way and his time. It is to enter into a Way of freedom.

There are many paths into this Way. One approach is to pack our bags like Abraham and Sarah, sever some of our ties with the past, and open ourselves to fresh possibilities from the future. Often, when we open ourselves to fresh insights from other religions and the Earth, for example, we are doing this. We are taking leave of past securities in order to discover new soils in which we might sink new roots. The precise ways in which these soils will shape our lives cannot be predicted. We must trust the process of dialogue itself and, beyond that, the Spirit who calls us into dialogue. Just as the Son of Man, like a fox, had no place to lay his head, so we have no place to lay our heads. We open ourselves to insights from Buddhists and sycamore trees, from Native Americans and buffaloes, from Hindus and rivers, trustful of a grace that is in the journey itself.

Another approach into the Way of freedom is not so much to disengage ourselves from the past, to leave home, as it is to stay with our pasts, and remember them, in fresh ways. At a personal level, this can take at least two forms.

One is to recognize the wounds we have suffered, sometimes at the hands of others and sometimes at our own hands; to accept the reality of our pain; and also to forgive those who have "trespassed against us," even when we ourselves are the trespassers. The alcoholic comes to grips with the pain she has caused others and herself; the abusive husband comes to grips with the pain he has caused his wife; the unfaithful lover comes to grips with her act of betrayal; the promiscuous male comes to grips with the ways he has harmed others and himself. A wise counselor was once asked by a student: "When do you know that your clients are healed?" Her answer was: "I know that they are healed when they can forgive those who have trespassed against them." Forgiveness is an act of creative re-membering.

Another way to creatively remember the past is quietly to recall the many faces of God that have already been at work in our lives in healing ways. We may well have forgotten them because we were not taught to recognize them as divine faces. To illustrate, I mention two faces that have been influential in my own life, both of them female.

One is that of my grandmother: Lillian Campbell from Camden, Arkansas. Born in 1898, she was both grandmother and friend to me. She raised three children of her own and a good many more out of the goodness of her heart. About age fifty she suffered a brain tumor which almost took her life, and yet she lived another forty years to shower love and affection on a host of others, including those who, like she, knew the trials of old age. She was a window through whom I saw God. While Nanny may not have been a goddess, she is nonetheless a living presence in my memory and her "face" shines on me today, even as it shined on me while she was alive. She is a female face of God, a female presence through which the very light of Holy Wisdom shines.

A second female face that nourishes my soul is the Guadalupe River in south Texas. I realize that not all people experience rivers as embodiments of female energy. Indeed, I know some rivers that are male. Still, for me and for others I have queried, the Guadalupe is female rather than male. She is not an "it" but rather a living presence imbued with strong, creative energy, and somehow this energy is female rather than male. Like the Ganges, the Guadalupe seems more a goddess than a god.

Along with my grandmother, the Guadalupe has been a spiritual guide in my life. Swimming in her as a child, I discovered the way in which dark, green water can nourish the soul and enliven the spirit. I especially enjoyed swimming beneath her surface, with goggles on, learning about the strange worlds of perch and catfish housed in her womb. From the Guadalupe's underwater depths I learned that I too have an underwater dimension, a side others cannot see but which bubbles up from my own inner depths. And I realized that other people too have inner depths that are more than the eye can see. Today I find myself grateful for two goddesses in my life, one human and one aquatic; both have been spiritual directors for me.

As the example of the Guadalupe River suggests, a "face of God" need not have eyes or a nose. It is any living presence, inwardly felt or outwardly perceived, that serves as a channel of grace in our lives. Faces of God may include a grandfather and a lake, a mother and a garden, a sister and a forest, a brother and a dog, a father and a farm, a cousin and a mountain, a friend and a cat, a lover and a star. Whatever our chosen channels, they are holy icons for us. Through them we have discovered green grace and red grace.

Green grace, we recall, is the healing we experience when we recover rich bonds with people, animals, and the Earth. Red grace is the healing we experience when we own our inner turmoil—suffering or guilt, fear or shame—trustful that we are embraced by God in our humanity. Both forms of grace are ecological in their way; they are from the Earth and of the Earth. And yet both are also divine. They are ways in which the healing energy of God can be part of our lives. My suggestion, then, is that the various faces of God that we find in our lives—some inside our own imaginations, some out-side our bodies—can be channels of both red and green grace.

My aim in the remainder of this chapter, then, is to show how selected dimensions of Hinduism might help us better appreciate diverse channels of grace. In the sections that follow, I offer three proposals:

1. That the polytheistic imagination of Hinduism might help us appreciate the manyness of God's faces, and thus relieve us of a shallow monotheism that confuses our preferred images of God with the true God.

2. That some of God's many faces manifest a female energy, itself divine, that can be found in sacred sites and in the natural world, and also in living presences within our own imaginations.

3. That some of the female faces of God—such as the ostensibly terrifying face of the Hindu goddess Kali—can help us better understand that God claims the terrain of death as well as life as a horizon of healing love.

My guide throughout the essay will be Diana Eck, who is professor of com-parative religion and Indian Studies at Harvard University and a long-time participant in the interfaith dialogue program of the World Council of Churches. I draw upon Eck for two reasons. First, her life and thought vividly show the way in which a practicing Christian can be deeply nourished by Hindu points of view, including Hindu images of divine, female energy. And, second, because, as a woman fully familiar with feminist critiques of male projection, she has a much better sense of female energy than I.

The Polytheistic Imagination

Eck is no stranger to green grace. She grew up in Bozeman, Montana, surrounded by the healing powers of Bear Mountain and the Gallatin River, the Spanish Peaks and the Blackfoot River. It was from her childhood and teenage years that she gained a sense of God's freedom to be present in moun-tains, campfires, prayer, and basketball. Her wings came from roots in Montana (1993, 4–5).

Eck's introduction to Hinduism came almost by accident. While a student at Smith College in the 1960s, she spent a year in Banaras, India. That year expanded her Christian faith considerably. Initially, things were not easy. Af-ter only a few days, she wrote home sharing her confusion and bewilderment:

Wandering half-scared through the side-walk narrow streets near the Chowk market today was an exhausting experience, exhausting because it was as if I had walked through all of India, seen, felt, tasted, smelled it all in three hours. There were too many people, too many faces, too many cows, too many catacomb streets and dead ends, too little air. The utter concentration of life, work, misery, odor, and filth in this area of the city was staggering (1993, 7).

And yet, she was immediately moved by the religiousness of Banaras. In Banaras, "religion was surely the most important observable fact of daily life. The whole city seemed to revolve on a ritual axis. There were temples everywhere, large and small, inhabited by images of gods and goddesses whose names I did not know, whose multi-armed forms I could not even distinguish one from the other, and whose significance was beyond my grasp" (1993,7).

Thirty years and twelve trips to India later, the multi-armed forms are more comprehensible to her. Today Eck is one of the foremost scholars of Hinduism in the United States, having authored two books that are used throughout colleges in the United States as basic texts on Hinduism: *Banaras, City of Light* (1982) and *Darsan: Seeing the Divine Image in India* (1981). The books have had a wide impact on many audiences, including college students.

Eck is also one of the few Christian "theologians of dialogue" who is willing to share the way in which another world religion, in her case Hinduism, has deeply shaped her life. Many theologians talk about the importance of dialogue with world religions, but they emphasize the principles of dialogue rather than the concreteness of the lessons learned. Eck is an exception. In a recent book, *Encountering God: A Spiritual Journey from Bozeman to Banares* (1993), she offers numerous lessons she has learned over the years, lessons from which we might learn as well.

If there is a single message that includes all others, it may be that "God has many faces." Eck's encounter with Hinduism has helped her realize that, in a Hindu context, polytheism and monotheism are complementary, not contradictory.

> The Hindu tradition is both monotheistic and polytheistic. Oneness and manyness are not seen as true opposites. In the Hindu tradition, matters of importance are thought of quite naturally in the singular and in the plural. There are many gods (devas), many divine descents of gods (avataras), many ways of salvation (margas), many philosophical systems (darshanas). There are also many scriptures: the ancient "wisdom," or Vedas, including collections of hymns, like the Rig Veda, and philosophical dialogues, like the Upanishads; the two Hindu epics, the Mahabharata and the Ramayana; the Bhagavad Gita, "Song of the Lord," which forms part of the Mahabharata; and the "old stories," the Puranas, which include mythologies of the gods as well as the lore of kings, heroes, and heroines. The profusion of gods and scriptures is matched by a polycentric religious life, social structure, and family structure. There is no one clear, unmistakable center. Manyness is valued; indeed it is seen as essential (1993, 60).

And yet the profusion of gods and scriptures is best understood in terms of the fecundity, the sheer abundance, of the one Sacred Whole of which all gods and goddesses are manifestations. This Sacred Whole is God, the "One Across Whom Space and Time is Woven" (1993, 53).

An analogy, borrowed from a German Indologist Betty Heimann might help (Eck 1981, 25). Imagine a crystal with an infinite number of facets, each of which reveal the whole of the crystal from a certain point of view, but none of which exhaust the crystal. Analogously, the Sacred Whole is an infinitely faceted mystery, and the gods and goddesses are its facets. They are faces of the Whole, points of view from which it can be approached, lenses through which it can be beheld. They appear to us in our imaginations, and yet they are more than us. They are faces of God, facets of the crystal, angles of approach to the Mystery.

This analogy is consonant with a Hindu perspective, yet it is also consonant with the Christian perspective I have proposed in this book. I have suggested that God is the Sacred Whole of the universe, appropriately conceived as "She" or "He" as well as "It." This Sacred Whole is living, in the sense that it possesses interiority of its own, and yet its life includes the entire visible universe: the plants and animals, the trees and stars, the mountains and rivers, the friends and foes. Like a man on a cross, who identifies both with those who mourn his death and those who cause his death, the Sacred Whole is Christlike, identifying with all living beings on the planet and in the universe. The divine One is not a skin-encapsulated ego residing off the planet, but a universe-including Life whose very body is the world. Each creature—from proton to paramecium, from penguin to human person—is a cell in its body, adding whatever richness it can to the divine experience, and also, if circumstances are right, serving as a channel of its grace.

What Hinduism adds to this point of view, I believe, is that objects within our own imaginations—gods and goddesses—can also be cells in the divine Body. The universe includes the invisible as well as the visible, the mythic as well as the factual, the inner as well as the outer. Already we Christians know that some such objects can be revelatory. We experience God through the internal images of "Father" and "Son" and "Holy Spirit." Some of us also find God in imaginatively entertained scenes from the Bible and in revelations from dreams. An encounter with Hinduism invites us to have even more expanded imaginations, to recognize that there can be many holy icons in our imaginative lives, some of which come to us from other religions, all of which are part of God's body, and none of which exhausts God's Mystery. Hinduism invites us to be open, not only to the gods and goddesses of our own lives, but to those of other religions as well. Just as the Hindu tends to see God in the living Christ, so the Christian is invited to see God in the living Kali.

To be sure, we will approach the less familiar faces through the lens of images with which we are familiar. As Eck explains:

Each of us brings religious or ethical criteria to our understanding of the new worlds we encounter. When I "recognize" God's presence in a Hindu temple or in the life of a Hindu, it is because, through this complex of God, Christ, and Spirit, I have a sense of what God's presence is like. Recognition means that we have seen it somewhere before. I would even say that it is Christ who enables Christians—in fact, challenges us—to recognize where we didn't expect to do so and where it is not easy to do so (1993, 79).

Still, there may be something distinctively Christian about moving from the familiar to the unfamiliar. After all, Jesus loved strangers. He unsettled the orthodox of his day by tending to those who were "too impure" or "too sinful" to be godly. He loved outsiders because he himself was an outsider. He knew what it was like to be rejected.

We too can be open to outsiders. Obedience to the Way can challenge us to find God outside the confines of the Christian church and outside the familiarities of our own imaginations. Hindus are among the "outsiders" we meet in our world. They are not outside the reality of God's love or the ecumenism of God's creation, but they are outside what the more conservative among us find familiar in Christianity. Faith in Christ challenges us to be open to them, and also to their gods and goddesses, as ways of encountering the Abba of Jesus.

At least this is the way it has worked with Diana Eck. The living Christ whom she met in Bozeman, Montana, took her to Banaras, India, where she discovered still broader horizons of divine grace. Recounting a visit to a temple for the god Vishnu in South India, she writes:

The image of Vishnu at Padmanabhaswamy both challenged and enlarged my own concept of God. I remember on the shelf of the library in the Methodist church in Bozeman: *Your God is Too Small*. And he was. As one theological liberation movement after another has discovered, "he" was also too male, too white, and too much at home in Western culture. India's theological gift to me has been the discovery that God can be addressed as Mother, can wear the ashes of the cremation pyre, or can beckon us to dance (1993, 79).

Plagued with overly masculine images of God, we too need to address God as Mother; tempted by overly sentimental images of God, we too best recognize that the divine Mother can sometimes wear ashes. Toward the end of this chapter I will show how one such Mother—the Hindu goddess Kali—helped Eck recognize the terrible tenderness of a motherly God. For now, let us consider in more detail the nature of the polytheistic imagination.

Eck uses the phrase "polytheistic imagination" to refer not just to a way of imagining the world, but to a Way of living in it (1981, 22). It is a Way that values manyness as well as oneness, diversity as well as unity, complexity as well as simplicity. It is sensitive to 1) the many faces of God, none of which is reducible to the others, 2) the many Ways in which people can approach God, all of which are tailored to individual needs and cultures, 3) the many ways in which people can organize their lives in relation to one another, some of which are foreign to us, 4) the many dimensions of our own unconscious lives, many of which appear to us in dreams and fantasies, and 5) the manyness of life itself, including the many forms of life that are not human but are nevertheless valuable and revelatory. The polytheistic imagination delights in many forms of manyness.

Even for a polytheistic imagination, however, there must be limits to certain forms of manyness. The polytheistic imagination at its best will not celebrate the manyness of a human population that already exceeds the carrying capacity of the planet and threatens the manyness of the rest of creation; or the manyness of inner-city violence that already exceeds the carrying capacities of our hearts. The world needs structure and order as well as manyness. But we learn from ecology that healthy ecosystems require diversity for their order, and a polytheistic imagination recognizes the same. It sees that diversity, both human and ecological, is essential to the well-being of the planet and the wholeness of God. It knows that, without many faces, even God would be impoverished. To denude God's body of manyness by a destruction of cultures and biotic communities is to nail the Christ to a cross. It is an act of violence against the world and against God.

What is the opposite of a polytheistic imagination? Eck calls it a "monotheistic consciousness," which emphasizes oneness at the expense of manyness. Unfortunately, she explains, such an emphasis has been part and parcel of much Western religion:

> It is a way of thinking equally pervasive in the three great monotheistic traditions of the West—Judaism, Christianity, and Islam. In monotheistic consciousness, the singular is the proper number for questions of truth: There is One God, one Only-Begotten Son of the Father, one Seal of the Prophets, one Holy Book, one Holy Catholic and Apostolic Church (1981, 22).

Even Westerners who lack faith in God, says Eck, can exhibit this one-over-many attitude. They can assume that individual human beings are self-contained units of oneness rather than relational webs of manyness; that there is, or ought to be, one overarching authority in matters of social organization; and that truth is one rather than many. Nietzsche was not wrong in saying that, in the West, monotheism has too often been the "rigid consequence of one normal human being—consequently the belief in a normal God, beside whom there are only false, spurious gods" (Eck 1981, 60).

Christians can learn to be less normal. A Christianity with roots and wings will appreciate the odd and the different, the strange and the bizarre, the surprising and the wild. We can recognize that "normalcy" is too often our way of projecting onto others what we worship in ourselves. A healthy monotheism moves beyond self-worship. It recognizes the multiplicity of our inner lives, the multiplicity of human cultures, the multiplicity of biotic life, the multiplicity of God's faces. In its attention to the various faces of life and God, it sees that some can indeed be channels of grace, vessels of Holy Wisdom's healing power.

In short, the needed shift in our time is from a shallow monotheism that elevates a few images to exclusive status and remains attached to them at all costs, to a still deeper monotheism that recognizes many images as revelations of the Sacred Whole but does not reduce them to objects of ego-based clinging.

One sign of ego-based clinging is exclusivity. When we single out our images as the only images, we commit idolatry. Our idolatry lies not in attending to the revelatory power of images, but in clinging to our images in ways that obstruct God's freedom to be present in other images as well. In being attached to our own at the expense of others, we violate the spirit of the polytheistic imagination and, therefore, of deep monotheism, which admits many images. Eck's journey from Bozeman to Banaras helped her move beyond idolatry into a deeper monotheism. She now sees God in mothers and ashes and dances, not just in fathers and sons and spirits. My suggestion is that we do the same.

The Female Energy of God

Given the dearth of female images of the Divine in Western monotheism, it is not surprising that, for Eck, the female images of the Divine offered in Hinduism have been uniquely attractive. She writes: "In listening for the language of this energetic, fiery mystery of Spirit in the Hindu tradition, I have often been moved by what they call Shakti—divine energy, female energy" (1993, 136). Eck emphasizes various ways in which Shakti can enrich Christian understandings of divine Breath or divine Spirit.

Eck notes that even in the West the original word for "divine breath" was feminine. "Remember that *ruach*, the generative breath that moved upon the waters at the dawn of creation, is a feminine noun." The history of Christianity involved a replacement of this originally feminine breath with a masculine alternative: "In the course of time, and no doubt in the interest of patriarchy, she became neuter in the Greek (*pneuma*) and eventually masculine in the Latin (*spiritus*)." Eck notes further that in the interests of preserving tradition, many more conservative churchmen now resist any use of feminine language for God's breath. "Some of the same church patriarchs who even today become indignant when the 'He' language of the Father and Son is tampered with by feminists in the church are nonetheless unapologetic about the linguistic sleight of hand that changed the gender of the Holy Spirit" (1993, 136). She finds herself turning to the Shakti of Hinduism, not only because it is powerful in its own right, but because a linguistic sleight of hand exhausted even God's breath of its femininity.

The word *shakti* means "energy" or "power." This power is not that of women, but the very power of the Divine, understood as a life force that runs through our veins, through plants and animals, through sun and stars, through the entire creation. Eck quotes the Indian poet Tagore to make the point:

> The same stream of life that runs through my veins night and day runs through the world and dances in rhythmic measure.
>
> It is the same life that shoots in joy through the dust of the earth in numberless blades of grass and breaks into tumultuous waves of leaves and flowers (Eck 1993, 140).

For Eck, the Holy Spirit of Christianity includes this "energy for life," which is "creative, generative, and always at work awakening us to the mystery and presence of the Divine" (1993, 140). It is perceived by many people in many traditions as feminine, and yet it is not the patriarchal feminine of pure, passive nurturance. "It is beneficent and life-giving energy, though not unambiguously so. The Spirit may be comforting, but she is also frightening; she may be gentle, but also restless; she may be the 'sweet, sweet spirit in this place,' as the old Gospel hymn has it, or a sense of seismic unsettling power" (1993, 37).

Indeed, the Spirit thus understood is like my own grandmother: creative, caring, nurturing, and outrageous. It is the divine, surging, mothering energy of the Guadalupe River, not only in times of rest, but even during floods when her holding capacity has been overridden. How shall we conceive this energy? In light of the crystal analogy offered earlier, we may be tempted to imagine Shakti as a facet of the divine Whole, a face of the Crystal. But a better analogy, I believe, is to imagine Shakti as the invisible energy of the Crystal itself, laced in the interstices of each and every face, distinctively but not exclusively expressed in the faces of mythic goddesses.

Or, to shift the analogy, we might imagine God not as a Crystal, but rather as a Power Source that illuminates many light bulbs. The gods and goddesses would be light bulbs, of course, but so would plants and animals, stars and rivers, men and women. All living presences—visible and invisible—would be empowered by the Power Source, and Shakti would be the electricity that ignites them. She would be revealed in a distinctive way in the female light bulbs: in women and goddesses. Without Shakti there would be no world and no functioning God. "Without Shakti, Shiva is shava" (1993, 137). Shiva is a god, and *shava* means "corpse." Our tradition is replete with metaphors that suggest the female depends on the male. The saying suggests the opposite is true as well. Without divine Femininity, there is no divine Masculinity.

Our problem as Christians, of course, is that we have lacked a healthy sense of divine Femininity. For some of us, Mary has been our female light bulb, our vessel of Shakti. Though sometimes Mary can seem all nurture without power, it nevertheless remains true that, for many people in many settings, her energy can be electrifying. As Eck observes: "Were my Hindu friends to visit the basilica [Our Lady of Guadalupe on the outskirts of Mexico City] I have no doubt they would . . . not hesitate to speak of the Virgin of Guadalupe as Shakti. Marian shrines throughout the world are filled with the 'feel' of Shakti" (1993, 139). Perhaps it is no accident that the river in whom I find sacred female energy—the Guadalupe in South Texas—is named after the site where the Mother appeared. Growing up a Protestant, I had no Black Madonna to shape my imagination, but I did have a Lady of Guadalupe.

Still, for me as for so many others, institutional Christianity has been overwhelmingly male. In worship, the very word "God" almost inevitably suggests a male presence: a puppeteer, or a clockmaker, or, at its best and richest, the father of adult children. This father means much to me. I pray to him often, and I love him. But he is not enough.

Eck proposes that we Christians need a healthy dose of Shakti to enrich our lives and imaginations. Whether male or female, we need to be enriched by the power of women's experience even as we honor the power of male experience, and we need to recognize that the female energy in women's experience is not itself exhausted by women. We find this energy, says Eck, in at least three additional places: in sacred sites, in nature, and in our own capacities to accept suffering.

Female Energy in Sacred Sites and the Earth

The Christian tradition has most often found revelation in words not places, in texts not buildings, in what is heard not seen. We have attended to the power of the ear at the expense of the eye, to the power of the word at the expense of the place. Eck shows how the Hindu notion of *jagrita* can correct this imbalance by reminding us God's Shakti can be part of the very spirit of a living place:

> Shakti is what Hindi speakers call *jagrita*, "wide awake," and her shrines are magnetic for that reason. They too are called *jagrita*. Shakti is immanent, present, near at hand. Her shrines are called *pithas*, "seats" or "benches," and they are located right in the midst of life, rooted in the earth of this shore, so to speak. Shakti is under the tree, on top of the hillock at the edge of town. Her shrines are ceaselessly visited with offerings and songs. She hears the cries of the poor, the concerns of the farmer, the prayers of the anxious or grieving. Hers are active shrines. They do indeed feel as if the Divine is "wide awake" there (1993, 138).

As Christians reading Eck's account, we naturally wonder if our own sacred sites—church buildings—exhibit such aliveness. In Eck's experience, many do not:

When I think of the churches in Boston, indeed most churches I know in the United States, I would not call many of them *jagrita*. We do not gravitate to them after work or in the evening. If we did we would often find them locked. Many churches, especially Protestant churches, are closed most of the week and there is a sense of sleep that settles upon them. On Sunday mornings there is activity, perhaps there is even a service every weekday morning; on the whole, however, the sense of power and presence that one feels in a great sanctuary of Shakti is not there, except in a few very energetic churches (1993,139).

Still, Eck recognizes that some churches do embody female energy. She mentions the Basilica of Our Lady of Guadalupe on the outskirts of Mexico City; the community of Taize in France; the parish church of Saint James Picadilly in London; the Cathedral of Saint John the Divine in New York; and Twelfth Baptist in Boston's Roxbury neighborhood. I would add Mount Pleasant Baptist Church in Conway, Arkansas, a black church where, as with the others just named, one senses the aliveness of divine energy in the sheer vibrancy of the place. Mount Pleasant is a place, a sanctuary, "where people throng for a sense of God's wakeful presence" (1993, 139) and find it.

Wilderness as Jagrita

Another kind of sanctuary, not specifically noted by Eck but in keeping with her tone, is the wilderness. If our local churches lack *jagrita*, then perhaps we can find it in the natural sanctuaries of the Earth and then introduce some of it into our churches. Participating in the "wide-awakeness" of God—either at Mount Pleasant Baptist Church in Conway or at Yellowstone National Park—involves attention to the entirety of our immediate surroundings, being mindful of the various living presences, visible and invisible, as they interact with one another and as they coalesce in our heart. Perhaps wilderness areas also can be basilicas of God, if we have eyes to see. And perhaps the divine energy we sense in them can be, at least for some of us, female in its presence.

Consider, for example, the following account of a wilderness experience told by Gerald May, a psychiatrist and spiritual writer in the United States.[1] Explaining that, for him, a "relationship with Jesus" never quite worked, he experimented for years with various forms of spiritual practice, only to find in the later years of his life the Way of wilderness. Wilderness was, as he put it, "my first direct encounter with God's immediate presence." And the God whose presence he felt was distinctively female:

---

1. Gerald May is Director for Research and Program Development at the Shalem Institute for Spiritual Formation in Washington, D.C. This organization's goal is to call forth a deeper spiritual life in both person and community through group retreats and training in spiritual direction. Its address is: Mount Saint Alban, Washington D.C. 20016.

At times I felt a physical touch, as if someone were taking me by the shoulders helping me be still or guiding me here and there, gently but powerfully showing me things, teaching me, even healing me in ways my mind could not understand. The very same presence simultaneously arose inside me as a slowing, centering, urging energy in my belly. It was at once me and not-me, transcendent and immanent, a presence both with me and incarnate inside me as me (1994, 5).

Seeking a name for this palpable presence, he allowed his own imagination to speak, trustful that its speech would be right for the moment.

The first name that came to me was "The Power of the Slowing," probably because the presence slowed my mind and body and opened my senses to being there more completely than I had ever felt before. . . . But the presence was far too personal to call "It." Nor was this the Father-God or the Son-Jesus that I might have expected. Instead, I found myself thinking of a "Her." In my experience the presence has been consistently, undeniably feminine. . . . Slowly I recognized Her from scripture as Wisdom: "Hokmah" in Hebrew, "Sophia" in Greek, the dynamically touching, guiding, creating, urging, and distinctly feminine presence of God in us and in the world. I cannot deny that these experiences might be hallucinations. But I also cannot deny that they are completely real for me, in many ways more real and certainly more intimate than any encounter I have ever had with anyone or anything (1994, 5).

For men who are tempted to envision female energy in overly domesticated terms, it is important to note that for May the female presence of God in wilderness is not only nurturing but wild. The energy within him was creative, wild, and free; it was also healing, guiding, and nurturing. It was, to use Eck's terminology, "powerful and surging" even as it was "mothering."

Eck's insights support the point. In addition to Shakti as *jagrita*, she says, "a second way in which the Hindu perception of Shakti might stretch our Spirit-consciousness is the linking of Shakti with nature." Her illustration of God's Shakti in nature is not a wilderness experience in Appalachia, but rather bathing in the Ganges. In the Ganges, she explains, God's female energy is experienced through the confluence of worship, bodily experience, and earth revelation: "The power of the dawn on the Ganges in Banaras is not simply the collective power of worship, but the seamless interpenetration of prayer, bathing, the river and sunrise" (1993, 140). The experience can be electrifying:

A Hindu friend, a professor in a women's university in Delhi, once told me what it meant to her to bathe in the Ganges at Hardwar at the time she brought her father's ashes there for immersion. "I felt as if an electric shock passed through my body. I felt completely transformed," she said. "When I came up out of the water, I felt as if I could now bear the death of anyone, even those people I loved most, even my own" (1993, 140).

In some ways the experience of Eck's friend parallels the insights of many Christians. Just as God sent his Son that we might be able to bear the deaths of our loved ones, trustful that we are embraced in divine Light even amid our sadness, so the Goddess sent a river to help Eck's friend bear the death of her father, trustful that he and she alike were embraced in divinity.

In her case, however, she *bathed* in it; in the case of many Christians, we but *believe* in it. Too often we are not "shocked" by God's love, because we do not really experience it directly. If we are disembodied Christians, stuck in our heads at the expense of our bodies, we may well envy her experience, and for good reason. Even though God became incarnate in Jesus, we cannot find God in the enfleshment of our own bodies.

What Hinduism may teach us, I submit, is that we need more "bathing." We need to discover the living presence of God in bodily ways: like Gerald May in the wilderness, or Diana Eck's friend in the Ganges.

One place to begin may be to include within our own daily practices activities such as walking in local parks or gardening in back yards. I know a man who walks daily in his back yard to attend to his plants and pet his dog. He considers it his morning prayer. This, I suggest, is a form of "bathing." It may not be shocking, but it is indeed healing. He came to grips with the death of his own loved one through such walks. It is the way he, and we, might pray to God, not by talking to God in our heads, but by listening to God through our senses.

Another place to begin may be to recognize the many ways in which the Earth is already present to our senses in our sacraments: in the wood of our pews, in the water of our baptismal fonts, in the bread and wine of the eucharist. Eating the bread and drinking the wine can be forms of bathing. We may not bathe in God, but we taste God in the very sensations of bread being swallowed and wine being drunk. The key is mindfulness: being present to the bread and wine and the divine energy in them. Again, the bread and wine may not be shocking, like the Ganges, but they are palpable like its waters. If received mindfully and prayerfully, they are faces of God in our lives: visible signs of invisible graces.

Female Energy in Visible and Invisible Presences

In the Hindu imagination, of course, Ganga is not only the river. She is also a living goddess. Even as she lives in the currents of the largest river in India, she also lives beyond those currents, both visibly and invisibly.

Visibly, Ganga permeates the whole of the natural world, particularly though not exclusively in sacred waters. As Lina Gupta, a contemporary Hindu writer, explains:

Whether it is the water of a lake, stream, pond, river, or ocean, touched with her holy name, ordinary water takes on her sacred nature. Therefore I am not without her. She is the energy, the life that permeates all of nature. By naming her I identify her divine essence in all things (1993, 102).

This means that as we bathe in our own sacred waters, we bathe in Ganga whether we realize it or not. She is in the Guadalupe of my own experience, and the Gallatin of Diana Eck's, even as she is in the Ganges of India.

Invisibly, Ganga lives in our imaginations. Or at least she lives in the Hindu imagination. Consider the following anecdote offered by Gupta:

I was talking to a very dear family member in India today. He is a Shiva worshiper. I was telling him about my project and some problems in writing a paper on Ganga. He said something quite interesting. He told me to ask Lord Shiva to release Ganga from his matted hair. I did, and I started my journey in writing. There was a sense of release from my own predicament. I do not know who released what and how it all came about. All I know is what I have experienced. That is, Gods and Goddesses are parts of us, parts of the divine essence. By appealing to them we name our predicaments, and by naming them psychologically we release our inner power and potential that are dying to appear on the surface (1993, 103).

Ganga, then, is one of the goddesses within Gupta's imagination. Ganga is part of her as a dimension of her own psyche, and yet Ganga is more than her, a guiding presence who enables her to discover her own "inner power and potential." Ganga is "the beacon of life that shows me the path I have forgotten and shines on the one I have chosen. She is the mother. She is a goddess. She is woman. She is a journey as simple as a river, as complex as life itself" (1993, 102).

I suggest that Christians no less than Hindus can be open to such goddesses. Like Gupta, we can understand them as parts of ourselves and also as parts of the divine Essence, or at least as channels of divine grace. And, like Gupta, we can dive deep into our inner natures through an exploration of our imaginations, in order to experience their healing graces.

Of course, if we are not from India, we will not call our own goddesses Ganga. That, after all, is a uniquely Indian image of the female face of God. The particular goddesses who appear to us, and our names for them, will be relative to the biographical, social, and historical circumstances of our lives. After all, this is the way the Beloved works. Holy Wisdom influences our lives, not by inflexibly imposing upon us pre-ordained faces, but rather by pouring forth her grace through faces we can appreciate and understand. The goddess may appear in my imagination as Holy Grandmother or Sacred River; another may acknowledge a Holy Sister or Sacred Pond. The particular contours of her face will be relative to languages we can understand, given the shape of our lives.

For some Christians male faces may be sufficient. The verbal icons of Father, Son, and Holy Spirit, all conceived as male, will be up to the task of helping produce inner wholeness and wisdom, and outer compassion. Certainly the history of Christianity is replete with people whose lives have been graced by these three icons alone. My own grandmother was one of them. She lived and died content with God the Father.

But others—for example, some women who have been abused by men—cannot trust such faces. If they do trust them, they do so out of fear not love. For these women there is a deep need for goddesses, not gods, as channels of grace in their imaginations, as conduits of healing energy. Moreover, there are many people who, while not abused, nevertheless feel a need to include female presence within their spiritual horizons. I am among them. I was privileged to have loving parents and loving grandparents as well, that were faces of God in my life. Still, perhaps because I was so blessed, I find my own inner life drawn to divine faces both male and female, to Black Madonnas and Brown Nazarenes, to Holy Grandmothers and Crazy Grandfathers, each of whom, in different ways, reveals the healing energy of God. Surely the heart of the universe—Holy Wisdom—is free enough and gracious enough to reach out to us, and into us, with such images.

As these images live in our imagination, they are not two-dimensional but rather five-dimensional. They possess the three dimensions of space, a fourth dimension of time, and a fifth dimension of interiority. Some of them were actual people in our lives before they became living presences in our imaginations; some just appeared to us in our dreams, with no discernible trace of people we have known in life. In any case, they speak to us; they hear us; they suffer with us; they enjoy with us.

Evangelical Christians who have truly personal relations with Jesus know what I mean. Jesus is not simply a figure who lived two thousand years ago and died a tragic death; he is also a real person, alive in the here-and-now, whom we can address as Lord and Savior or Friend and Brother. He has feelings of his own, just as we do. He is real. More liberal Christians, whose imaginations have been impoverished by de-mythologized worldviews, have much to learn from the living Jesus of evangelical piety. At Mount Pleasant Baptist Church in Conway, Arkansas, I have met this living Jesus. He is real and powerful. I have known him in my own life as well, and still do.

Still, Jesus is not the only living presence in our imaginations through whom the healing spirit of God can work. That healing spirit can also work through remembered grandmothers and beloved rivers, through outrageous grandfathers and animal spirits, through tender virgins and even bloodthirsty goddesses. Some of these five-dimensional images in our imaginations can be vessels for the distinctive kind of healing energy that we no longer experience in the living Jesus, albeit with a very different face. It is to the latter possibility—that of experiencing the red grace of Jesus on the cross through

images of a terrifying goddess—that I now turn. Here again, Diana Eck will
be my guide.

The Red Grace of Kali

There are two manifest forms of evil in our world: untimely deaths and
gratuitous suffering. By "untimely deaths" I mean the occasions when a living being's possibilities for rich experience are cut short by death. In many
instances, the death at issue is physical. It is the death of a cholera-ridden
child or a teenager gunned down in a drive-by shooting; of a woman stabbed
to death by a rapist or a man tortured by jailers. But the death may also be
psychological. It may be the gradual death of the substance-abuser, whose
possibilities for meaningful relations with friends and family are cut off by
drugs and alcohol; or that of the compulsive careerist, whose possibilities for
meaningful relations with her own inner life are cut off by an addiction to
work. Untimely deaths may be physical or psychological, sudden or gradual.
In either instance we realize that meaningful possibilities for connection and
creativity, for roots and wings, were extinguished.

By "gratuitous suffering" I mean suffering that is without justification,
that is uncalled-for. I mean the suffering experienced by the person tortured
by jailers, or by the child dying of cholera, or by the addict suffering from
self-hatred. I mean also the suffering of animals as they are abused by callous
humans, and of the Earth as it is assaulted by industrial civilizations. From
some points of view, I realize, all suffering is called-for. Some Hindus believe that every bit of suffering in the world is an unfolding of karmic justice;
and some Christians believe that it is an unfolding of the divine will. From
the vantage point of this book, however, neither karma nor God can justify
some of the suffering we see in our world. As we look upon it, we cannot help
but realize that the world would be better without it. It is gratuitous, uncalled-
for, and tragic. It is evil.

These two evils—untimely death and gratuitous suffering—come together
in one of the most poignant stories in Eck's spiritual autobiography. The story
concerns the brutal death of her brother, Laury. In what follows I will consider how, inspired both by Kali and by the Holy Spirit, Eck learned to see the
feminine energy of God even in the presence of death. Then I will reflect
upon the relation between the feminine energy of God and evil.

Kali: The Mother Who Handles Death

Eck first met Kali in Calcutta, the city named for her temple on the banks
of the Hooghli River.

Her four armed image is everywhere on the streets approaching the
temple—black, with huge eyes and a lolling red tongue, her neck circled

with a garland of skulls and covered with fresh offerings of red hibiscus, holding a cleaver in one hand and a severed head in another, yet somehow incongruously with her other hands gesturing not to be afraid and holding a lotus flower (1993, 141).

Kali's worshipers were clearly not afraid of her. "Indeed they come before her with folded hands, saying 'O Mother, Mother Kali,' as if she were as life bearing as the Ganges" (1993, 141).

For many years Eck's attitude toward Kali was ambivalent. On the one hand, she could not empathize with the severity of Kali's image. It seemed too violent to her Christian imagination. And yet, on the other, there seemed almost to be a truth in the violence: "It was the truth of a divine power claiming the terrain of both life and death, difficult as it might be to look death in the face. Bearing the lotus in one hand and the cleaver in another, she clearly signals that the fullness of life includes both the flowering and the finality."

The finality was imposed upon Eck with the death of her brother. Laury was only forty-eight when he died in a jail in Juarez, Mexico. He had gone to Juarez to work with the poor. The authorities had arrested him, detained him, and beaten him. He limped around for a few days afterward with a rupturing spleen. Most of his time was spent alone in a dingy hotel room, in agony. When he finally was taken to the hospital, he died within thirty minutes.

Eck describes how she, her mother, and Laury's son went to Juarez to get his body. "We spent days retracing his steps," she says, "the desk clerks, the cashiers, the doctor sitting at a card table in a parka, the streets of the poor among whom he had decided to live." Then they went to the morgue, where a doctor described to them the blows that Laury had suffered. Eck had seen several deaths in her life, but this one—that of her beloved brother—was almost unparalleled in its tragedy. Her description of entering the morgue—of confronting the tragedy face-to-face—requires repeating in depth:

> As we entered the large cold room, the three of us did not know if we would be able to stay or would have to flee. . . . I saw nothing in the morgue but Laury. Six foot five, cold, wrapped in a large sheet and plastic. Completely peaceful. His face is imprinted clearly and forever in my memory.
>
> We had gone to graduate school at Harvard together in the fall of 1969, driving tandem in our Volkswagen Beetles from Montana to Boston. He was an attorney and man of real Christian faith. He probably didn't really understand my keen interest in Hindu temples, he surely did not understand Kali. Neither do I.
>
> But I know I did not run away from that moment. As Mom and Bryan and I held fast to one another, I opened the *Book of Common Prayer* and read slowly and carefully the words of the Twenty-third Psalm and the prayers for the dead. "Even though I walk through the valley of the shadow

of death, I will fear no evil, for Thou art with me. . . . " I have no idea how long we stood there in the morgue, but it was a time in which the Holy Spirit hovered with immense wingspan over us (1993, 143).

In these words Eck has captured the sense of horror that can accompany our encounters with untimely deaths and unwarranted suffering. Often it is not our own untimely death or unwarranted suffering that is most horrible, but that of others we love. Eck captures the kind of grace that can empower us in our encounter with tragedy, if we are very, very fortunate.

The grace at issue is red not green. It is not the grace of being richly bonded with people, animals, and the Earth in ways that are obviously healing; rather, it is the grace of being able to face the suffering of our loved ones, and our own suffering, with a sense that somehow they and we alike are sheltered by Holy Wings. Such grace does not make everything all right, but it does give us the courage not to run away.

Unfortunately, many in our world do not experience the red grace of courage. Their loved ones suffer violent or untimely deaths, and they crumble. In many ways crumbling is an honest response. There is wisdom in despair, in falling apart. It is the other side of our interconnectedness. We would not crumble were we not so connected to those we love. Indeed, the world would be a better place were more people capable of crumbling. The problem in our time is not that people are too prone to crumble, but that they have anaesthetized themselves from the sufferings of others so that they are incapable of vulnerability.

The kind of courage Eck found, in facing her brother's death, was the courage to look horror in the face, to be present to it, with a full capacity to crumble, and yet with empathy and strength. Where did she get this strength, this inner peace?

Eck tells us that she got it from the Holy Spirit, and I believe her. I have tried to say that the very Wisdom by which the universe was called into existence is within each of our hearts as a source of strength in time of need. This Wisdom not only *calls* us to courage in times of crisis, she *energizes* us with courage.

Eck explains that Kali offers a similar kind of strength to her followers. The Indian poet Ramprasad ends one of his songs to Kali with the question, "What will you do, bound by Death?" His answer, explains Eck, is: "Call the Mother, She can handle Death" (1993, 142). Somehow, says Eck, the Holy Spirit whose wings gave her the strength to handle death in the morgue was this Mother. In reading the Twenty-third Psalm, Eck was calling the Mother, and through the quiet peace she felt, the Mother responded.

Evil and the Feminine Energy of God

If Ramprasad were Christian, he might have said, "Call the Father, He can handle Death." At the heart of Christianity we have the image of a fatherly God who loves the world so much that he dies for it, on a cross, with blood dripping from his legs and arms and water coming out his side. The image is as violent in its way, as is that of Kali in its way. In the case of Jesus on the cross, the image is of one who suffers death; in the case of Kali, it is of one who claims death as terrain and hence who seems to have power over it.

Christianity also offers the image of a God who has power over death. This is the image of resurrection, of a God who appears anew to people, freshly, amid and after their darkest hours. "Repent," we read in Acts, "that times of refreshing may come from the presence of the Lord" (3:19). Christianity offers a God who both shares in our sufferings and offers solace from them. He both undergoes and helps bring wholeness out of the tragedies of our lives and all lives.

Some Christians say that the sufferings we face, and that other living beings face as well, are caused by God or at least preventable by God. They say that the gratuitous sufferings and untimely deaths that we see around us are part of a cosmic game-plan, designed or at least envisioned by God, within which we play our appointed roles. Thus God's power over death is one of complete control. From the beginningless past God has known exactly what will happen, and when it will happen. In God there are no surprises.

I have proposed an alternative way of understanding God's relation to gratuitous suffering and untimely death. I have suggested that there are things that happen on Earth that are not foreseen by God and that even God cannot prevent. The power of Holy Wisdom is not that of a script-writer who knows our lines in advance and watches us utter them with full knowledge of what we will say. Rather, it is that of a divine Lover who beckons us to speak lines that yield wholeness for ourselves and others, and who shares in our sufferings, and the pain of those whom we victimize as well, even when we speak uncalled-for lines.

One purpose of this chapter has been to suggest that the divine Lover can be experienced, not only as an inward call to wholeness in community with others, but also as an energy in the Earth and ourselves. We experience this energy as the *jagrita* of communities that are wide-awake, as the sacred presence of rivers and streams, as the internal goddesses of our imaginations. The goddesses, the rivers, and the sacred sites can be channels of grace in our lives, faces of God.

But what about the gratuitous suffering and untimely deaths? Are they too faces of God? In some deep way the answer must be yes. At least they can be faces through which we discover God. We discover the Lover in cholera-ridden children and brutally beaten prisoners, in self-hating alcoholics and in the families that suffer their torments, in abused animals and in an ever-despoiled Earth. Somehow, in and through them, we can discover a Mother who "handles" death.

How does she handle it? Two possibilities emerge. One is to say that she handles it by generating it. This is to view the Mother as the underlying cause, not only of *jagrita* and rivers, but also of gratuitous suffering and untimely death. Her female energy empowers not only life but death, not only happiness but sadness, not only compassion but hatred. The analogy offered earlier—that of a Power Source that illuminates light bulbs—encourages this perspective. From this point of view, all the power in the universe is divine power, and all that happens is the dance of God.

The other possibility, and one that I recommend, is different. It says that the Mother handles gratuitous suffering and untimely death, not by generating it, but rather by sharing in it, and by exhibiting a strength to endure it, not only for her sake, but also for that of the living beings whom she loves. In this view, not all things that happen are her dance. There are some serious missteps, which emanate from creative powers not her own, in relation to which she responds with strength and compassion. If we use the metaphor of the Power Source, we must say that the bulbs can resist the power of the Source, acting in ways that block the Generator's healing currents. If the Mother is a generator, she is not all-powerful.

And yet, as Eck says, God claims terrain even over death, even over the resistance of recalcitrant light bulbs. Her power lies in her capacity to be present to the resistance, to be present to the gratuitous suffering and untimely death, to survive it without crumbling. Her healing energy is that of cross-bearing and resurrection, not control.

Is this the God we find in Kali? With Eck, I cannot say. It is clear that Kali invites us to be present to the dark side of life and to survive it not by going around it, but by going through it. Kali invites us to pass through the cross on the way to resurrection. But it is not clear, at least to me, whether Kali herself causes the crosses or just gives us the strength to endure them.

The cross-bearing and resurrecting God is, however, the God we find in the Nazarene. His face is important to us, not because it promises a life free of gratuitous suffering and untimely death, but because it reveals a Lover who joins us in that life and gives us the energy to become whole within the very conditions of finitude. Eck's encounter with God through Hinduism suggests that this energy can be felt as feminine, as Shakti. From her story we are invited to recognize that our Lover—revealed so poignantly in the life, death, and resurrection of Jesus—may indeed be our Mother as well as our Father. However the Hindu might see things, we see Christ in Kali, and Kali in Christ. We can be grateful to Hinduism, and to Holy Wisdom, for stretching our imaginations in just this direction.

Chapter 10

Communion with Spirits and Ancestors

Selected Lessons from North American Native Traditions for Remembering Our Roots in the Earth

I have a few ecologically sensitive white students who wish they were Hopi or Navaho or Sioux. In part, they are expressing a legitimate spiritual hunger. They sense that native traditions are more spiritually attuned to the Earth than most Western traditions, and they want to be similarly attuned. However, these students are also doing an injustice to native peoples. They carry around peace pipes and participate in sweat lodges, but they have little if any interest in the struggle for survival that characterizes so many native peoples today. They are rendering unto Indians that which belongs to archetypes.

It is no accident that some native peoples are angry. Consider Andy Smith, a Cherokee and member of Women of All Red Nations. In an article called "For All Those Who Were Indian in a Former Life," she strongly criticizes "New Age feminists" and others who "sell sweat lodges or sacred pipe ceremonies which promise to bring individual and global healing," or who "sell books and records that supposedly describe Indian traditional practices so that you, too, can be Indian." She writes:

> The "Indian" ways that these white, new age "feminists" are practicing have little grounding in reality. . . . White "feminists" want to become only partly Indian. They do not want to be part of our struggles for survival against genocide, and they do not want to fight for treaty rights or an end to substance abuse or sterilization abuse. They do not want to do anything that would tarnish their romanticized notions of what it means to be Indian (1993, 168).

Needless to say, Smith's critique also applies to non-feminists—male and female—who wish to appropriate native ways without taking the time to know native peoples and their communities. Such appropriation amounts to a kind of spiritual materialism. Native ways become commodities in the spiritual marketplace, which we buy as consumers, without regard for the integrity of their owners. Smith's rebuff is simple: "Our spirituality is not for sale" (1993, 171).

Wanting to avoid spiritual materialism, I try to invite native speakers to my college so that they can speak for themselves and describe their communities on their own terms. One such speaker was Martin Brokenleg, an enrolled member of the Rosebud Sioux Tribe in South Dakota and professor of Native American Studies at Augustana College in Sioux Falls. Brokenleg is active in education and counseling programs among Sioux in South Dakota, serving as a consultant to Gifted and Talented American Indian Children of the Northwest and Midwest, the South Dakota State Penitentiary, the South Dakota Indian Affairs Commission, and the South Dakota Children's Home Society. I mention these activities to indicate that he is not the kind of "Indian" who is more interested in selling Indian spirituality than in working with his people. He is a sociologist turned activist, who seeks to rebuild broken lives among his people.

My students came to his lecture in droves. He gave a fascinating talk on Sioux approaches to family and life, spirituality and community. He told many stories about his grandfather and grandmother, about the changes he had seen in his own life, and about the changes he expects to see. Later, in answer to questions, he also described how he tries to integrate the ways of his elders with his Christian faith, without diluting the power of Sioux ways. He was, and is, an Episcopal priest.

After his talk I was left with a question. Mindful of the problem of spiritual materialism, and yet inspired by his example of being both Christian and Native American, I wanted to know if there was a way for non-native Christians to learn from native cultures without pretending that we were Indians in our former lives. I talked with him on the way to the airport and then called him in South Dakota. My question to him was straightforward: "Is there a way for non-native Christians to learn from Lakota and other native ways *with respect?*"

Brokenleg's answer was equally straightforward, and went something like this: "Yes, you can learn from our people, and we from yours. It all hinges on the idea of kinship. At a deep level, we Lakota believe that all creatures are our kin, our family. We believe that you can learn from us *with respect* if you act like a relative to us; we can learn from you if we do the same. We act like relatives to one another if we spend time with each other; if we help each other out; if we take the time to build relationships."

In this chapter, then, I hope to follow his advice. My aim is to identify and discuss some spiritual lessons that I think white, non-native peoples might learn from native peoples *if* we "act like relatives" to them.

In the current cultural context, acting like a relative must be political as well as spiritual. If we are "relatives" to our native friends, we will build relationships by supporting native aspirations for survival and self-determination, for community and cultural preservation. This will involve time, money, and energy. But our help will not be arrogant. Contrary to times past, we will not think of ourselves as saviors. Rather, we need the wisdom to realize that, in many instances, native peoples do not seek greater assimilation into white culture, but rather greater independence from that culture. The same applies, of course, to African Americans, Asian Americans, and Hispanic Americans. If we are white, we will have the wisdom to relativize our cultural norms and accept our place as one among many.

Presuming such engagement with native causes, we can then allow our lives to be transformed by native wisdom. Following the advice of Smith, we ought not appropriate specific ceremonies and ritual practices unless we are invited to do so by respected elders. Such elders are not easy to find. As Smith explains: "Many non-Indians express their confusion about knowing who is and who is not a legitimate spiritual teacher. The only way for non-Indians to know who legitimate teachers are is to develop ongoing relationships with Indian communities. When they know the community, they will learn who the community respects as its spiritual leaders. This is a process that takes time" (1993, 171).

But let me be honest. Many of us will not take this time. Either we are separated from reservations by long distances and cannot make contact with local communities, or we are so overwhelmed by other activities that our energies are depleted. We can still support native causes with our time and money. But we ought not pretend that we know native communities and their elders.

Martin Brokenleg said that even those of us restricted by distance and time can learn from native traditions. He urged us not to give up on making contact with local communities, no matter how minimal. "Even a little contact is better than none," he said, "not only because you need it, but because we do as well. Our numbers are so small—less than one half of one percent of the United States population—and we need our non-native friends." Given at least aspirations for contact, however, he said that we can indeed learn from native ways by opening ourselves to the more general attitudes toward life that characterize many native cultures, and then ask how such values, if internalized, might change our own lives.

This is my intention in the remainder of this chapter. I identify three attitudes toward life that are found in many if not all traditional native paths, and I try to show how these attitudes might change the lives of white, middle-class, non-native Christians such as I. The attitudes are 1) that authentic spirituality lies in being bonded with, and indebted to, a specific geographical place or life community, on which our survival depends and which partly forms our own spiritual identity; 2) that the inhabitants of a given life community include not only the visible creatures but also invisible spirits and ancestors who can be encountered in dreams and visions; and 3) that we make peace with the visible and invisible dimensions of life not only by wisdom and vision but by bodily rituals. At the end of the chapter I suggest that the eucharist can be one such bodily ritual.

One brief caveat before proceeding. It is difficult, if not dangerous, to generalize about Native American attitudes toward life. Oren Lyons, a faithkeeper of the Onondaga Nation in upstate New York, estimates that there are five hundred distinct cultural traditions which still maintain sacred relations with diverse bioregions on the North American continent (Grim 1993, 41). If this is the case, most non-natives know but a little about a few of the five hundred. Certainly this true of me. I can only hope that the three attitudes I identify are common to many of the five hundred traditions. They are generalizations, not universalizations.

Fidelity to Place

To the outsider, one thing that is striking about many native ways is their sensitivity to specific life communities. By "specific life communities" I mean identifiable geographical regions—replete with animals, plants, and people— that serves as a source of survival and spiritual identity. I mean the Arctic coast for the Eskimo, or the boreal regions of the subarctic for the Algonquin, or the Eastern woodlands for the Ojibwa-Chippewa, or the plains and prairie grasslands for the Lakota, or the desert Southwest for the Navaho and Pueblo. For most Native peoples, it seems, specific life communities of this sort are essential to the spiritual life. Spirituality cannot be separated from survival, and survival cannot be separated from geography. We make contact with the Great Spirit when we know and love where we are.

Already many of us who are white and middle class are challenged. Do we know where we are? Let the reader recall the sense of place test offered in Chapter 2. There I proposed that we know where we are if we can respond with facility to the following kinds of questions and challenges:

- How many days 'til the moon is full?
- What was the rainfall in your area last year?
- Name five native edible plants in your region and their seasons of availability.
- From what direction do winter storms generally come in your region?
- How long is the growing season where you live?
- On what day of the year are the shadows the shortest where you live?
- When do the deer rut in your region, and when are the young born?
- Name five grasses in your area.
- Name five resident and five migratory birds in your area.
- Trace the water you drink from precipitation to tap.

If you are a white, middle-class American living in a suburb or apartment, my guess is that you, like I, do not do well on such a test. Rootless consumerism has taught many of us to be upwardly mobile at the expense of knowing when the deer rut in our environs, or what grasses grow naturally in our area, or even where our water goes when it leaves the tap.

Equally lamentable, many of us are not troubled by our ignorance. Our problem is twofold: one cultural and one religious.

"Indoorism"

The cultural problem might be called "indoorism." Indoorism is a way of thinking in which we take the experience of being indoors, in relatively comfortable and controlled settings, as normative for the nature of reality. Our world is that of central air, of walls and windows, of comfort and convenience. The avoidance of pain is one of our primary concerns; we assume that life is supposed to be easy and pain-free. Nature is something "outside" that we visit and enjoy on occasion, but whose elements we never really get to know except on vacations and retreats. Usually we gravitate only toward the "pretty" areas, those that offer scenic beauty. Except when we "get away for a while," rutting deer and edible grasses, resident birds and waning moons are not real to us. Reality is what happens amid indoor comfort.

To be sure, some of us are less indoorist than others. Those of us who take regular walks, or who garden, or who do manual labor in the hot sun, are less indoorist than those of us who work at computer terminals or shuffle paper all day. Still, if we live in the city, we are all seduced by indoorism to one degree or another. Migratory birds and growing seasons are not part of our frame of reference. Only when we are reminded of them, through specials on television or in books, do they become part of our world. The fact that we need to be reminded bespeaks our indoorism.

Our religion has accentuated the problem. For many modern Christians, Christianity is a text-based, creed-centered, human-preoccupied, indoor religion. Often our worship is symptomatic of the problem. It almost always occurs in an indoor setting, separated from the out of doors by stained glass windows and controlled temperatures. Moreover, the sermons we hear almost always stress human-divine and human-human relations at the expense of human-Earth relations. While decorative plants may grace our sanctuaries, animals are left outside, where they "belong." It is assumed, by contrast, that we belong inside. Our task, it seems, is to know the name of God's only begotten Son, but not the names of wild grasses and resident birds.

Traditional Native ways rightly challenge indoorism. In the first place, they invite us to have more worship services outside, in the great cathedral of the open sky, where we can honor our kinship with the animals and wild plants. Equally important, however, they invite us to recognize that our spiritual identities are partly formed by the very geographies and life communities in which we are situated.

Knowing Our Place

To illustrate the connection between a spiritual identity and local geography, consider the following story in the life of Oren Lyons, the Onondagan faithkeeper mentioned earlier. The story is told by Huston Smith.

> Oren Lyons was the first Onondagan to enter college. When he returned to his reservation for his first vacation, his uncle proposed a fishing trip on a lake. Once he had his nephew in the middle of the lake where he wanted him, he began to interrogate him. "Well, Oren," he said, "you've been to college; you must be pretty smart now from all they've been teaching you. Let me ask you a question. Who are you?" Taken aback by the question, Oren fumbled for an answer. "What do you mean, who am I? Why, I'm your nephew, of course." His uncle rejected his answer and repeated his question. Successively, the nephew ventured that he was Oren Lyons, an Onondagan, a human being, a man, a young man, all to no avail. When his uncle had reduced him to silence, his uncle said, "Do you see that bluff over there? Oren, you are that bluff. And that giant pine on the other shore? Oren, you are that pine. And this water that supports this boat. You are this water" (1991, 371).

If we are urban Christians, most of us need uncles of this sort. We need people who will remind us that our very identities are defined, not only by the people we know and the God we love, but also by the bluffs and pines and waters that have nourished our souls.

Moreover, as Oren Lyons's uncle made clear, it is not just *any* water or *any* pine or *any* bluff that makes us who we are. Rather, it is *this* water and *this* pine and *this* bluff. It is that portion of the Earth in which we and our ancestors have lived; to which we feel bonded; and to which we are indebted for our very survival. Our souls are properly defined not simply by our loyalty to "the Earth" as seen in photographs taken from space, but by loyalty to local places. We find ourselves when we come home to our local bioregions, when we let them form us and make us more human.

Before the advent of the European onto the North American continent, there were plenty of bioregions to go around. Individual tribes could live generation after generation in particular life communities, establishing their own distinctive relations with the flora and fauna around them and with fellow members of their tribes. To be sure, there was warfare among tribes fighting for land. But there was nothing compared to the wars over land that resulted from white conquest.

In our time, by contrast, most bioregions are not, and cannot be, home to exclusive cultural groupings. There are too many people and not enough bioregions to go around. Except for cultural groups whose very survival depends on exclusive inhabiting of particular lands, as is the case with native peoples in the United States and indigenous peoples throughout the world, exclusionary attachments to local bioregions are neither possible nor desirable. Different peoples with different histories and different customs need to share the same bioregions. They—we—must learn to live together.

Still, we can learn from traditional native ways. Just as their spiritualities have taught them to be faithful to particular portions of the Earth, so ours can teach us as well. We are faithful to our local bioregions, not when we require that all other people follow our cultural and religious ways, but when we learn to share the land with them, and to share ourselves with the land. Sharing ourselves with the land is somewhat analogous to a marriage. We approach the land with genuine needs for intimacy and communications, but we also approach it with a deep desire to help keep it healthy, to help sustain it, and to nourish it. We care for it because, to paraphrase Oren Lyons's uncle, it is who we are.

In Chapter 3 I tried to spell out some practical implications of being faithful to the land. I suggested that we are faithful to the land when we make peace with it, understanding ourselves as kin to the flora and fauna that surround us and working to develop local communities that are humane and sustainable. As a general rule of thumb, I suggested that such communities might embody ten key values: grassroots democracy, economic self-reliance, nonviolence, respect for diversity, global awareness, personal and social responsibility, political decentralization, future focus, ecological wisdom, and post-patriarchal attitudes. Certainly not all native peoples subscribe to these values, but these values represent our way of internalizing that fidelity to place that we so often see in native traditions.

In addition to committing ourselves to such values, however, we must learn another lesson from native traditions. This is a lesson that many native peoples today are seeking to learn themselves. We must learn to "stay put" and "stay at home," even when we are tempted to move on to greener pastures. For many of us, this will not be easy. We have been conditioned by consumer culture to think that upward mobility and material improvement are moral obligations, almost commandments from God. As a result, most of us who are white and non-native, along with many who are native, do not live within walking distance of our parents and grandparents, or of the place we were born. Native traditions tell us that we and our families must live in a place for many generations before it truly becomes home. Most of us will not give our places this chance.

We need to see through the illusions of upward mobility and "come home" to our native places, wherever they are. We need to "stay put" even when dreams of material improvement encourage us to leave. We will not be universal people who are at home anywhere on the planet; we will be particularized people who love learning about many places on the planet, but who are also at home in local places that we have grown to love. To the degree that we experience such homecoming, we will find our true identities. Along with

Oren Lyons and his uncle, we will know, in our own way, that we are *this* bluff and *this* pine and *these* people.

Communion with Spirits and Ancestors

If fidelity to place represents one lesson we can learn from native peoples, a second concerns the invisible dimensions of life: the worlds of spirits and ancestors. By "spirits" I mean immaterial presences that we cannot see with our eyes, but which we can nevertheless encounter in dreams, visions, and ceremonies. And by "ancestors" I mean human beings and other creatures who have died, but who nevertheless live among us in memory, imagination, and vision.

It is not fashionable for scientifically minded, liberal Christians to be interested in spirits and ancestors. We sometimes call such interests superstitious or naive. If this is the case, then native peoples are indeed superstitious and naive. However, the naiveté may lie with us, not them.

In native societies, as in most indigenous traditions, it is taken for granted that reality includes immaterial as well as material presences. The universe is not limited to the visible plane of existence; rather, it includes many planes of existence, some visible and some not. The invisible planes constitute the spirit worlds. Such worlds are not necessarily supernatural, as if separated from nature by an unbridgeable gulf. Rather, they are part of nature itself. This means that for native and other indigenous peoples, the Earth is not just what we see with our eyes. It is also what we know through dreams and visions. This is why Western-trained ecologists cannot really know a local place or a life community as a native person knows it. The ecologist has been trained to look at the plants and animals but not the spirits and ancestors.

In some native tribes certain people—shamans—are thought to be experts at making contact with these invisible planes. They travel to the spirit worlds, some above and some below the visible plane, encounter various kinds of guiding spirits, and then bring back reliable knowledge for healing and social guidance. They are adventurers of the spirit. In most native traditions, however, access to the spirit world is not limited to the shaman. All people are to some extent able to experience the spirits and the ancestors, often in the context of public ceremonies. Consider the following account of a prayer ceremony held among members of the Onondagan Nation. The ceremony lasted about fifty minutes, during which no eyes were closed.

On the contrary, everyone seemed to be actively looking around. As the prayer was offered in native tongue, I could understand nothing of it. When I later asked its content, I was told that the entire prayer had been devoted to naming everything in sight, animate and inanimate, with the invisible spirits of the area included, inviting them to join the occasion and bless it (Huston Smith 1991, 371).

The spirits and ancestors were not simply present, they were participants in the ceremony, active members of the life community. Without them, the ceremony would have been incomplete.

The Communion of Saints

For Christians, this inclusion of spirits in a worship service may at first seem strange. Perhaps we are like the ecologist who has been taught to limit reality to what can be seen by the eyes, measured by instruments, and controlled by technology.

On further consideration, however, we might also recognize our own parallels to the ceremony above. In worship services, for example, we usually affirm a communion of saints, whose members include departed ancestors, who somehow join us in the act of worship. In some traditions these saints are limited to the extraordinarily God-centered Christians who have come before us and become church-sanctioned saints. In others, however, the saints of the past are understood more generally as all the Christians who have come before us, whose joys and sufferings are parts of our lives, and who form a cloud of witnesses to God's grace.

The native emphasis on a kinship of all creatures invites us to extend our understanding of saints still further to include *all* the departed relatives to whom we are indebted: the four-leggeds and the winged creatures as well as the two-leggeds. At least this is the direction in which a Christianity with roots and wings will move. Ecologically sensitive Christians number among the departed saints of our lives the first generation of stars after the big bang; the first living cells on our planet; the early amphibians; the first mammals; the ancient hunters and gatherers; the first farmers; and, of course, our own great-grandparents. At some deep level we recognize with the Native American that we are all related, and hence that the communion of saints is a communion of kin.

Regardless of how narrowly or widely we wish to define saints, however, native traditions invite us to recognize that in some prayerful circumstances we might actually encounter our departed ancestors in vivid and palpable ways. As an example of such an encounter, consider what happened at a worship service in Dallas, Texas, at Perkins Theological Seminary. As described by Ruben Habito, who teaches at the seminary, it shows how, even for Christians, departed ancestors can be "right here."

The occasion was a worship service commemorating the deaths of martyrs for justice in Central America. Habito writes:

As the participating congregation went up in two files to the altar to receive the communion bread, a deacon standing beside the communion minister handed each of us a small wooden cross made out of two popsickle sticks pasted one across the other, and with it a small slip of paper to bring back to our pews and keep. On each slip was written a name, a country, and a date. On mine was the small inscription: Victoria de la Roca, Guatemala, Jan. 6, 1982.

After we were all settled back in our pews and after the usual momentary silence, we were invited to stand up one after another and, holding the small wooden cross up high with the right hand, to recite the name of the person written on the slip of paper we received, saying, " . . . Presente!"

It was indeed an event that cut through barriers of time and space as we stood up, one after another, cross uplifted, reciting, "Victoria de la Roca, Presente!" "Jose Bernardo, Presente!" "Estrella Consolacion, Presente!" . . . At that moment of "Presente!" the images of all those men and women, young and old, still living or already deceased, that I had met in my many visits to my own country, the Philippines, struggling for their very survival under situations very similar to those of grass roots communities in Central and Latin America, came to the fore to me in a rather vivid way. They were all right here, with all their struggles and their wounds and their tears, as well as their hopes and their joys and their laughter, "Presente" (Habito 1993, 110-11).

In some ways, of course, what happened at Perkins Chapel may seem different from what happened at the Onondagan ceremony in upstate New York. Habito speaks of the presence of images from the past, whereas the Onondagan speak of the presence of spirits. The people who appeared to Habito lived hundreds if not thousands of miles away; those who appeared to the Onondagan were closely connected with the local landscapes. Still, for Habito as for the Indians, living people from the past were palpably present as fellow participants in a religious service. They were "presente!"

But were they really present? Or were they mere projections?

Shortly I will offer a speculative answer to this question. I will propose that, with the help of Jungian psychology and process theology, we might recognize that spirits and ancestors are surfacings from the memory banks of a collective unconscious, and/or that they are actual beings who inhabit a spirit world. To approach this more speculative concern, however, we best consider still one more example of how spirits and ancestors can be encountered. Let us consider the vision quest.

The Vision Quest

The vision quest is sometimes called democratized shamanism. In the Plains Indian traditions, for example, any and all can partake of it, though, according to Joseph Epes Brown, men did so more frequently than women (1990, 15). It is an occasion when, in isolation, a person encounters spirits and ancestors that offer guidance for self and in many instances for community. Some native peoples consider it the most important aspect of Native American religions. As one Sioux Indian, Mary Crow Dog, puts it:

Dreams and visions are very important to us, maybe more important than any other aspect of Indian religion. I have met Indians from South and Central America, from Mexico and from the Arctic Circle. They all pray for visions, they are all "crying for a dream," as the Sioux call it (quoted in Comstock 1995, 77).

In Mary Crow Dog's case the visions came with the help of peyote, understood not as an artificial drug but rather as a dimension of the Earth itself. Describing her first experience with peyote, she writes:

I became part of the earth because peyote comes from the earth, even tastes like the earth sometimes. And so the earth was in me and I in it, Indian earth making me more Indian. And to me peyote was people, was alive, was a remembrance of things long forgotten (quoted in Comstock 1995, 77).

In most other instances among North American Indians, however, plant hallucinogens are not used. Visions generally come with fasting, drumming, dancing, sweating, isolation, and the endurance of physical pain rather than with herbs.

To give us a feel for the concrete content of a particular vision, we might consider the first vision quest of John Fire Lame Deer, a Sioux elder who shared his experience in *Lame Deer: Seeker of Visions* (1976). Lame Deer describes how, after fasting and doing a sweat lodge as a young boy, a medicine man named Chest took him to a hole dug in a hill and left him there for four days without food or water. It was his first *hanblechia*, his first vision-seeking. "If Wakan Taka, the Great Spirit, would give me the vision and the power, I would become the medicine man and perform many ceremonies" (quoted in Comstock 1995, 51).

Lame Deer did indeed become a medicine man and leader of his local community. Among the many realities he experienced in his first vision were numerous animal spirits, including birds. Isolated in his vision hole, he perceived that a voice was trying to tell him something. The voice was that of a bird and, all of a sudden, he found himself in the sky with birds, looking down on the hill where his hole was. The birds said to him:

We are the fowl people, the winged ones, the eagles and the owls. We are a nation and you shall be our brother. You will never kill or harm any of us. You are going to understand us whenever you come to seek a vision on this hill. You will learn about herbs and roots, and you will heal people. You will ask them for nothing in return. A man's life is short. Make yours a worthy one (quoted in Comstock 1995, 53-54).

After his vision of the birds, his great-grandfather then appeared to him:

Then I saw a shape before me. It rose from the darkness and the swirling fog that penetrated my earth hole. I saw that this was my great-grandfather, Tahca Ushte, Lame Deer, old man chief of the Minneconjou. I could see the blood dripping from my great-grandfather's chest, where a white soldier had shot him. I understood that my great-grandfather wished me to take his name (quoted in Comstock 1995, 54).

Lame Deer's grandfather had been killed at Wounded Knee, an uprising in 1890 provoked by failure of the United States government to keep treaty promises. Even though dead, he was somehow also alive, offering guidance to his great-grandson, soon to be a medicine man.

What Really Happened?

What are we to make of a vision such as this? Are we to assume that the bird spirits and great-grandfather actually presented themselves to Lame Deer's experience? Or are we to assume that they were apparitions or hallucinations projected by Lame Deer's brain, having no agency of their own? Did Lame Deer *receive* them, or did he *project* them?

In most of our experiences reception and projection occur together. The dichotomy between discovery and generation is a false one. When someone walks into our field of vision, for example, that person is both "given" to us as someone to be perceived and also "interpreted" by us in light of our previous experience. We say to ourselves, "Here comes Mary," and we also are aware of the various things we feel about Mary, which shape the "Mary" we experience.

The same dynamic applies to invisible realities. We both receive them and interpret them. They come to us and we to them simultaneously. Consider our own dreams. Living beings and landscapes appear to us from a night world not of our making, and, as they do, we respond to them emotionally. No less than Mary, they are given to us and yet we also interpret them.

After the dream, of course, we may conclude that some of the things that came to us were but figments of our imaginations, as if our own egos had projected them onto a blank screen at a movie theater. This is the way sense-bound, mono-dimensional visions of reality encourage us to look at things. They encourage us to say that Lame Deer was "just projecting" when he saw the bird spirits and his great-grandfather.

But perhaps such a view is too narrow. It fails to honor the truth of Lame Deer's vision on *his* terms. My suggestion is that a Christianity with roots and wings will seek a more generous interpretation of Lame Deer's experience. It will recognize the fact that things *present themselves* to us in our dreams and visions, and that there is more to reality than meets the physical eyes. There are at least two movements in contemporary Western thought that can help move us in this direction: Jungian psychology and process theology.

Jungian Psychology

Jung invites us to take a first step in honoring the truth of Lame Deer's vision by helping us recognize that the human mind is much more than ordinary waking consciousness. According to Jung, our minds include unconscious as well as conscious dimensions, the former invisible to the visible eye yet deeply influential of our innermost feelings.[1] We encounter the unconscious dimensions in visions and dreams, the latter of which are, to quote Jung's teacher Freud, a royal road to the unconscious.

From Jung's point of view, as from Freud's, most of our experience is unconscious rather than conscious. Our ordinary waking consciousness is to our unconscious experience as a tip of an iceberg is to the iceberg beneath it, or as a cork floating on an ocean is to the ocean itself. Our minds or psyches are the entirety, not just the tip but the whole iceberg, not just the cork but the cork and the ocean. Our task as humans, says Jung, is to allow for integration between the conscious and unconscious dimensions of our minds so that we can live creatively and compassionately. When a genuine dialogue between the conscious and unconscious dimensions of our minds occurs, we are slave to neither but open to both. We know the truths of ordinary waking consciousness and also the truths of dreams and visions. For some people, such integration occurs naturally through the ordinary course of life; for others, it never occurs; and for still others, integration requires conscious effort or "inner work."

With what do we work when we do inner work? From Jung's point of view, we work with energies and forms of intelligence that lie beneath the surface of our conscious life, but that nevertheless shape our innermost feelings, moods, and motivations. Drawing upon the analogy of cork and ocean, we can imagine these energies as buried treasures or coral reefs lying under the surface, yet encounterable in dreams and visions. The treasures appear to us in symbolic form: birds and clowns, monsters and friends, animals and buildings. Yet they are charged with forms of energy and insight that lie within us, and that may appear to others through different symbols.

Assume, for example, that we all carry within us a potentiality for innocence that is part of who we are, but that is lost to our more jaded, conscious life. One person may experience this potentiality through the image of an innocent child, another through a vulnerable lamb. In each instance we experience a dimension of ourselves, but we do so in "languages" appropriate to our own life experiences.

Behind this Jungian theory of the unconscious lies a more general theory of memory. The buried treasures and coral reefs of our unconscious minds are themselves ways in which the past lives in the present. Our innermost energies and forms of intelligence are living memories.

---

1. Much of my discussion of Jung is drawn from Johnson 1986, 5-12.

Some of these memories come from our past experience. In my own life, for example, memories of being at the Guadalupe River at age six are of this sort. They are unique to me. My friends do not share them. They are part of my personal unconscious.

Other memories that shape my life may have more collective origins. The wisdom of innocence, for example, is a living memory that I share not only with friends, but with many people the world over. In all of us there is a "small child" or "innocent lamb" that is part of who we are, at least in potential. It is that side of us which looks at the world, or can look at the world, with soft eyes, trustingly. Somehow, in seeing actual children and lambs, we "remember" a time when we were ourselves innocent, either in this life or a previous life. Such memories form part of a collective unconscious that we share with others, which may be encoded in our genes or transmitted in more direct ways, or both.

The memories within the collective unconscious that we share with others can be of two sorts. Some are distinctive potentialities that we share with other members of our race, or our culture, or our ethnic tradition. Their collectivity is limited to "our people," whoever we are. Other memories, however, we share with all humans. These are energies and forms of intelligence that we share with others on the basis of a common heritage that extends back to the hunters and gatherers, the first hominids, and the forms of life from which they emerged. Indeed, this more collective past extends back to the very history of the Earth, the solar system, and the universe. We carry within us memories not only of *our* people but also of *all* people; and not only of *all* people, but of *all* creatures. In the house of the collective unconscious there are many mansions.

If we assume that there is truth in Jungian ideas such as these, then it seems to me that they offer a very helpful first step in honoring both the idea of kinship that we find in Native traditions and also in honoring the particularities of Lame Deer's vision. They help us honor the idea of kinship by suggesting that we are indeed kin to all other creatures and, more important, that we carry within ourselves feelings of such kinship. Somehow, at levels too deep for words, we have feelings for what it would be like to be birds and reptiles and amoeba and shooting stars, because their experiences are part of our own collective unconscious. Native traditions allow those feelings to surface, so that we might be better integrated as human beings. They remind us that we know something of what it is like to be a bird, because we carry within us the energies of birds themselves.

Jung's ideas help us honor the particularities of Lame Deer's vision by suggesting that his vision was indeed an encounter with the collective unconscious of his own experience. On the one hand, the great-grandfather was probably unique to him and his tribe, to those who had actually known the man. He was a living memory for Lame Deer, but not for us. On the other hand, the bird spirits may have been forms of animal intelligence from which, as just noted, we all inherit. The difference is that Lame Deer knew that he was a bird as well as a man. Most of us who are white and Christian have not yet evolved to such integrated knowledge. We still talk about human nature as if it excluded birds and plants and stars.

Process Theology and Spirit Worlds

If Jung's ideas help us take a first step in recognizing the truth of Lame Deer's vision, process theology helps us take a second. It invites us to honor the *possibility* that the Earth itself is richer than the secular world imagines, that it includes spirits and ancestors as well as plants and animals.

Along with Jung, process theologians believe that conscious experience is but the tip of the iceberg; that our unconscious minds contain within them forms of wisdom and energy from the near and distant past; that these intelligences and energies can be directly perceived in dreams and visions. In addition, so we learn from Jung and from process theology, there is a healing presence at work in our lives: in our dreams as well as our ordinary waking consciousness, in our fantasies as well as our reflections, in our bodies as well as our minds. We can call this healing presence God or Holy Wisdom or, as Jung sometimes does, the Self. Whatever name we use, the presence is a Lure toward wholeness in community with others. The Lure beckons us to make peace with the worlds around us and within us, with our external neighbors and our internal archetypes.

Process theologians suggest further that some of these "internal energies" may not be "internal" at all, but rather external, part of our own natural and cosmic surroundings. Some of the spirits and ancestors may be *real*, not only in the sense of being living memories in our unconscious minds, but also in the sense of being living presences, contemporary to our own lives, who inhabit other planes of existence. Perhaps a story can illustrate.

Many years ago I was taking a course on process theology from John Cobb, perhaps the leading process theologian of his generation. While teaching the course, he was forced to miss several days of class to attend a conference, "The Rights of Nature." Several Native elders attended the conference, and they chose to participate by taking participants to a wilderness area which was, for them, sacred ground. As the participants sat together in this remote area, the elders explained to the white participants that they could actually hear their ancestors dancing on the ancestral grounds. As they placed their ears to the ground, their ancestors were present, singing and dancing.

Cobb returned to class after the event and described the experience. I remember asking why he was not skeptical of the elders' point of view. He explained that, from a process point of view, living beings that perish do not become nonexistent. Rather, they continue to exist as objectively immortal in the conscious and non-conscious memories of those who succeed them. Their various forms of wisdom and energy are not invented by us, they are given to us in the very depths of our own experience as mediated by the universe. Various dimensions of the universe—sacred soils of our ancestors, for example—may trigger such memories. If we put our ear to the ground, we may indeed make contact with such memories.

Cobb further explained that, from the perspective of Whiteheadian cosmology, it is *possible* that the living beings continue to exist after death, not only as objects in the memories of those who come after them, but even as self-conscious subjects. This is because, for Whitehead, reality itself is multi-dimensional. There is nothing absolute about three-dimensional space. It is one plane of existence, which may well be complemented by others of different nature, some overlapping and some not.

I was not expecting to hear such speculations from an esteemed professor. As I was taking a course on process theology, I was taking a course in biblical studies, in which we were learning to "de-mythologize" biblical stories. Cobb's approach seemed to "re-mythologize" a cosmos that I was learning to "de-mythologize."

Still, I understood his logic and, over the years, I came to agree with it. I am struck by the fact that Whitehead, a well-known philosopher of science and mathematician, was open to possibilities of a more enchanted universe. Perhaps it had something to do with Whitehead's mathematical mindset. As a mathematician, Whitehead was fully aware that humans can develop well-defined geometries for universes we cannot see with our eyes but can imagine in our heads. He knew that we can articulate in some detail the geometry for a forty-four dimensional cosmos, or the algebra for an eighty-eight dimensional universe. Accordingly, he found it natural to assume that universes very different from our own are possible. He left open the question as to whether or not such possible universes are actual.

Perhaps native peoples offer some evidence. Perhaps in their vision quests and ceremonies they see things that we do not see, but could see if more of our perceptual doors were opened. Christians with roots and wings can and should be open to this possibility. With Whitehead and process theologians, we can recognize the *fact* that alternative universes—spirit worlds, if you will—are empirically possible. We should take the testaments of Native Americans and indigenous peoples the world over that at least some of these worlds are actual. If this is the case, then Lame Deer was right. When he saw his great-grandfather, he was not simply witnessing a surfacing from his unconscious mind. Rather, he was being visited by his great-grandfather, who died long ago, but who still lived at the time of his vision, and perhaps still lives today.

Jesus as Departed Ancestor

Lame Deer's experience ought not be so odd to believing Christians. In the Christian tradition we also have stories of departed ancestors who survive death. Jesus was one of them. He was, and is, a departed ancestor who now resides in a very mysterious spirit world, uniquely close to God. He "sits at the right hand of God."

For many white, non-native Christians, however, this living ancestor has been reduced to a doctrine. Factually, Jesus may be a departed ancestor who lives in our collective unconscious or in a spirit world; functionally, he has become a doctrine, creed, and abstraction. The liberal talks "about" the historical Jesus, insisting that he not be reduced to a god; the conservative talks "about" the Christ, insisting that he not be reduced to a man. Neither approaches Jesus as a native might. As a Comanche once put it: "The White Man talks about Jesus; we talk to Jesus" (quoted in Tedlock 1975, xx).

Perhaps Native Americans can help us talk to Jesus again. We do this departed ancestor no service by reducing him to doctrine. More important than establishing his ontological status is encountering his living presence, directly, in the here-and-now, whatever christological ascriptions we may or may not attach to him. If there is a uniquely Christian vision quest, it probably lies in "talking to Jesus."

Our modes of talking will differ. Some will do so with feelings, some with silence, some with song, and some with words. We have many forms of communication, many forms of "talking." Each can be a language through which we talk to Jesus.

Moreover, the Jesus to whom we talk may appear to us in different ways. In our dreams and visions he may appear to us as a young child, as a cross, as a lamb, as a mother hen, as a great-grandfather, as bread and wine. Or, if our internal states are less visual in orientation, he may appear to us as a song, or a sound, or a feeling, or a sensation in our bodies. Wherever there is healing and wholeness there, for the Christian, is the departed Nazarene. He will be with us always. His "face" assumes a language we can understand, guiding us toward a *shalom* we need.

Finding the Holy in Body and Ritual

As a departed ancestor, Jesus can appear to us in still more palpable ways. While he may indeed be encounterable in internal states of consciousness, we can also find him in the Earth itself. Just as natives sometimes find their departed ancestors in the wind and dust of their surroundings, so we can find the departed Christ in the elements of our own lives: old letters, old buildings, old trees, an old Earth. One contemporary Christian who indicates this possibility is Kathleen Norris, author of the best-selling *Dakota: A Spiritual Geography*.[2]

The essays in *Dakota* recount Norris's own conversion back to Christianity after having abandoned it for much of her adult life. A professional essayist

---

2. I discovered Norris's work in two ways. Martin Brokenleg recommended her to me, and about the same time, a review of *Dakota* by Debra Bendis appeared in *The Christian Century* (Bendis 1994). My description of her work parallels Bendis's review.

and poet, Norris and her husband moved to Lemmon, South Dakota, from New York in order to settle the affairs of her grandparents, who owned a family farmhouse in the area. They had intended to stay only for a year, but gradually they found themselves drawn to the landscapes and the people.

Theirs was not a romantic projection. In many ways the people of South Dakota were less open-minded and the landscapes much barer than anything they had known in New York. But there was something real, something palpable, about both the landscapes and the local people. Somehow the quietness and slower pace of South Dakota helped them find a quietness and a freshness in their own hearts. They discovered the joy of allowing a life community full of finite people and rugged landscapes to shape their spirits.

Norris credits the landscape itself for much of her spiritual growth. She writes: "The Plains have been essential not only for my growth as a writer, they have formed me spiritually. I would even say they have made me a human being." Her words remind us of the sense of place that is so important to many native traditions.

Norris also credits local churches. She had originally left Christianity because of its narrowness and superstition. Moving to South Dakota, Norris had no intention of going back to church. But she gradually got to know some local ministers in the community, and almost by accident, she came to attend church again. In the process, she realized, she would have to confront "the crap I learned in Sunday School." A Presbyterian pastor, steeped in Russian Orthodox spirituality, helped her see through the "crap" to the depth.

Part of the depth lay in a simple discovery of community and character. She recognized that potlucks and service projects have their own ways of binding people together in holy communion and of giving them strength of character.

But part of the depth also lay in a renewed encounter with the eucharist. She found that she could meet other people and Jesus in the simple act of eating bread and drinking wine. Her poem "The Room" describes the process (1994, 720). It begins with a line from a letter Emily Dickinson wrote to Samuel Bowles in 1877: "I went to the Room, as soon as you had gone, to confirm your presence." Then it reads:

> Once you had gone,
> your absence filled the room.
> like changing light,
> like song.
>
> You were everywhere
> I looked—unloseable
> friend—river's edge
> wind on water,
> leaves all green aflame . . .
>
> O, dear Jesus, I am learning to say,
> and the face of Christ you left me—not stern

but sad, you said, very Russian—gazes back at me
with human eyes.

He said:
I am with you always, when
all I wanted was to see you again.
I tasted you
in the bread and wine.

Like any poem, "The Room" can be read in many ways. On one reading, the "you" who left the room seems to be a departed friend, perhaps one who gave her an icon, a "face of Christ" that seemed "very Russian." The friend died; she bemoaned his absence; and yet the things he left behind, including lands he loved, confirmed his presence. He *became* the land and the icons. To use the language of process theology, he became "objectively immortal" in the very objects into which his spirit diffused.

On another reading, the "you" can also be the departed Jesus. It can be Jesus as incarnate in the departed friend or as companion to that friend. In any case, the Nazarene's face appears in icons left behind—the items people learn to love and revere. And it appears also in the river's edge and the wind on the water. On this reading, Jesus too became the land and the icons. Whereas in his life his presence was focused, in his death his presence became more widely available. Wherever people remembered and felt him, he was present.

Of relevance here is the fact that departed ancestors, Jesus and otherwise, can be *tasted* in the palpable elements of the Earth. They become holy spirits who can be directly apprehended: "I *tasted* you in the bread and wine."

This gets at a final lesson to be learned from native traditions. It can be divided into two points. The first is succinctly articulated by Huston Smith. It is that in many native traditions "the holy, the sacred, the wakan as the Sioux call it, need not be exclusively attached, or consciously attached at all, to a distinguishable Supreme Being" (1991, 378). The second is that in meaningful ritual the holy can be directly "tasted" in a bodily way. I conclude with a comment on each of these points.

The Holy as Detached from a Distinguishable Supreme Being

Many if not most native traditions involve belief in a Supreme Being of one sort or another. There is *Tirawa* of the Pawnee; *Wakan Tanka* of the Sioux; *Takanakapsaluk* of the Eskimo; *Poshayaanki'i* of the Zuni; *Ma'ura* of the Winnebago (Tedlock 1975, xvii). Smith's point, however, is that people can experience the holy or the sacred in this world, without explicit reference to that Supreme Being. Belief in the Supreme Being is not as important as it is, for example, in Christianity. Experiencing the holy can be more important.

One scholar of native traditions, John Grim, speaks of this experience as an "intuition of the sacred" (1987, 5). Here the sacred is not unlike the Shakti of Hinduism as described in the previous chapter. It is a divine energy that can be part of holy objects, but that is not precisely identified with the natural energy of those objects. Objects partake of this energy if, as one Dakota chief puts it, Wakan has "stopped":

> The sun, which is so bright and beautiful is one place where he has stopped. The moon, the stars, the wind he has been with. The trees, the animals, are all where he has stopped (quoted in Grim 1987, 5).

In places where Wakan has stopped there remains a kind of sacred energy. We can feel its presence and gain power from it. We may or may not think about a Supreme Being as we experience the power; the experience is more important than theology.

No less than sacred places, sacred rituals can be occasions for experiencing divine energy. While much can be said of the role of ritual in human life, the point I wish to highlight is simply that rituals are bodily. They are things people do with their bodies, together.

Consider the peace pipe ceremonies of the Plains Indians (Brown 1990, 17-18). A peace pipe is passed. Each grain of tobacco has been carefully placed in the pipe, representing a part of creation. When the bowl is full, it is understood to contain all of time and space. The fire burns the tobacco with the help of human breath. The smoke is exhaled east and west, north and south, above and below, and then the smoker blows the smoke on himself. The bodily sensations of mouth on pipe, of breathing in and breathing out, of smoke on the skin and in the air, of other people in one's immediate field of vision: all are part of a sacramental act in which the people become present to one another and to the universe in the immediacy of a timeless moment. The intentions of the participants are quite important. They need to understand the spiritual significance of the ceremony. But the bodily experiences are also important. Without the body there would be no ritual.

Moreover, many kinds of bodily experience can be included within ritual, including self-inflicted pain. Recall the Sun Dance of the Plains Indians. A large circular lodge is constructed, an analogy of creation itself. At the center is placed a tree toward which, and away from which, dancers dance.

> Some dancers make specific vows to pierce the muscles of their chests. Into these cuts are attached thongs that have been tied to a high point in the tree, so that the dancer is now virtually tied to the center and must dance until the flesh breaks lose. Through the rigors and sacrificial elements of these rites the individual participants often receive powers through vision experiences, and the larger community gathered in support of the dancer participates in the sacred powers thus generated (Brown 1990, 16-17).

Clearly the pain is part of the ceremony; without the pain the ceremony would not be effective. But the pain has meaning. The pain is endured not only for the personal gain of the individual but as an act of helping to renew all life and of sharing in the suffering of all life. Were the pain not endured, so the Plains Indians believe, the very energy of the universe would run out.

For many white Christians, the importance of body and ritual have been forgotten. Either we grew up in sacramental traditions that are now meaningless to us, or we grew up in non-ritualistic traditions in which all emphasis was placed on right belief, not right ritual. Either way, we assume that the primary way to experience the holy is through the mind, not the body.

Moreover, for many of us the idea of rituals that involve self-inflicted pain seems downright crazy. Consumer culture has taught us that convenience and pleasure are gods and that inconvenience and pain are devils.

Native defenders of the Sun Dance tradition are familiar with these criticisms. Lame Deer, for example, responds in the following way to white people who criticize the "piercing" of the Sun Dance.

> Some white men shudder when I tell them these things. Yet the idea of enduring pain so that others may live should not strike you as strange. Do you not in your churches pray to one who is "pierced," nailed to a cross for the sake of his people? (quoted in Comstock 1995, 65).

And, of course, he is right. If we are Christian, we do indeed see a man who was pierced for the sake of his people as holy. Ours is not a tradition that identifies happiness with maximal pleasure and minimal pain, but with the meaning found in sharing in the pleasures and pains of others, trustful that both are shared by the very heart of the universe, Holy Wisdom.

Christianity is, or can be, a tradition that celebrates experiencing the holy wherever it can be experienced. While most Christians, like most Sioux, do not separate the holy from the Great Spirit who manifests it, some Christians today find it difficult to believe in that Spirit, at least understood as an all-powerful, all-good Creator who seeks the well-being of each and all. In this book, of course, I have offered a different image of the Spirit. I have proposed that it is all-good but not all-powerful, at least if the latter is understood as all-controlling. I have proposed that there are some things that happen in life that even the Great Spirit cannot prevent.

Still, I understand the indelibility of the monarchical image. Many people have been taught that the only legitimate meaning for the word *God* is that of a Great Spirit who is, or could be, all-controlling. Some then find themselves unable to believe in this Spirit, because they see too much in the world that, in their view, such a Spirit *should* have controlled, were it all-good. For people such as this, I suggest, native emphases on body and ritual can be healing balm. So can traditional emphases on body and ritual in more sacramental forms of Christianity. They can come to recognize that the holy itself can be experienced in ritual and community, even if not exclusively or consciously attached to images of a Supreme Being.

I recall an older graduate student I once knew. We both worked as busboys at a local restaurant and talked often. He had seen much suffering in his life and no longer found belief in God a possibility. And yet he was very active in a local Episcopal church. The liturgy and community and music meant much to him. His own life showed a kind of tenderness and honesty that I found deeply Christian. He traced his own kindness to the gratitude he felt for the local community in which he was privileged to participate. Like Kathleen Norris, he was not that interested in theology. And yet he loved the church more than I did.

At the time I did not understand him. I thought that true Christians must "believe" in Christian basics: God the Father, Son, and Holy Spirit. I imagined that God had only one mode of access to people's lives, namely, through their intellectual assent to the proposition "God exists." Here was a man who did not assent. How could God reach him?

Years later I look back with different eyes. I have met too many people who do not "believe" in orthodox ways, and yet who bear witness to the living Christ in their lives. I have learned from native traditions that the holy can be experienced without attachment to the image of a Supreme Being and that we can experience it with our bodies as well as our minds.

Many who cannot believe in God find the holy in nature. They find sacred presence in the trees and stars, and they do not name it God. For my graduate-school friend, however, the holy had a slightly different location. He found it in ritual and community. He found it in the sounds and silences of the worship service, in the kneeling at the altar for bread and wine, in the affection of friends for one another, in the fun of the potlucks after service. He found it in the soup kitchens sponsored by the church for the homeless in the area, and in the visitations he made to others, and others to him, in times of crisis and need. For him, this was the very stuff of Christianity. It was holy and perhaps even mystical. But it was not dependent on "God the Father."

Did his unbelief matter to God? I cannot answer. I do not know God well enough. But I somehow doubt it. I imagine that the God of Jesus is more interested in being eaten than being flattered. At least we know that Jesus wanted to be eaten: "For my flesh is food indeed, he who eats my flesh and drinks my blood abides in me and me in him" (Jn 6:55-57). My guess is that God wants to be eaten as well.

To eat God is to taste the holy in the ordinary and extraordinary experiences of our lives, taking on the healing power of God when possible, and sharing in the healing suffering of God when necessary. Sometimes, as Sun Dancers well know, the sharing of suffering can be immensely meaningful. Perhaps some of us need to rediscover the truths of ritualized, self-inflicted pain. For others, however, there may well be enough pain as it is. We have no need of more. What is important is that we learn to taste God in the ways appropriate to us. For many of us religion has become a disembodied, de-ritualized affair. It has been reduced to a matter of private belief, as if the holy can reach us only through our minds. From native traditions we are reminded that the holy can also reach us through our bodies: through things we taste, touch, smell, see, and hear. We remember that religion can be danced as well as believed. We discover the earthiness of a Palestinian Jew who once said of bread and wine, in ways more literal than we might ever imagine: "This is my body given for you. Take. Eat."

Conclusion

"Find a Community and Follow a Practice!"

Final Reflections on Community and Prayer

This book has been written for people seeking an alternative to consumerism and fundamentalism. Consumerism tells us that we are saved by shopping alone; fundamentalism tells us that we are saved by ignoring fresh revelation. With many others, I seek a third Way. I seek a path that is rooted in the Earth, open to other religions, and centered in the healing power of the Spirit. I seek a Way with roots and wings.

Roots and wings are metaphors for connectedness and creativity, groundedness and freedom. In the previous chapters I have tried to identify some of the healthy soils into which we might sink our roots and the healing skies into which we might fly. My aim in this conclusion is to review and weave together some of the basic themes I have proposed throughout the book; share some practical advice on spiritual nourishment that I have received from a Buddhist writer; and offer final reflections on community and prayer. Without community and prayer, the ideas in this book remain abstract and disembodied. With them, we just might find our roots and wings.

The Way of Roots and Wings

I have spoken of a third Way between fundamentalism and consumerism. My approach to this Way is Christian. In general, I have found Christianity a nurturing context for spiritual growth and practical peacemaking. But what I find most meaningful about Christianity is not what I learn from the Nicene Creed or the Bible. Rather, it is what I have seen in hardworking mothers and loving fathers, cross-bearing prisoners and courageous addicts, compassionate nurses and kindly housekeepers, outrageous monks and funky poets. The Christian paths they seek to walk, sometimes successfully and sometimes not, speak to me more than the creeds of the church and quotations from the Bible. With them, I would like to walk the Way of Jesus.

215

But we Christians are not the only family on Earth. Our path is neither right for all people nor the best for all purposes. Many Buddhists are better at awakening to interconnectedness, many Jews at finding God through tradition, many Hindus at honoring diversity, and many Native Americans at being bonded with the Earth. In an age of ecology and dialog, those of us who are Christian had best assume a humble place in the larger family of life. Only when we listen and learn from others have we any right to invite them to listen and learn from us. And often we best remain silent.

I have a friend in the environmental movement who is Buddhist, and from whom I have learned much about wisdom and compassion. She does not simply talk Buddhism, she lives it—kindly and gently and mindfully. She is not a saint, and she would laugh at the very idea that she was. But she is at least as saintly as most good Christians I know. She is active in local causes to help the Earth and the human poor. I think Jesus would like her.

Once, in a moment of sharing, she told me of a vision she had while walking on a beach. She is not the visionary type, but she had been taking a course at a local college on the historical Jesus. The approach to Jesus was Jungian, and it had gotten her interested in dreams and visions. As she walked on the beach, she felt the presence of four figures walking alongside her: a Goddess, a Coyote Trickster, the Buddha, and Jesus. She said that each figure had a different presence, a different ambience. They did not seem competitive, but rather friendly to one another and to her. What was unique about Jesus, she said, was that he seemed loving and caring, deeply identified with "the least of these." She said he felt like "a brother." She asked what I thought about the Jesus who had appeared to her. I said, "Yes, this is the Jesus that I love, too." And it is.

At the time of our conversation, her father was very ill. After she asked how I felt about her vision, she asked if she might be able to pray for her father in the name of Jesus, even as she walked her Buddhist path. "Is that all right?" she asked. I said I thought it was fine. "And would you help me pray?" I said I would. So we stood by a tree and prayed for her father, mindfully, in Jesus' name.

Our relationship illustrated interreligious dialogue at its very best. Each of us had something to offer the other, and neither demanded that the other abandon what was dearest. I did not ask that she "become a Christian" and she did not ask that I "become a Buddhist." Our paths were different, but our truths complementary. We helped complete one another.

But let me offer a confession. After we prayed together, I almost added a sermon. I almost said: "And if you'd like to 'become a Christian,' you need not abandon the Goddess or Coyote or the Buddha." I believe this. I believe Buddhists can "become Christians" without denying the truth of Buddha; that Hindus can "become Christian" without denying the many faces of God; and that Native Americans can "become Christian" without denying the wisdom of their elders. Still, I held my tongue. I feared I was trying to convert her.

I do not mean to dismiss the value of individual conversions. I have read *The Autobiography of Malcolm X*. It is one of the most influential books of my life. It helped me understand the rage of some black people against white society, and also the promise of Islam as an empowering religion. I am quite moved by the way in which Malcolm's life came together by his conversion to Islam. I have seen analogous conversions in several African-American friends of mine.

I have also known people whose lives have been made whole by converting to Judaism, Buddhism, and Christianity. I have a former student, born Presbyterian, who converted to Judaism, and whose life is much the better for it. He felt that his heart had always been Jewish and that Christianity was like a foreign set of clothes. I believe him. And I have another student, born Methodist, who converted to Buddhism, and who is now free from chemical addiction thanks to Buddhist meditation. He was "saved," not by Jesus, but by *zazen*.

Indeed, I have many students, born nothing, who have converted to fundamentalist Christianity as a way of finding direction amid life's tragedies. Their parents gave them no religious training at all, and the truths of Christianity—embraced with the whole of their hearts—helped get them off drugs and violence. Their theological nozzles are too narrow for my liking, but with the help of such narrow nozzles, they are able to get their lives together.

My point is that the religions and non-religions into which we are born are not necessarily the best for us to follow all our lives. Sometimes God calls us to change course, to adopt a new path, to become new people. We experience God through fresh possibilities for healing and wholeness, relative to the situations at hand. For some, Christianity can be such a possibility, for others Islam, for others Judaism, and for others Buddhism.

But it is God who calls, not us. Had I issued an altar call to my Buddhist friend, I would have been doing it for my sake, not for hers or for God's. I would have been trying to convert her so that I might feel more secure about the "rightness" of my Christianity. I know myself too well. I have some evangelist in me, some missionary. Too often it is ego-based.

But perhaps I also know my tradition too well. If we are Christian, we best admit that our tradition has been overly aggressive, almost violent, in its impulse to make the world over into our image. We have said that we are "making the world over" for God's sake, but I fear we have been doing it for our own. We have a hard time trusting that God might be in the lives of others quite apart from our interventions. We have a hard time letting others be.

Accordingly, my aim in this book has been to help us become more generous in our attitudes toward the Earth and people who are different from us. With regard to the Earth, I have encouraged us to read the Bible with the eyes of a mountain; to tell the biblical story as if it were an ongoing, unfinished creation story; to honor God's covenant with all creatures; to make peace with our local bioregions; and to be sensitive to the green grace of dark forests even as we are receptive to the red grace of the Christ's cross. I have suggested that we humble ourselves before an unfolding cosmic process that is fifteen billion years old, and that we learn to see God in the stars and the planets as well as the poor and powerless of our city streets.

With regard to other religions, I have suggested that we learn from Jews and Buddhists how better to commune with trees and sea pirates; from Hindus how better to commune with rivers and goddesses; and from Native Americans how better to commune with spirits and ancestors. I have proposed that we partake of the quiet mindfulness of Zen meditation, the sensuous sacramentality of Hindu bathing, and the visionary receptivity of Native American shamanism.

In making these recommendations, my conviction has been that God's guiding spirit has been influential throughout the entire planet, not just in the Christian part of it. The Holy Wisdom we see enfleshed in the peacemaking Christ has also graced the lives of coyotes and Buddhists, mountains and Hindus. Her creative yet healing winds are much more wide-ranging than we Christians have often imagined. Holy Wisdom blows where she wills.[1]

I must admit I did not learn all this in Sunday School. My childhood catechisms were more human-centered and exclusivistic. The sermons I heard spoke of God not the Goddess, of Jesus not the Buddha, of the Bible not the Earth. I have many fundamentalist friends who will cringe when they hear me recommend openness to goddesses and rivers. I know Christians who do not think God hears the prayers of Buddhists. I hope that we can grow beyond such insensitivity.

In allowing our imaginations to be stretched, it helps if we realize that our tradition is a multi-generational journey. When we think that the journey is finished, that our faith has been fully defined once-and-for-all, that nothing new can be revealed under the sun, then we have become idolatrous. We have substituted the achievements of the past for God's call from the future. This is the problem of fundamentalism. It worships the past.

But neither do we want to worship the future. Worshiping a utopian ideal can be just as damaging as worshiping a golden age. Just as we ought be open

---

1. Perhaps one way for us to be mindful of the Spirit's wide-ranging winds is to recognize a difference between church and Church. Perhaps we best let the word *church* with a lower-case "c" represent the Christian family, now scattered throughout the world, with more than sixty percent of its members in Asia, Africa, and Latin America. If we are white middle-class Christians, it is very important for us to remember that we are a minority, even among Christians. Most of our Christian sisters and brothers, like their non-Christian neighbors, do not have white skin or video-cassette recorders. Many do not even have full stomachs. As affluent Christians in the West, our claim to membership in the church of Jesus is pure travesty unless we join the struggle to help make peace in, and bring justice to, the global village. We should begin, but not end, in our own backyards.

In addition, however, we can also recognize the larger context in which we and our peacemaking struggles are nested. Let Church with an upper-case "C" be the Earth itself, and beyond that the Universe, both of which form the body of God. The coyotes and hummingbirds are part of this larger Church, as are the planets and the galaxies. Likewise the archetypes and energies of our collective unconscious are part of Church, as are the spirits and ancestors of the spirit worlds. The Church is cosmic as well as earthly, unconscious as well as conscious, extraterrestrial as well as terrestrial. When we gaze into the starry heavens on a cold winter's night, or when we encounter departed ancestors in our dreams, we are being introduced to larger dimensions of God's body. We are looking at Church.

to the past without clinging to it, so we ought be open to the future without clinging to it. In truth, there is no end of time to which we, as Christians, ought commit ourselves. The only true end of time is the present moment itself—the here-and-now—in which past and future come together in memory and hope. And the immediacy of this present moment is always impermanent. For good or ill, we never catch impermanence taking a holiday. Every moment of our lives is a birth and death. If there is a heaven, and I hope there is, I imagine that the situation is similar there, and also in hell. The only Ultimate End is God's life itself, which is fluid and changing like a river, forever weaving tapestries out of the pieces of our lives. Our lives find their deepest meanings, moment to moment, in that larger tapestry.

A Word to People of Other Paths

But enough advice to my fellow Christians. If you are not a self-identified Christian, I hope that you too have gained from this book. For you, this book has been an experiment in interreligious dialogue, with my voice as an "other" with whom you have been in dialogue. If you are a Buddhist, be a Buddhist with roots and wings; if you are a Jew, be a Jew with roots and wings; and if you are a "none of the above," be a "none of the above" with roots and wings.

I have many friends who are "none of the above." They are serious seekers who want to be centered in the healing wisdom of the Spirit, but who do not find "religion" a helpful context for spiritual pilgrimage. They feel enslaved by labels such as "Christian" or "Buddhist" or "Jew" or "Hindu." As I see it, the body of God includes unaffiliated spirits, too. Not only can they be kind and creative people, but they remind us labels are so often misleading. At some level none of us is Buddhist or Christian or Hindu. We are just ourselves.

Whatever your religious identification or dis-identification, however, I suspect that we—you and I—have at least one thing in common. When it comes to spiritual growth, I suspect that our minds and imaginations are slightly ahead of our lives. We can imagine what it might be like to be more whole, more wise, more compassionate than we are; and yet our lives cannot quite live up to what we imagine. To one degree or another we fall short of the better self we would like to be. In Christian language, we miss the mark. We sin.

From the point of view of this book, missing the mark is not always bad. It is bad when it harms others, human and nonhuman. And it is bad when it harms us. But it also evokes in us an awareness of a better self we would like to be. This better self is both a possibility and a presence. It is one way that God is present in our lives. Following process theology, I have suggested that, at each and every moment of our lives, Holy Wisdom reaches into our lives by offering possibilities for growth and development, relative to the situations at hand. We feel these possibilities at a very deep level, with sighs too deep for words. They represent a better self that we can become. They are fresh possibilities for responding, or at least coping with, the situation at hand. We might also call them prayers.

The prayers belong both to God and to us. They belong to us because they embody our deepest yearnings, our deepest desire for who we would like to be. And they belong to God because they embody God's deepest yearnings, God's deepest desire for who we can be, if we are to realize our potential. At a level deep within our hearts, we are always participating in God's prayer. Our task is to hear God's prayer and respond to it.

Our failures to hear this prayer, to become our better self, are sometimes painful, both to God and to us. Much violence in our world results from people being out of touch with their own deepest desires, alienated from their better selves, neglectful of God's prayer in them. And yet God never gives up: not in this life, or the next, or the next. St. Paul advised us to "pray without ceasing." Certainly this is good advice. We pray without ceasing when we live in constant mindfulness of God's presence in the here-and-now, as revealed in the faces of friends and enemies, visions and archetypes, plants and animals.

But my point is that God too prays without ceasing. God is always becoming incarnate in our lives through fresh possibilities for healing and wholeness. Every moment has its opportunity, if not for happiness then at least for coping. There is grace sufficient to the moment, and it is God's ongoing prayer in our lives.

Getting Practical

What can we do to better respond to God's prayer within us? There are no simple answers, no formulas for wholeness. When we cling too zealously to techniques for becoming whole, we miss the fact that life itself is our teacher. And we forget that wholeness most often arrives not when we aim at wholeness itself, but rather when we aim at other things—like service to others and fidelity to truth.

Still, we need starting points. Many of us might benefit from finding a group of spiritual friends whom we can support and be supported by, even when times are tough; and following a daily practice of prayer and meditation, to which we adhere even when we do not feel like it. Find a Community and Follow a Practice! That's what it seems to come to.

This advice comes from the Buddhist peace activist, Joanna Macy. Macy travels throughout the world giving "despair and empowering workshops" to community activists. She helps activists come to grips with the pain they feel for the sufferings of other people and other species; she helps them become more effective peacemakers in their local communities. Her Buddhist-influenced insight is that the despair we feel over the suffering of others is the flip side of our connectedness with them. We would not suffer with them, she says, were we not so connected to them. Once we awaken to these connections, we become capable of being creative healers in a broken world.

It is significant to me, as a Christian, that Macy sees this as a Christian as well as a Buddhist truth. She writes: "The cross where Jesus died teaches us that it is precisely through openness to the pain of our world that redemption and renewal are found" (1991, 21-22). I once called her and thanked her for that insight into Christianity. She responded that she feels identified with Christianity even as she travels a Buddhist path. "Even as I sit on the Zen meditation cushion," she said, "I sit at the foot of the cross."

Often, at the end of workshops, people ask Macy what they might do to "keep on keeping on" in their activism, even when their efforts to make a difference in the world seem to come to naught. "How can personal energy and compassion be sustained," they ask, "when it is so easy to burn out?" Drawing upon her own experiences as an activist in the First and Third Worlds, she responds:

Two ways that I know are community and practice. The liberation struggles in Latin America and the Philippines have demonstrated the efficacy of spiritually-based communities for non-violent action. These tough networks of trust arise on the neighborhood level, as people strive together to understand, in their own terms and for their own situation, what they need to do to live without fear and injustice. These groups need be neither residential nor elite, just ordinary people meeting regularly in a discipline of honest searching and mutual commitment.

In addition to such external support, we need, in this time of great challenge and change, the internal support of personal practice. I mean practice in the venerable spiritual sense of fortifying the mind and schooling its attitudes. Because for generations we have been conditioned by the mechanistic, anthropocentric assumptions of our mainstream culture, intellectual assent to an ecological vision of life is not enough to change our perceptions and behaviors. To help us disidentify from narrow notions of the self and experience our interexistence with all beings in the web of life, we turn to regular personal practices that range from meditation to the recycling of our trash (1991, 37-38).

Macy's recommendations concerning community and practice take us full circle, back to Chapter 1, where I proposed that there are four healthy soils in which we might sink our roots: the Earth, the wisdom of ancestors, meaningful relations with other people, and the still small voice of God as discovered in silent prayer and meditation. Community and practice are dimensions of the latter two soils. Without them, the ideas in this book remain abstract. With them, perhaps we begin to answer God's prayers in our lives.

Community

Like many others in consumer society, I yearn for more community than I know. It is easier to say the word *community* than to live it. To be sure, I have friends and family, coworkers and neighbors who are community to me. Without them I would be nothing. They are faces of God in my life.

And yet, like most of us, I have also been caught up in the individualistic ethos of modern Western culture. I often ask "What's in it for me?" at the expense of asking "What can I do for you?" As a result, I need a community that teaches me how better to live in community: one that helps me dis-iden-tify with the performance-based, individualistic ethos of modern life, so that I can be a better husband and father, neighbor and friend, coworker and school board member, teacher and recycler. Sometimes I turn to the out-of-doors for this community: to the birds and trees and sky. But they are not enough. I need human models, too.

One place to which I have turned—which I offer as an example but not norm—is a local Episcopal church in the town where I live. On Wednesday evenings at seven o'clock at St. Peter's there is a healing and eucharist service that I often attend, along with about fifteen or twenty others. Some of us are men and some women, some adults and some children, some rich and some poor, some heterosexual and some homosexual, some conservative and some liberal, some extroverted and some introverted, some happy and some sad. There is no dress code and no pretense. Our service is led by a female priest, a former counselor, who gives the whole atmosphere a feeling of calm and grace.

The healing ceremony consists of a laying on of hands, amid which the priest anoints our foreheads with oil in the sign of the cross. We can lift up the names of people for whose healing we yearn, or we can remain silent and simply seek healing for ourselves. For many, the healing at issue is psycho-logical not physical. Our bodies are all right, but our souls are not. We want to become our better selves.

As we walk down the aisle for healing, we move slowly, almost waddling. I sometimes imagine us as beautiful yet vulnerable ducks, walking in a line. We are not doctors or lawyers or housewives or gas station attendants or sec-retaries or construction workers who strut nobly to receive God's blessing. Rather, we are green-headed mallards, half-whole and half-broken, who waddle with vulnerability and beauty. As we approach the altar, we anticipate receiv-ing a healing prayer, itself more like an energy than an idea, from the priest, who is herself a waddler. After she lays hands on us, we do the same for her. The touch of the hands, hers on us and ours on hers, is most important. Through touch we come together, whatever is happening in our lives.

The touch is also important later in the service, when we receive eucharist. Here the concern is not so much healing as wholeness. We celebrate a whole-ness that we feel with each other, healed or not. Together we eat the bread and drink the wine, each in our own way; together we bring our souls to the table. There is a vivid sense of unity in diversity and diversity in unity. We are like one body with many organs, none superior to the others, all essential to the whole.

For my part, I try to be mindful in the Zen sense during the service. Too much of my ordinary life is lived in distraction, in not being present to the present. I am too often preoccupied with things to be done, some worthwhile and some not. I often have "more important" things to do than being awake in the here-and-now.

Accordingly, I look forward to the Wednesday evening services as an occasion just to be, not do. I try to be present to the people around me, to the oil on my forehead, to the bread in my mouth, to the wine on my tongue. Even the Nicene Creed, which we recite in unison, seems more like a chant than a theology. The service consists of both sounds and silences. Often I find God in both.

But let me be truthful, lest I paint myself as more pious than I am. I am not *fully* present at *all* the services I attend. Even in church, and sometimes because it is church, I think of other things. I think of what I must do when I get home, or what I must do at work the next day, or how to get out of washing the car. And yet, strangely enough, it seems all right to be distracted. The first rule of Zen Buddhism is "Be fully present to the present." The second rule is "If you cannot be fully present, be fully distracted." Sometimes I follow the second rule.

When I follow the first, however, I sometimes get a feeling of deep communion. As I chant the creed, pray for forgiveness, touch the shoulders, and eat the bread, I have the sense that the whole of creation, with its pain and its joy, is somehow gathered into the unity of the sanctuary, and that the moment belongs to all of creation, not just to us. Dimly and deeply I feel a kind of communion that is closer to sacred community than anything I know. It is divine in its universality and yet wholly ordinary in its concreteness. It is the "holy ordinary."

As I leave the service, I would like to take some of this divinity, this holy ordinariness, into the rest of my life. I would like to take it into my relationships with my wife and children, with my fellow workers and neighbors, with the battered women in my city, with the men who batter them, with the drug addicts and their families, with the homeless on the streets, with the workers in the soup kitchen, with my dogs, with the forests to the north of the city, the grasslands to the south, the lake to the east, the mountains to the west. I would like to be communion to them as God has been to me.

I realize that it is rare to find such meaning in Christian worship services. In much of my life I've not found such meaning either. And I do not necessarily recommend Episcopal churches. Sometimes they can be deadly dull, as can any church.

My point is that each of us, in our own way, needs to find forms of local community where we taste communion at its deepest and richest, so that we are energized to be healers in a broken world. Where we find communion will differ. For some of us, our local communion may be a small group in a local synagogue; for others, a weekly gathering of spiritual friends; for still others, a weekly meditation group; and for still others, a weekly meeting of Alcoholics Anonymous. I know people whose most intimate tastes of communion occur in coffee shops, bookstores, and even bars. Wherever two or three are gathered together, in a spirit of healing love, God is present.

The phrase "two or three gathered together" comes from Matthew 18:20. The passage reads: "For where two or three are gathered in my name, there am I in the midst of them." In my experience at the Episcopal church, we do indeed gather in Jesus' name. And yet, I have seen some gatherings in which the spirit of Jesus has been present even though the name of Jesus has been absent. Some of these gatherings have been Buddhist, some feminist, some Native American, and some "none of the above." What is most important is that we find *some* context in which we let our pretenses and roles drop, acknowledge our vulnerability, celebrate our commonalities but also respect our differences, and learn to trust a mystery of Interbeing deeper than words. In my view, Jesus is indeed present in those gatherings, and it does not matter that much to him whether we use his name or not. I understand "in my name" to mean "in my spirit."

If imbued with the spirit of Christ this worshipful community will then energize us to be healers in a broken world, to make peace with our local bioregions, to befriend the friendless, to cast our lot with the poor. At the Episcopal church that I attend, the worship services are complemented and inspired by ministries to people with AIDS, people in jail, people in nursing homes, people on the streets, fellow congregants, and, in some ways, the Earth itself. This is as it should be. Whatever our most meaningful local communities, they need to give us a sense of internal communion and also prod us to look beyond ourselves to that larger communion which is the Earth itself.

Daily Practice

Community is not enough. Most of us also need a daily spiritual practice, a quiet time, a time of prayer. The French philosopher Pascal is alleged to have said that all the problems in our world would be solved if every person would learn to sit in a room alone for thirty minutes each day. Many of us probably need an hour.

My aim is not to encourage slavish devotion to inflexible schedules but to encourage a discipline. Most of us need to spend some time each day "doing nothing" except finding our heart in God, each in our own way. Some of us may do it through Bible study, others through Zen meditation, poetry writing, journal keeping, practicing yoga, working with dreams, spiritual dance, or walking in the park. If done mindfully and with spiritual intent, any of these activities can be a form of prayer and meditation.

We may also need a spiritual director or spiritual friend, someone with whom we meet once a month to discern the promptings of God in our lives and who holds us accountable to our desires to grow spiritually.[2] Among Christians, such a person is more common in Roman Catholic and Anglican traditions than in Protestant traditions. He or she is not a counselor who helps us solve personal problems, or even a pastor who gives us teachings of a tradition, but a friend who understands our spiritual pilgrimage and walks with us along the way.

Whatever practices we choose, they should be *unproductive* by consumer standards. They ought not earn us money, offer us prestige, or make us "better looking." We ought not approach them as if they made us "holier" or "more spiritual" than others. Holier than thou attitudes are spiritual materialism at its worst. They parallel secular materialism, which tells us that we are worth something when we look good in the eyes of others. Prayer tells us just the opposite. It says that we are worth something when we can relax, let go, and be ourselves in God's presence. We become our better selves by accepting ourselves.

On Being Too Busy

The problem, of course, is that many of us are too busy to be ourselves. Praying can seem a waste of time, given all the things that "need" to be done. In truth, our obsessive busy-ness is itself a form of violence, harmful both to ourselves and to others. This is the case even if we are obsessively busy doing constructive things, like helping others or making peace in our local bioregions. Thomas Merton puts it this way:

> There is a pervasive form of contemporary violence to which the idealist fighting for peace by non-violent methods most easily succumbs: activism and overwork. The rush and pressure of modern life are a form, perhaps the most common form, of its innate violence. To allow oneself to be carried away by a multitude of conflicting concerns, to surrender to too many demands, to commit oneself to too many projects, to want to help everyone in everything is to succumb to violence. The frenzy of the activist neutralizes his work for peace. It destroys the fruitfulness of his own work, because it kills the root of inner wisdom which makes work fruitful (Edwards 1980, 88).

Without prayer, we lack the self-awareness and inner depth that make love authentic.

As we seek our own forms of personal prayer and meditation, we can benefit from the experience of others. Good books abound on the many options that have been tried over the centuries in all parts of the world (cf. Edwards

---

2. A common pattern is to meet with a person once a month for an hour. For information on the history and nature of spiritual direction, see Edwards (1980) and Leech (1977).

1980; Goleman 1988). If we are Christian, many of us must turn to such books, because our own clergy are unfamiliar with the techniques of prayer and meditation. Strangely enough, most seminaries in the United States do not have courses called "How to Pray and Meditate." It is presumed that we already know. Most of us do not.

Prayer

This book is not the context to review the myriad methods of prayer that are available to us. Still, I realize that some of you may be interested in the implications of this book for prayer. At least this is the case with many of my students. "If we can't pray to God," they ask, "what good is God anyway?"

I agree. Many of us know more about God through prayer than through reflections. I once heard a prayer that goes: "Dear God, I have never believed in you, but I have always loved you." In this book I have wanted to offer a God in whom we can believe. But I am more interested in a God whom we can love. "Talking to God" and "listening to God" can be forms of love, of communion. I conclude with reflection on each.

Prayer as Talking to God

If talking to God is to make sense, we must imagine God as a reality who listens. This does not mean that God has a physical body with ears, or that, as the poet Gary Snyder puts it, "God resides off the planet." But it does mean that God is more than a blind force or power, and more than a mere aggregate of the objects in the universe. It means that God is an inclusive reality with awareness and sensitivity, with what Thomas Berry calls "interiority."

This is the image of God that I have recommended in this book. I have proposed that we imagine God as a living Communion with interiority of her own, whose very body is the universe itself. This interiority is not located in a particular region of space or time. It is everywhere and nowhere at once. I have compared it to an Ocean in which all living beings live and breathe and have their being. Along with countless other creatures, we humans are like fish swimming in this Ocean, dimly aware of it as a horizon in which we swim, yet connected to it in the innermost depths of our hearts. My proposal is that we can actually experience this Ocean in many ways: 1) as an inwardly felt lure toward wholeness offering grace sufficient to the moment; 2) as a healing energy—a surging, mothering power—that is within us and around us; 3) as a revelatory presence in our dreams and visions; 4) as a revelatory presence in the Earth and Cosmos; and 5) as a Companion to our joys and sufferings. Talking to God begins with the latter awareness. It begins with the recognition that our deepest feelings are felt and shared by the widest context of our lives, by an Ocean of Empathy, by a gentle Listener, by God.

There is more than one way to imagine the personal empathic receptivity of this gentle Listener. Some find it helpful to imagine the Ocean of Empathy as heavenly Father, some as powerful Mother, and still others as beloved Lover. Like a Buddhist boddhisattva, the Ocean is omni-adaptive; it actually *becomes* the image that is needed by the person at issue. To those who need a father, it becomes a father; to those who need a mother, it becomes a mother; to those who need a friend, it becomes a friend; to those who need a lover, it becomes a lover. It becomes God the Father and Sophia the Mother and Jesus the Friend and Christ the Lover, relative to our needs. God becomes the face we need, that we might speak to God face-to-face.

Talking to God is speaking to God face-to-face. It is turning to the Ocean of Empathy, who shares our deepest joys and sorrows, and responding as a lover to a beloved. The languages we use can vary. Some of us talk to God with words, others with feelings, body movements, laughter, tears, and silence. Each of us has preferred forms of communication.

The messages we offer God will vary from circumstance to circumstance. Sometimes we will want to say "Dear God, I love you" or "Dear God, I need you" or "Dear God, I am sorry for what I've done to you." And sometimes we will need to say "Dear God, I am mad at you" or even "Dear God, I hate you." For some of us, some of the time, prayers of argumentation and protest can be as important as those of love and affection. Many grievers have found their hearts in God by admitting, to God, that they are angry with God over the death of a loved one. From the point of view of this book, God does not cause the death. There are things that happen in the universe that even God cannot prevent. But God is certainly gracious enough to absorb the anger and frustration. Our Beloved receives our pain with understanding.

However we talk to God, we need not always seek results. Often we are not asking for anything, we are simply communing with the Heart of the universe. It is as if, in the depths of our heart, we are sitting with our Lover by a warm fire on a winter's night. Or resting in our Father's arms after we have been hurt by friends. Or visiting with a Friend over bread and wine. There is no place to go, because we are already there. The communion is an end in itself.

For most of us, however, there will also be times when we wish to petition God. Our prayer will be: "Dear God, please be with my son as he battles with depression!" or "Dear God, I lift up my mother who is dying of cancer!" or "Dear God, please help the terrified children in war-torn countries!" or "Dear God, please don't let them destroy still another forest!" We may not know what needs to happen, but we know that *something* must happen if those we love are to find healing and wholeness. Our prayer is an act of hope.

From the vantage point of this book, our hopes are justified. There *is* a difference between the way the world ought to be and the way it is. Sometimes the fish in the Ocean do horrible things and suffer horrible tragedies that ought not occur. Even Holy Wisdom cannot prevent them. Still, Holy

Wisdom is influential in the universe as a lure toward what can be and ought to be. Only God knows the fullness of what ought to be. Often we are unclear on the matter, confusing our ego-based will with God's more inclusive will. Still we pray that the will of God, whatever it is, be done "on Earth as it is in heaven." To our Beloved we cry, "Not their will, or even my will, but *your* will be done."

Two words of caution are in order. First, we best not imagine that our petitions initiate a divine influence that would otherwise be absent. The Empathy at the Heart of the universe is present within all living beings on the planet, praying for them and in them, regardless of our prayers. God prays without ceasing. Second, we ought not think that because God hears our prayers, miracles will of necessity occur. Precisely because God is a Christ-like Lover rather than a Cosmic Puppeteer, there are things that happen on this planet that even God cannot prevent.

Still, petitionary prayers can play a very important role in our lives. They are not magic wands. Rather, they are like yeast that we scatter into the universe and into God, in hopes that "holy bread" can be made. By "holy bread" I mean circumstances that are more whole than broken, more creative than stagnant, more peaceful than violent, more wise than confused. I mean well-fed children and non-abused animals and violence-free teenagers and protected rainforests. These are breads worth praying for.

The problem, of course, is that the baking process is unpredictable, because all the variables cannot be controlled. Even as we offer our prayers, countless other creatures in the universe are adding their ingredients to the mix, some healing and some harming. Sometimes, even we ourselves are adding other ingredients that contravene our prayers. We pray for a sick friend, but we do not visit the friend for whom we pray; we pray for protected rainforests, but we do not work to protect them; we pray for personal wholeness, but we do not alter the behavior that leads to our addictions. Many ingredients go into every mix. Yeast-like prayers are but one.

The good news is that God is adding God's ingredients to the mix, always healing but never controlling. God's ingredients are the lures toward wholeness that are part of each and every life, the healing energy, and the listening. While petitionary prayers cannot overpower the countless powers of the world, they can add leavening influence to God's healing love. As we utter them, often with wordless sighs that are more like hopes than demands, they enter into the collective unconscious of humanity, into the depths of our own inner lives, and into the very heart of God, offering freshness to the divine life.

Recall the prayer I uttered with my Buddhist friend for her father. Our prayer was like yeast. Because the universe is a network of interbeing, it became part of her father's life in some small way. It also helped give rise to greater mindfulness on my friend's part, and on my part, for the value of her father. It was our way of cooperating with and participating in an ongoing, everlasting Prayer of God that all be whole, each in its own way. As it turns out, her father survived the crisis. I do not attribute his survival solely to our prayer. Certainly the doctors and nurses helped, along with the immediate support of loved ones. But I do not think the prayer was meaningless either. It added a healing hope to the mix. It was leaven for life.

Prayer as Listening

One of the most powerful ways to participate in the ongoing Prayer, however, is not by talking but by listening with the heart, in silence, putting on the mind of God and hearing as God hears.

For many of us, such hearing does not come easy. Our minds are bursting with the noise and chatter. Buddhists compare them to monkeys in a cage, jumping from side to side, rattling each side incessantly. To recognize this for ourselves, we need but attend to our own stream of consciousness for a while. "What am I doing here? What is he saying? When can I eat? Where is the catsup? What time can I leave?" Psychologist William James calls it a "blooming, buzzing confusion."

The internal energy behind this confusion is inherently creative. It is the power of our own freedom, our own selfhood, our own individuality. But this psychic energy needs to be channeled in healing directions if it is to be fruitful. In order to let it be channeled, we must settle down for a bit, come to our senses, let the rattling subside, and simply hear God's prayer in the depths of our existence. This is the purpose of silent prayer: to hear God's prayer and God's presence.

God's prayer is the called-for action relative to the situation at hand. God's presence is the silence, the spacious freedom that emerges in our own inner lives when our chattering has subsided and we rest in the still point of the turning world.

This prayer of silence has a long tradition in Christianity. It begins with the Desert Fathers, works its way through John of the Cross and Teresa of Avila, and finds its way to Thomas Merton and others in our time who find God in what has come to be called centering prayer. In order to find the silence, writers often recommend that we focus on simple words or sounds that help free us from distractions, but then let go of the sounds themselves in order to rest in the silence. Amid such rest, there is no sense of a "self" or an "ego" that is enjoying the prayer or doing the listening. There is just the silence itself. In a letter to a Muslim friend, Merton described his own experience of it this way:

> Now you ask about my method of meditation. Strictly speaking I have a very simple way of prayer. It is centered entirely on attention to the presence of God and to his will and his love. That is to say that it is centered on faith by which alone we can know the presence of God. One might say this gives my prayer the character described by the prophet as "being before God as if you saw him." Yet it does not mean imagining anything or conceiving a precise image of God, for to my mind this

would be a kind of idolatry. On the contrary, it is a matter of adoring him as all. . . . There is in my heart the great thirst to recognize totally the nothingness of all that is not God. My prayer is then a kind of praise rising up out of the center of Nothingness and Silence. If I am still present "myself," this I recognize as an obstacle. If he wills he can then make the Nothingness into total charity. If he does not will, then the Nothingness actually seems itself to be an object and remains an obstacle. Such is my ordinary way of prayer, or meditation. It is not "thinking about" anything, but a direct seeking of the face of the invisible, which cannot be found unless we become lost in him who is invisible (Hall 1988, 50).

For Merton, imagining something in prayer or conceiving an image is idolatry. The prayer of silence is a wholesale assault on idols both inner and outer.

I suggest that many of us need some taste of this inner silence. It is not the silence of tears or anguish, nor even of joy and ecstasy. It is deeper than that and more creative. It is the silence of God as present in the depths of our inner lives. God is not a "thing" among things, but rather a "no-thing"—more like a spacious sky than a cloud among clouds. This creative Sky is around us at all times, as the Listener who understands our joys and sufferings and who beckons us into the fullness of life. But the Sky is also within us, as a "living Christ" who is pure wisdom, pure compassion, and pure freedom.

Like the rest of us, Thomas Merton probably did not taste this freedom with the depth he wished. In life on Earth we but glimpse it occasionally, when we are momentarily released from our monkey minds. To the degree that we taste it, however, we know the meaning of what in Christianity is called resurrection. It provides our ordinary life with a freshness and spontaneity that is new at every moment and that can give us the courage to face crosses day by day.

Resurrection

It seems fitting to end this book with the theme of resurrection. A story from the life of Thomas Merton makes the point. Merton died while at a conference for monks in Thailand. On his way to the conference he was able to visit many Tibetan Buddhists, including the Dalai Lama. His visits were arranged by a young convert to Catholicism, Harold Talbott, who accompanied him.

At one point, according to Talbott, Merton met a somewhat "wild" Tibetan lama who impressed him deeply, but who had serious reservations concerning Christianity. He called Merton "a Jesus Lama." The lama then confessed:

You know, I have never been able for the life of me to get a handle on Christianity so I'm glad you're here this morning. . . . The center of your religion concerns a man who comes back to life after death; and yet, in Tibetan Buddhism, when you have one of these people, a rolog, or a walking corpse, we call our lama to put him down. So I want to know what kind of a religion is Christianity which has as its center a dead man coming back to life (Talbott 1992, 23-24).

The lama did not question the literal reality of Jesus rising from the dead. From a Tibetan perspective, such rising did not seem that extraordinary. What troubled him was the fact that the early followers of Jesus did not "call in a lama" to send him on his way, to another plane of existence where he rightly belonged.

Merton did not respond defensively. Instead,

Merton explained the Resurrection in tantric terms about the overcoming of fear and the utter and complete power of liberation which is at the center of Christianity . . . freedom from all constraints and restraints. A man has died and he has come back in a glorious body and he has freed us from fear of death and fear of life. That's freedom (Talbott 1992, 23-24).

According to Talbott, the Tibetan lama was satisfied by Merton's response. For once in his life, Christianity made sense.

Christianity may or may not make sense to you, the reader, but perhaps resurrection can make sense. It is a process of being reborn, moment-to-moment, in a freedom that is wise in its sensitivity to the interconnectedness of all things, compassionate in its empathy for all living beings, and centered in the very mystery of God. We understand resurrection when we taste a freedom and freshness that lies in the very depths of our lives. From my perspective as a Christian, this freedom and freshness is the living Christ, the resurrected One. You may name it differently. In any case, "he" is not exactly a "him" anyway. "He" does not have a body that is located in space and time. "He" is more like the wind, or our own breathing, or the sky. The resurrected One is the very freshness of God, the very freedom of Holy Wisdom, as a Center that is within us and beyond us, ever-present yet ever-new. There is a freshness and freedom in the very center of things. In this freshness and freedom, we find our roots and wings.

Works Cited

Adams, Carol, ed. 1993. *Ecofeminism and the Sacred.* New York: Continuum.

Ariarajah, Wesley. 1985. *The Bible and People of Other Faiths.* Geneva: WCC Publications.

Austin, Richard Cartwright. 1988. *Hope for the Land: Nature in the Bible.* Louisville: Westminster Press.

Baker, John Austin. 1990. "Biblical Views of Nature." See Birch et al., 1990, 9-26.

Beck, Charlotte Joko. 1993. *Nothing Special: Living Zen.* Ed. Steve Smith. San Francisco: Harper.

Bendis, Debra. 1994. "Dakota and Other Holy Places: The Writings of Kathleen Norris." *The Christian Century* (July-Aug.): 720-23.

Berry, Thomas. 1988. *The Dream of the Earth.* San Francisco: Sierra Club Books.

Berry, Thomas, and Brian Swimme. 1992. *The Universe Story: From the Primordial Flaring Forth to the Ecozoic Era: A Celebration of the Unfolding of the Cosmos.* San Francisco: Harper.

Berry, Wendell. 1977. *The Unsettling of America.* San Francisco: Sierra Club.

_____. 1981a. *The Gift of Good Land: Further Essays Cultural and Geographical.* San Francisco: North Point.

_____. 1981b. *Recollected Essays.* Berkeley: North Point.

Birch, Charles, William Eakin, and Jay B. McDaniel, eds. 1990a. *Liberating Life: Contemporary Approaches to Ecological Theology.* Maryknoll, N.Y.: Orbis Books.

Birch, Charles. 1990b. "Chance, Purpose, and the Order of Nature." See Birch, et al., 1990.

Black Elk. See Neihardt 1972.

Borg, Marcus. 1987. *Jesus: A New Vision: Spirit, Culture, and the Life of Discipleship.* San Francisco: Harper.

Brown, Joseph Epes. 1990. *The Spiritual Legacy of the American Indian.* New York: Crossroad.

Brown, Robert McAfee. 1981. *Making Peace in the Global Village.* Louisville: Westminster/John Knox.

Buber, Martin. 1958. *I and Thou.* Trans. Walter Kaufmann. New York: Scribners.

Callicott, J. Baird. 1989. *In Defense of the Land Ethic: Essays in Environmental Philosophy.* Albany, N.Y.: State University of New York Press.

233

_____. 1991. "Genesis and John Muir." See Robb and Casebolt, 1991. *Co-Evolution Quarterly* 32 (Winter 1981-82), 1.

Cobb, John B., Jr. 1982. *Beyond Dialogue: Toward a Mutual Transformation of Buddhism and Christianity.* Philadelphia: Fortress Press, 1982.

_____. 1991a. *Matters of Life and Death.* Louisville: Westminster/John Knox Press.

_____. 1991b. "Economism or Planetism: The Coming Choice." *Earth Ethics.* Vol. 3, no. 1 (Fall).

_____. 1992. *Sustainability: Economics, Ecology, and Justice.* Maryknoll, N.Y.: Orbis Books.

Comstock, Gary L. 1995. *Religious Autobiographies.* Belmont, Cal.: Wadsworth.

Cooey, Paula M., William R. Eakin, and Jay B. McDaniel. 1993. *After Patriarchy: Feminist Transformations of the World Religions.* Maryknoll, N.Y.: Orbis Books.

Corless, Roger. 1989. *The Vision of Buddhism.* New York: Paragon House.

Crow Dog, Mary. 1990. *Lakota Woman.* New York: HarperCollins.

_____. 1995. See Comstock, 69-89.

Daly, Herman, and John B. Cobb. 1989. *For the Common Good: Redirecting the Economy Toward Community, the Environment, and a Sustainable Future.* Boston: Beacon Press.

Dunfee, Sue. 1982. "The Sin of Hiding: A Feminist Critique of Reinhold Niebuhr's Account of the Sin of Pride." *Soundings* (Fall), 316-27.

Durnig, Alan B. 1989. "Poverty and the Environment: Reversing the Downward Spiral." *Worldwatch Paper #92.* Worldwatch Institute: Washington D.C.

_____. 1991. "Taking Stock: Animal Farming and the Environment" *Worldwatch Paper #103.* Worldwatch Institute: Washington, D.C.

Eck, Diana L. 1981. *Darsan: Seeing the Divine Image in India.* Chambersberg, Penn.: Anima Press.

_____. 1982. *Banaras, City of Light.* New York: Knopf.

_____. 1993. *Encountering God: A Spiritual Journey from Bozeman to Banaras.* Boston: Beacon Press.

Edwards, Tilden. 1980. *Spiritual Friend: Reclaiming the Gift of Spiritual Direction.* New York: Paulist Press.

_____. 1987. *Living in the Presence: Disciplines for the Spiritual Heart.* San Francisco: Harper & Row.

Fellmann, Jerome, Arthur Getis, and Judith Getis. 1985. *Human Geography: Culture and Environment.* New York: Macmillan.

Goleman, Daniel. 1988. *The Meditative Mind: The Varieties of Meditative Experience.* New York: Tarcher.

Green, Thomas. 1987. *Weeds Among the Wheat.* Notre Dame, Ind.: Ave Maria Press.

Grim, John. 1987. *The Shaman: Patterns of Religious Healing Among the Ojibway Indians.* Norman: University of Oklahoma Press.

_____. 1993. "Native North American Worldviews and Ecology." See Tucker and Grim 1993, 41-54.

Gross, Rita. 1993. *Buddhism After Patriarchy: A Feminist History, Analysis, and Reconstruction of Buddhism.* New York: State University of New York Press.

Guenther, Margaret. 1992. *Holy Listening: The Art of Spiritual Direction.* Boston: Cowley.

Gupta, Lina. 1993. "Ganga: Purity, Pollution, and Hinduism." See Adams 1993, 99-116.

Habito, Ruben. 1993. *Healing Breath: Zen Spirituality for a Wounded Earth.* Maryknoll, N.Y.: Orbis Books.

Hall, Thelma. 1988. *Too Deep for Words: Rediscovering Lectio Divina.* New York: Paulist Press.

Hanh, Thich Nhat. 1987. *Being Peace.* Berkeley: Parallax Press.

_____. 1993. *Interbeing: Fourteen Guidelines for Engaged Buddhism.* Berkeley: Parallax Press.

Hick, John, and Paul F. Knitter. 1987. *The Myth of Christian Uniqueness: Toward a Pluralistic Theology of Religions.* Maryknoll, N.Y.: Orbis Books.

Jackson, Wes. 1987. *Altars of Unhewn Stone.* San Francisco: North Point Press, 1987.

Johnson, Robert. 1986. *Inner Work: Using Dreams and Active Imagination for Personal Growth.* San Francisco: HarperSanFrancisco.

Joranson, Philip N., and Ken Butigan, eds. 1984. *Cry of the Environment: Rebuilding the Christian Creation Tradition.* Santa Fe: Bear & Company.

Kasulis, Thomas. 1980. *Zen Action/Zen Person.* Honolulu: University of Hawaii Press.

Kavanaugh, John. 1991. *Following Christ in a Consumer Society.* Revised. Maryknoll, N.Y.: Orbis Books.

Kaza, Stephanie. 1985. "Towards a Buddhist Environmental Ethic." *Buddhism at the Crossroads* 1(1), 22-25.

_____. 1993a. "Acting with Compassion: Buddhism, Feminism, and the Environmental Crisis." See Adams 1993, 50-69.

_____. 1993b. *The Attentive Heart: Conversations with Trees.* New York: Fawcett Columbine.

Keating, Thomas. 1986. *Open Mind, Open Heart: The Contemplative Dimension of the Gospel.* Amity, N.Y.: Amity House.

_____. 1988. *The Heart of the World: A Spiritual Catechism.* New York: Crossroad.

Knierim, Rolf. 1981. "Cosmos and History in Israel's Theology." *Horizons in Biblical Theology,* vol. 3 (1981), 59-123.

Knitter, Paul. 1985. *No Other Name? A Critical Survey of Christian Attitudes Toward the World Religions.* Maryknoll, N.Y.: Orbis Books.

_____. 1987. "Toward a Liberation Theology of Religions." See Hick and Knitter 1987, 178-200.

Lame Deer, John Fire. 1976. *Lame Deer: Seeker of Visions* (with Richard Erdoes). New York: Simon and Schuster.

_____. 1995. See Comstock 1995, 51-68.

Leakey, Richard E. 1981. *The Making of Mankind.* New York: E.P. Dutton.

Leech, Kenneth. 1977. *Soul Friend: The Practice of Christian Ministry.* San Francisco: Harper.

_____. 1992. *The Eye of the Storm: Living Spiritually in the Real World.* New York: HarperCollins.

Leopold, Aldo. 1949. *A Sand County Almanac.* New York: Oxford University Press.

Macy, Joanna. 1991. *World as Lover, World as Self.* Berkeley: Parallax Press.

May, Gerald. 1982. *Will and Spirit: A Contemplative Psychology.* San Francisco: HarperSanFrancisco.

_____. 1988. *Addiction and Grace: Love and Spirituality in the Healing of Addictions.* San Francisco: HarperSanFrancisco.

_____. 1994. "I Met Her on the Mountain." *Shalem Newsletter,* vol. 18, no. 2 (Spring-Summer). Mt. Saint Alban, Washington, D.C. 20016.

McDaniel, Jay B. 1980. "Zen and the Self." *Process Studies* (Fall).

_____. 1989. *Of God and Pelicans: A Theology of Reverence for Life.* Louisville: Westminster/John Knox Press.

_____. 1990. *Earth, Sky, Gods and Mortals: A Theology of Ecology for the Twenty-First Century.* Mystic, Conn.: Twenty-Third Publications.

_____. 1993. "A God Who Loves Animals and a Church That Does the Same." See Pinches and McDaniel 1993, 75-102.

_____. 1994. "Revisioning God and Self: Lessons from Buddhism." See Birch et al. 1990a, 228-58.

McFague, Sallie. 1993. *The Body of God: An Ecological Theology.* Philadelphia: Fortress Press.

Morton, Nelle. 1985. *The Journey Is Home.* Boston: Beacon Press.

Neihardt, John G. 1972. *Black Elk Speaks: Being the Life Story of a Holy Man of the Oglala Sioux,* as told through John G. Neihardt. Lincoln and London: University of Nebraska Press.

Norris, Kathleen. 1993. *Dakota: A Spiritual Geography.* Boston: Houghton Mifflin.

_____. 1994. "The Room." *The Christian Century* (July-Aug), 720.

Oelschlaeger, Max. 1991. *The Idea of Wilderness.* New Haven: Yale University Press.

Orr, David. 1992. *Ecological Literacy: Education and the Transition to a Postmodern World.* Albany: State University of New York Press.

_____. 1994. *Earth in Mind: On Education, Environment, and the Human Prospect.* Washington, D.C.: Island Press.

Pinches, Charles, and Jay B. McDaniel. 1993. *Good News for Animals? Contemporary Approaches to Animal Well-Being.* Maryknoll, N.Y.: Orbis Books.

Plaskow, Judith. 1993. "Transforming the Nature of Community: Toward a Feminist People of Israel." See Cooey, et al. 1993, 87-105.

Prager, Dennis, and Joseph Telushkin. 1983. *Why the Jews? The Reason for Antisemitism.* New York: Simon and Schuster, Inc.

Robb, Carol S., and Carl J. Casebolt. 1991. *Covenant for a New Creation.* Maryknoll, N.Y.: Orbis Books.

Robinson, H. Wheeler. 1946. *Inspiration and Revelation in the Old Testament.* Oxford: Clarendon Press.

Ruether, Rosemary Radford. 1983. *Sexism and God-Talk: Toward a Feminist Theology.* Boston: Beacon Press.

_____. 1992. *Gaia and God: An Ecofeminist Theology of Earth Healing.* San Francisco: HarperSanFrancisco.

Scholtes, Peter. 1966. "They Will Know We Are Christians by Our Love." F.E.L. Church Publications, Ltd.

Schüssler Fiorenza, Elisabeth. 1983. *In Memory of Her: A Feminist Reconstruction of Christian Origins.* New York: Crossroad.

Schweitzer, Albert. 1933. *Out of My Life and Thought.* London: Allen and Unwin.

Seamands, David. 1989. *Healing Grace: Let God Free You from the Performance Trap.* Wheaton, Ill.: Victor Books.

Shopping for a Better World (Council on Economic Priorities). 1991. New York: Ballantine.

Smith, Andy. 1993. "For All Those Who Were Indian in a Former Life." See Adams 1993, 168-71.

Smith, Huston. 1991. *The World's Religions.* San Francisco: HarperSanFrancisco.

Snyder, Gary. 1990. *The Practice of the Wild.* Berkeley: North Point Press.

Speiser, E. A. 1981. *Genesis: A New Translation with Introduction and Commentary.* Garden City: Doubleday.

Spretnak, Charlene. 1991. *States of Grace: The Recovery of Meaning in the Postmodern Age.* San Francisco: HarperCollins.

Talbott, Harold. 1992. "The Jesus Lama: Thomas Merton in the Himalayas." *Tricycle: The Buddhist Review* (Summer), 14-24.

Tedlock, Barbara, and Ted Tedlock, eds. 1975. *Teachings from the American Earth: Indian Religion and Philosophy.* New York: Liveright.

Tobias, Michael. 1993. "Jainism and Ecology: Views of Nature, Nonviolence, and Vegetarianism." See Tucker and Grim, 1993, 138-49.

Tucker, Mary Evelyn, and John A. Grim, eds. 1994. *Worldview and Ecology.* Maryknoll, N.Y.: Orbis Books.

Tucker, Mary Evelyn. 1989. "New Perspectives for Spirituality," *Religion and Intellectual Life* (Winter), 48-56.

United Methodist Hymnal. 1989. Nashville: United Methodist Publishing House.

Watts, Alan W. 1957. *The Way of Zen.* New York: Vintage.

Whitehead, Alfred North. 1967. *Adventures of Ideas.* New York: Free Press.

Wiesel, Elie. 1993. *Sages and Dreamers: Portraits and Legends from the Jewish Tradition.* New York: Touchstone.

World Almanac and Book of Facts. 1992. New York: Pharos Books.

Wouk, Herman. 1987. *This Is My God: The Jewish Way of Life.* Boston: Little, Brown and Company.

Index

Actions, peace and, 19
Agriculture, the Fall and, 123-24
Ancestors, 200-14
Anthropocentrism, 124-25
Baker, John Austin, 88-89
Banares, City of Light (Diana Eck), 175
Basho, 51
Beck, Charlotte Joko, 166
Berry, Thomas, 3, 42-43, 77, 78-88, 110-12; panentheism and, 103-4
Berry, Wendell, 50
Bible, 76
Big Bang, 80
Bioregion, definition of, 67
Bioregionalism, 46-47; Native Americans and, 68
Bioregions, 197-99
Birch, Charles, 104-5
Bodies, awareness of, 48-49, 208-14
Body of God, The (Sallie McFague), 77, 99-100
"Born-again" experience, 94
Brokenleg, Martin, 193-94
Brown, Robert McAfee, 59, 60-61, 63
Buber, Martin, 155-58
Buddhism, 31, 55, 117, 147, 159-70; animals and, 48; ecology and, 161-62; interconnectedness and, 6-7; meditation and, 49; the self and, 164-66
Buddhist mindfulness, 18
Callicott, J. Baird, 1-2, 51-52, 123-25
Campbell, Colin, 66
Campbell, Lillian, 173

Ceremonies, Native American, 211-14
Christ, 113-14; as name for God, 99-100; ecology and, 127-28; life in, 125-28; naming, 114; pain and, 212
Christian heritage, 16-17; Paganism, 12-13
Christianity, approach to other religions, 144; as community, 63; as path, 3-4; as pilgrimage; 38-39; as Way, 40-41; blood imagery in, 52-54; death and, 189-91; ecology and, 101-2; exclusivism in, 142-43; goal of, 95; goddesses and, 185-87; grief and, 14-15; lessons from Hinduism, 171, 176-79; normative, 8; pain and, 189-91; peacemaking and, 60-74; purpose of 23; red and green grace in, 58; stories in the tradition of, 78; teaching, 59; the Way of, 60-61; tragedy and, 9; uniqueness of, 144-46; violence and, 53; world pain and, 54-55
Christians, self-identified, 4
Church (capital "C"), church and, 218
Classical Phase, 84
Cobb, John, 71-74, 77, 123, 144, 150, 206-7
Communal living, 71
Communion, 148; creation and, 48, 92; dialogue and, 149; experiences of, 1-4; Native Americans and, 199-200; principle of, 86-87; with others, 28-30

Also in the Ecology and Justice Series

Claremont
3/97